D1205862

Reinventing the Left

Reinventing the Left

Edited by
David Miliband

Polity Press

This collection copyright © Polity Press 1994
Each chapter copyright © the author

First published in 1994 by Polity Press
in association with Blackwell Publishers.

Editorial office:
Polity Press
65 Bridge Street
Cambridge CB2 1UR, UK

Marketing and production:
Blackwell Publishers
108 Cowley Road,
Oxford OX4 1JF, UK

238 Main Street
Cambridge, MA 02142, USA

ISBN 0 7456 1390 x
ISBN 0 7456 1391 8 (pbk)

A CIP catalogue record for this book is available from the British Library.

Library of Congress Cataloging-in-Publication Data

Reinventing the Left/edited by David Miliband
    p.   cm.
    Includes bibliographical references and index.
    ISBN 0-7456-1390-x (cloth).——ISBN 0-7456-1391-8 (paper) (alk. paper)
    1. Right and left (Political science) 2. Post-communism.
    3. Social change. 4. Economic history – 1990– I. Miliband, David.
JA83.R455 1994
320.5'13'094–dc20
                                                              94–20713
                                                              CIP

Phototypeset in 10 on 12 point Stempel Garamond
by Intype, London
Printed in Great Britain by T.J. Press, Padstow, Cornwall

This book is printed on acid-free paper.

Contents

Contributors

Perry Anderson is Professor of History at the University of California at Los Angeles, and author most recently of *English Questions* and *A Zone of Engagement*.

Jos de Beus is Professor of Political Theory at the University of Twente and Assistant Professor of Economics at the University of Amsterdam. He was co-author of the 1994 election programme of the Partij van Arbeid, the Dutch social democratic party.

Gordon Brown is Labour Member of Parliament for Dunfermline East and Shadow Chancellor of the Exchequer.

Anna Coote is Paul Hamlyn Fellow of Social Policy at the Institute for Public Policy Research, author of *Power and Prejudice*, and editor most recently of *The Welfare of Citizens*.

James Cornford is Director of the Hamlyn Foundation and was formerly Director of the Institute for Public Policy Research.

Manuel Escudero is Associate Director of the Instituto de Empresa in Madrid and a member of the Federal Committee of Spain's governing PSOE (Spanish Socialist Workers' Party).

Gøsta Esping-Andersen is Professor of Political Economy at the University of Trento, and the author most recently of *The Three Worlds of Welfare Capitalism*.

Frances Fox Piven is Professor of Political Science at the Graduate School and University Centre of the City University of New York and co-author most recently of a revised version of *Regulating the Poor*.

viii Contributors

Anthony Giddens is Professor of Sociology at the University of Cambridge and the author most recently of *The Transformation of Intimacy* and *Beyond Left and Right: The Future of Radical Politics*.

David Held is Professor of Politics and Sociology at the Open University and the author of *Models of Democracy* and *The Principle of Autonomy and the Global Order* (forthcoming).

Patricia Hewitt is Head of Research at Andersen Consulting and Deputy Chair of the Commission on Social Justice. She was formerly Deputy Director of the Institute for Public Policy Research.

Margaret Hodge is Labour Member of Parliament for Barking. She was for ten years Leader of Islington Borough Council in London, and then a consultant at Price Waterhouse.

Will Hutton is Economics Editor of the *Guardian* and the author of a forthcoming book on British political economy.

Robert Kuttner is Editor of *The American Prospect*, a columnist for *The Boston Globe* and *Business Week*, and author most recently of *The End of Laissez-Faire*.

David Marquand is Professor of Politics and Director of the Political Economy Research Centre at the University of Sheffield. He is the author of *The Unprincipled Society* and *The Progressive Dilemma*.

Elizabeth Meehan holds the Jean Monnet Chair in the Department of Politics at the Queen's University of Belfast.

David Miliband is Research Fellow at the Institute for Public Policy Research, Secretary of the Commission on Social Justice, and co-editor of *Paying for Inequality: The Economic Cost of Social Injustice*.

Tariq Modood is a Senior Fellow at the Policy Studies Institute in London, and co-author of *Changing Ethnic Identities*.

Susan Owens is a Lecturer in the Department of Geography at the University of Cambridge, a Fellow of Newnham College, and co-author of *Environment, Resources and Conservation*. During the year 1993–4, she held an ESRC Global Environmental Change Programme Fellowship.

Bhikhu Parekh is Professor of Political Theory at the University of Hull, and was formerly Deputy Chair of the Commission for Racial Equality. He is author most recently of *Colonialism, Tradition and Reform* and four volumes of *Critical Assessments of Jeremy Bentham*.

Anne Phillips is Professor of Politics at London Guildhall University, and author of *Engendering Democracy* and *Democracy and Difference*.

Raymond Plant is the Master of St Catherine's College, Oxford, Labour Party spokesman in the House of Lords on Home Affairs, and author most recently of *Modern Political Thought*.

Michel Rocard was Prime Minister of France from 1988 to 1991.

Joel Rogers is Professor of Law, Political Science and Sociology at the University of Wisconsin, Madison. He is author (with Joshua Cohen) of *On Democracy* and (with Thomas Ferguson) of *Right Turn: The Decline of the Democrats and the Future of American Politics*.

Wolfgang Streeck is Professor of Sociology and Industrial Relations at the University of Wisconsin, Madison, and author most recently of *The Social Institutions of Economic Performance* and *Governing Capitalist Economies: Performance and Control of Economic Sectors*.

Stephen Tindale is Policy Advisor to Chris Smith MP, Shadow Secretary of State for Environmental Protection, and writes here in a personal capacity.

Acknowledgements

This book arises from a conference organized by the Institute for Public Policy Research and held in September 1993. The majority of the chapters in the book were first presented at the conference, and have been amended in the light of discussion there. Grateful thanks are due to the Friedrich Ebert Stiftung (London) who bore half the costs of the conference, and also to the Socialist Group of the European Parliament and the Lipman Trust for their financial contributions to its success.

Introduction

David Miliband

Politics in the advanced capitalist world has rarely been held in lower esteem. Whether measured by opinion polls or by the rise of protest parties, the formal institutions of politics, and the politicians who populate them, are held in low regard. At best, they are seen as impotent in the face of economic complexity and social change; at worst, they are part of a conspiracy to defraud the general public.

This scepticism of politics runs deeper and wider than any natural resistance to proposals for social and economic change.[1] Perhaps its most extreme manifestation is the post-modernist denial that there is any structure to the present or any way of organizing the future. More broadly, however, there is a pervasive sense that even as democratic reform triumphs across the globe, political systems in western Europe are not functioning effectively. Important issues seem ill-served by the traditional definitions of Left and Right; for example, feminism and the women's movement have over the last twenty years effected an enormous shift in the politics of gender, and posed fundamental questions to conventional conceptions of class, social structure and progressive political strategy.[2] Similarly, green politics is a central challenge to the commanding ideologies of the century, and demands of all major parties a reorientation of priorities and policies. And there is a disjunction between the short-term calculus of electoral politics and the long-term nature of economic and social problems, between hierarchical and rigid political institutions and new demands for decentralization of power and flexibility of response, and between the weakness of international political structures and the realities of international interdependence.

I am grateful to David Held, Anton Hemerijck, Anthony Giddens, and Ralph and Edward Miliband for detailed comments on earlier drafts of this chapter.

The crisis of politics that is widely diagnosed is not in essence a technical matter, but an ideological one. It is above all a reflection of the recent weakness of the political Left, which has for the last hundred years been the repository of ambitions for economic and social change, and for the use of politics to secure them. In the wake of communist collapse in the East, it became immediately fashionable to argue that the industrialized world had reached the end of the era of transformative political activity. But well beyond the ranks of those already committed to the liberal capitalist status quo, there has been serious questioning of the relevance of the Left's political project. John Dunn (1993: 122) argues that a new feature of the political environment

> is the effective disappearance of any systematic, or even widely credited, conception of how, for many generations to come (or even for ever) it [capitalism] could stand in any danger of being replaced by anything more edifying or less dismaying. What has been deleted from the human future, almost inadvertently but still with remarkable decisiveness, is any form of reasonable and relatively concrete social and political hope.

The final collapse of communism in the revolutions of 1989 – revolutions which Christopher Hitchens (1993: 1) calls the 'axis, pivot and subtext of all [political] commentary since' – revealed a bankrupt political and economic system. It also removed a heavy burden from the west European Left, which might have expected to reap a political dividend: an important bogey of the Right was finally removed from the scene (Eley, 1992); high military expenditure could no longer be justified by the Cold War; and most importantly, the revolutions of 1989 marked the end not just of a seventy-year challenge to capitalism as an economic system and liberal democracy as a political order but to the reformist orthodoxy predominant on the west and north European Left. In fact, the weakness and final collapse of communism during the 1980s was coterminous with the virtually universal recognition on the west European Left that the assumptions of *its* post-war settlement – the broadly social democratic admixture of Keynesian demand management, universal public services, and a mixed economy of public and private sectors – were an incomplete basis on which to address the social, economic, environmental and political challenges of the 1990s. This is the core issue: the Left needs a radical and new identity if it is to do more than rail against the (many) injustices of the present, and provide realistic hope of change in the future. It is the purpose of this book to contribute to the development of that identity.

In the post-war period, the Left in western Europe and Scandinavia constructed a model for social analysis, and a compelling prescription for social change, on the basis of an understanding of the nation-state as a political community, the working class as a political movement, and the state as a political agency. Today, however, the primary site of political power, the nation, has seen its autonomy reduced by the globalization of economic decision making, and the parallel decentralization of industrial organization – the 'double shift' of advanced capitalism. As Daniel Bell has put it, the national level is indeed too small for the big problems – control of currency speculation, environmental protection, defence and security – and too big for the small problems, from regional development to public service delivery. Similarly, the core of socialist and social democratic support in the industrial working class has shrunk, and the class map of industrial societies has become increasingly complicated. Finally, the state machine itself – in its Fabian form in the UK, in its *dirigiste* French incarnation, in its steerage role in the social market economies, or in its role as a partner in corporatist concertation in Scandinavia and the Low Countries – has itself become a source of frustration, as a result of either failure or impotence. 'Government failure' is now, after more than a decade of neo-liberal hegemony, as potent a slogan as 'market failure' in the lexicon of modern politics.

The result is that thirty-five years after Anthony Crosland (1956) argued in *The Future of Socialism* that Britain had become a post-capitalist society, it is today more usual to hear talk of 'post-socialism'.[3] Crosland's confident assertion that the British Conservative Party lacked 'the essential attribute of a counter-revolutionary party – a faith, a dogma, even a theory' (1956: 27) has been more often applied to the European Left. In the 1980s, the Left, rather than the Right, appeared unable to cope with social and economic change, and was deprived of ideological confidence and political office. Today, however, after a decade of experiment, the remedies of the Right have rapidly diminishing appeal.

A crisis of anti-politics?

The intellectual and ideological assault on the institutions of the post-war settlement has been led by the revived neo-liberalism of the New Right. In the 1970s, the theories of Hayek and Friedman were used to diagnose economic failure in 'government overload'; in the 1980s, they were used to prescribe a regime of privatization and deregulation. This highly political credo is, ironically, the quintessence of anti-politics. Employment policy in the New Right design is reduced to freeing up the labour market to the play of market forces. Economic policy involves bearing down on inflation, and letting the market do the rest. Industry policy is anathema, energy policy a contradiction in terms.

Today, however, New Right certainties strain the credulity even of true believers. Pounded by the accumulated weight of up to fifteen years' evidence, the claims of neo-liberal intellectuals and politicians seem not just implausible but dangerous. In Britain, the neo-liberal record is miserable. Growth has slowed rather than quickened. The tax burden has risen, instead of fallen. Dependency on state benefits has increased, rather than the opposite. Personal security has declined, as crime has soared. And the state has become more repressive and centralized, rather than less. Partly as a consequence, the neo-liberal project which revived conservatism in the 1970s is now causing warfare within conservative ranks. John Gray has written a 'radical critique of neo-liberalism from the standpoint which I believe to be that of traditional conservatism' (Gray, 1993: x). The *Economist* magazine has rediscovered market failure and the virtues of active government.[4] The head of the Health and Welfare Unit of the Institute of Economic Affairs has written that the social policies of the Thatcher years were 'dominated by a hard-boiled economic rationalism which failed to do justice to human character and potential' (Green, 1993: viii). And people who see themselves as genuine conservatives are waking up to the dangers posed by the neo-liberal agenda. Nevil Johnson (1992) poses the same question asked by Benjamin Disraeli in the second half of the nineteenth century, namely 'what will you conserve?'. The answer he finds is that 'there may no longer be any substantial social or moral foundation for a body of practice and thought that can realistically be designated "conservative".'

Of course, the ebb and flow between more or less liberalized forms of capitalist organization is not new. Schumpeter, Keynes and Polanyi all argued fifty years ago that unfettered market rule will corrode precisely the values and institutions on which the social order rests.[5] To borrow from Norberto Bobbio, nothing risks killing off capitalism more effectively than an excess of capitalism.[6] The increasingly obvious reality is that 'anti-politics' is a dead end: the problems besetting the advanced capitalist world, from familiar economic maladies to new social and ethical concerns, are not capable of resolution by the power of market forces and deregulation, and demand settlement through the political and collective realm. The task for the Left is in this context less to show that reform is necessary than that it is possible. That is why this book takes very seriously the challenge not just of proposing new ways of organizing and regulating society and economy, but also of showing that such interventions can be successful.

What Jurgen Habermas (1990) has called a 'fallibilist consciousness' permeates the volume. The uncertainty and complexity that define modern social and economic relations are a constant refrain in the chapters that follow. The globalization of economic competition, the customization of production, the revolution in the life-chances of women, or the demands for a new political settlement between governors and governed are not straightforward, either in their meaning or in their implication. But rather than abandon politics in the face of new demands on its traditional structures and ideologies, the authors of the essays in this book assert the need for its reinvigoration. Instead of proclaiming the redundancy of the political sphere, we stress not just its legitimacy but its increasing necessity. What is, however, beyond doubt is that we need a new model of political change. The certainties of what Anthony Giddens calls here the 'cybernetic model' – the model of directive control that characterized not just communism, but also various forms of top-down Fabianism – have little purchase today.[7] This kind of 'scientific' social and economic engineering is neither feasible nor desirable. But equally all is not chaos, unknowable and incomprehensible. We do live in societies whose organizing structures can be discerned, whose similarities and differences can be understood, and whose relations of power are amenable to social analysis; understanding the world is the basis for changing it.

The foundations for the analytical work pursued throughout the book are laid in chapter 1. Anthony Giddens argues that three interconnected processes – globalization, detraditionalization, and social reflexivity – are transforming everyday life, and above all inducing a quantum change and increase in risk and uncertainty. Globalization refers to what he calls 'action at distance' – the global and rapid effects of single decisions, from interest rates to nuclear safety. Detraditionalization refers not to the end of tradition, but the demand that it be justified – evidenced in the British case by the debate about the monarchy, or the thoroughgoing challenge to traditional assumptions about the role of women in society. Finally, social reflexivity constitutes the growing demand that people make more and better informed decisions for themselves, about everything from education to pensions.

It is important in this context to draw a distinction between what might be called 'blueprint politics' and what Giddens calls 'generative politics', one the politics of end-states, the other the politics of process. The politics of end-states is an essentially static conception in which political competition is defined by competing blueprints for the future. For a long time, socialists have stood squarely in this tradition. From Robert Owen to the Webbs, reformers dedicated themselves to the design of what a socialist society would look like. Today, market socialists are engaged in debate about whether an economy without private ownership but driven by market allocation would be both efficient and just. However, the politics of end-states, which envisages socialism as an end and not a process, or rather views socialism as the end of a process, too often ignores the realities of life today, and the mechanisms for changing it. This is not just intellectually incredible, but politically undesirable. As Brian Barry puts it: 'It is, precisely, the objection to all utopias that they leave no room for any human creativity except that of their inventor. The only worthwhile utopia is an open-ended one' (Barry, 1993: 2). The essays in this volume put their faith in the politics of a constant and continuing reapplication of a set of values to changing circumstance. Generative politics is above all committed to the creation, development and sustenance of economic opportunities and social commitments in the context of the plural reality in which we live. It is based on the view that the need for the Left is evidenced every day in the manifest failure of the advanced capitalist world to come to terms with the challenges of economic, social and environmental change, and it is from its analysis and engagement with these failings that the Left must derive its identity.

The chapters which follow try to give substantive meaning to this commitment by addressing the pressing problems that face advanced industrialized societies, and tackling some of the weaknesses of traditional approaches on the Left to their reform. Four themes dominate the book. The first is the view that the Left's traditional emphasis on the value of equality and solidarity needs to be supplemented by renewed commitment to the extension of personal autonomy in an increasingly interdependent world. The Right has made hay by arguing that equality means uniformity, but it is the development of a coherent understanding of the relationship between equality and diversity that is attempted here. Second, the authors are united in their view that it will be through an integration of public action and market decisions, rather than their counterposition, that the social interest will be best secured. The role of politics is not to abolish markets, but to organize and regulate them. Third, there is here an insistence that while conflicts at the workplace are a central feature of capitalist societies, politics is defined by relations of power beyond the labour process as well as within it, and the Left must reflect them in its practice. Finally, there is common recognition of the need to overcome traditional modes of political organization both within and beyond the nation-state. The value of politics lies in the process as well as the result; democracy is an end in itself, as well as a means to an end.

Each chapter is followed by a shorter 'comment'. The purpose of these contributions is not to deconstruct the argument of the chapter, but instead to take forward some of its ideas, as well as to introduce new (though related) ones. The comments therefore stand in their own right, though they will be most profitably read in conjunction with the main chapter.

The politics of autonomy

For over a hundred years, the objects of attack for the project of social and economic reform have been the same – privilege, inequality, unaccountable power, unregulated markets. The Left exists today, and needs to exist, because advanced industrialized societies are corrupted in fundamental ways by inequalities of income, opportunity and perhaps above all power. These inequalities are not accidental by-products of economic and social relations, but are integral to them. David Held's essay is important because it argues that an attack on illegitimate asymmetries of power and opportunity must be the central ambition of the Left. Held places at the centre of political debate the autonomy and life-chances of citizens, in his words the demand that 'they should be free and equal in the determination of the conditions of their own lives'. It is this emancipatory credo that generates the moral power of progressive politics, for the reality is that autonomy is structured through power.

Personal autonomy is not the same as personal autarky: it is based on a recognition that the growth of personal independence is matched by an increase in social interdependence. It is the relationship – or to use an old phrase, the dialectic – between individual and society that is of concern here. In capitalist societies, scarred by unequal relations of power, the demand for equal autonomy is clearly in various ways and to different degrees not met, whether at work, in the community or in the home. Crucially, Held says that to argue for the democratic right of all citizens to determine the course of their own lives is to argue against the social practices and institutions which determine the distribution of power at present, and for the just allocation of power and authority in and across the key sites of power. As he puts it, the basis of a substantive and enduring settlement between freedom and equality, and therefore the establishment of democratic autonomy, depends on the creation of equal participative opportunities, rather than on the achievement of strict equality *per se*. Held argues that the development of political, civil, social and economic rights represents an enabling condition for political participation; whether or not a rights-based strategy is sufficient, his analysis goes to the heart of a modern definition of the Left's project.

In chapter 3, Elizabeth Meehan pursues one of Held's themes, and argues that political equality cannot be understood, as it has been by some sections of the Left in the past, as a by-product of socioeconomic equality. In fact, socioeconomic change depends on political activity – it cannot be handed down to passive citizens by a benevolent state, but instead hinges on political participation. Fair and legitimate conclusions depend not only on the outcome, but also on the procedure by which they are decided. Meehan calls for an 'active pluralism' as the only way to reconcile the competing rights of individuals in the communities in which they live. She argues that the state exercises its functions in a context of radically unequal access to power, and thus 'active pluralism' demands that the state takes special responsibility to include in decision making marginalized groups. Only in this way can it ensure the precondition of a viable polity, namely a popular recognition that while citizens will not always get what they want from the political process, everyone believes participation to be fair and worthwhile.

Tariq Modood takes the argument about equality and difference a stage further, and examines how racial and religious difference and discrimination interact with more generalized social and economic inequality. He examines the challenge posed by multiracialism and multiculturalism to traditional definitions of egalitarian politics, and therefore links back to David Held's argument about the connection between different sites of power. Modood argues that racial discrimination is linked to other forms of disadvantage, that it is experienced in different forms by different groups, and that some groups and individuals prosper despite discrimination. These dimensions of discrimination and its effects pose difficult questions for traditional views of racial equality. Modood argues that while 'colour-racism' – the division between black and white – is the most commonly understood form of prejudice and the foundation of racial discrimination, it is not the whole story. He advances in an original way the challenging thesis that differences between groups within the 'black' community can be as significant as divisions between black and white, and that forms of racism targeted on particular ethnic minority groups (what he calls 'cultural racism') demand special attention. Modood concludes that programmes to eliminate racial disadvantage and extend equality must be both more general (linked to attacks on class inequality, for example) and more specific (recognizing differences within the 'black' community) than existing conceptions of 'colour-racism' allow.

The politics of economics

Where do these demands for autonomy leave the Left's commitment to collective and communal values? This is Gordon Brown's concern in chapter 5. His is the search for a diverse yet egalitarian socialist individualism. The Left has never gained the mass of its support on the basis of altruism, or what it promised to do for others; it has won elections when its programmes have combined the promise of improvement in personal circumstance with the prospect of collective progress.

Brown's essay applies in a radical way the hundred-year socialist commitment to the emancipation of individual potential. He argues that an unselfish individualism can be derived from a commitment to the equal right of all citizens to develop their talents to the full, and that a broad and pluralist notion of community can be rescued from the straitjacket of state control. In a new settlement between the individual, the market and the state, Brown argues that by attacking unaccountable concentrations of power, developing a thoroughgoing economic egalitarianism at the workplace, decentralizing power to reinvent government and integrating economic and social policy to build routes for social mobility, the Left can regain the political high ground. Brown draws four conclusions: that the Left must both rethink the ways in which it extends social control of the economy and at the same look beyond the productive economy to emancipate individual potential; that public ownership is not the only way to establish the public interest; that while the existence of markets is not antithetical to the public interest, the challenge is to ensure that markets do work in the public interest; and that the individual must have rights against all vested interests, public and private.

After a decade in which the imperialism of the economic realm has been all-conquering, the second substantive theme of the book therefore concerns the reassertion of the primacy of the political and the institutional spheres not only as the guardians of the public interest, but as the guarantors of economic prosperity. Social institutions and regulations are the traffic lights and traffic laws on the roads of modern economies; without them, the system would collapse. The essays in chapters 5, 6 and 7 emphasize that in contrast to the traditional debate about the boundaries of politics and economics, and the contest between them, there is an increasing interdependence of the two, and it is to the politics *of* economics that we must turn our attention.[8]

Capitalist societies are not of a piece, whatever their common features, and it is the differences that are as instructive as the similarities (Esping-Andersen, 1990; Albert, 1992). There is therefore acceptance throughout the book of the role of markets in allocation and production, but an insistence that they are social institutions, subject to social regulation and the demands of the social interest. The notion of a 'free market' is a contradiction in terms. Markets and market economies are political, in the broadest sense. They are shaped by political rules and collective institutions. European and east Asian experience show that it is nonsense to argue that government is always part of the problem, and never part of the solution. The debate we seek to take forward is about what that social interest is, and how it can be furthered.

It would be foolish, however, not to recognize that the economic context for the assertion of the social interest through politics has radically changed over the last fifty years. Changes in the international political economy have called into question the very promise of national economic change in an egalitarian direction. Fritz Scharpf (1991: 274) has argued in his powerful book on the trajectory of post-war social democracy: 'Unlike the situation in the first three post-war decades, there is now no economically plausible Keynesian strategy that would permit the full realisation of social democratic goals within a national context without violating the functional imperatives of a capitalist economy.' Joel Rogers and Wolfgang Streeck take on this argument head on. They agree that while national demand management is no longer the lever for full employment and equity, there exists a post-Keynesian equivalent of effective demand on the supply side. They say that while in a capitalist society the Left must stand against market diktat, it must if it is to secure power and achieve social reform contribute to the growth of productive capacity. In other words, it must seek to establish an egalitarian economic contract – an egalitarian productivism – in which direction of the economy in the social interest is achieved through the public institutions and regulations that structure the economic performance of firms.

Streeck and Rogers argue that the Left cannot concern itself exclusively with the redistribution of the proceeds of economic growth, but must involve itself in the processes of wealth generation themselves. They say that in an economic world of decentralization and specialization, coordination and cooperation are at a premium. As informal contacts grow within and between firms, so trust becomes crucial. In other words, modern capitalism needs a social infrastructure of collective goods, from shared norms about reward for contribution to cooperative research and development, that free markets cannot generate. The public good of training, which boosts economic efficiency and social justice, is an obvious example, but not the only one. Institutions for technology diffusion and joint marketing fall into the same category. But these institutions, which constrain and shape the economy, must themselves be constrained and shaped by democracy itself; within the firm, Streeck and Rogers argue that works councils are one route to greater equity and productivity.

In chapter 7, Michel Rocard takes forward the debate about how best to insert longstanding progressive values in the fast-changing context of the global marketplace. Rocard's analysis is sombre, but his long-term scope ambitious. He says Europe is engaged in a 'civilization contest', based on its values of human rights and social protection. He links central economic concerns to questions of human need, power and democracy, and thereby introduces the third theme of the book, namely that the Left's historic commitment to the economic reform and transformation of capitalist societies cannot be divorced from a commitment to wider social and environmental change, a broader practice than that encapsulated in the relationship between capital and labour. In other words, the Left must pursue not just a class 'settlement', but a new relationship between men and women, and an ecological contract between generations too. This is the politics of citizenship – civil, political and social citizenship in Marshall's famous troika – taken to its logical conclusion. The ambition of the Left is in this design better summarized as the 'free association of citizens' than the 'free association of the producers'.

Politics beyond economics

The work of Gøsta Esping-Andersen has made new links between the labour market, the welfare state and the family; each is dependent for its effective functioning on the others. Esping-Andersen has schematized in a new way half a century of social and economic policy, and in the process laid open some of the most fundamental relationships of social and economic life. His essay in this volume takes forward a central tenet of his work, namely that decisions about the welfare state are crucial for families, and that attitudes towards the family, and the gender division of labour in particular, are crucial for the welfare state. Just as the high point of European social democracy has been linked to the apogee of Fordism in the economic sphere, so it traded on a traditional family model, and above all unpaid female labour, in the social sphere. This has to change. As Ulrich Beck (1992: 109) has put it: 'The equalisation of men and women cannot be created in institutional structures that presuppose their inequality.'

A central dilemma facing the welfare state today concerns the costs of socializing these caring functions. Whether in the public or private sector, it is expensive to start paying for services that have traditionally been performed at home and without payment. Perhaps more important, the links between work and welfare are becoming stronger than ever. As Esping-Andersen points out, whereas the post-war welfare state was socially active when people were economically passive – providing child benefits for children, unemployment benefits for the unemployed, pensions for retired people – today the welfare state must be continually active, above all arming people with the skills and capacities to earn a living and achieve social mobility in the labour market. This is a good example of generative politics in action. Esping-Andersen argues that to achieve a new synthesis of equality and full employment, the Left must recognize that the growth of service sector work is not going to be reversed, but that it need not lead to the creation of a new 'service proletariat', mainly consisting of women, in the secondary labour market. If the Left embraces social mobility as the central goal of education and employment policy, entry into a low-status job at the beginning of the life-cycle need not entail a life of low wages and poor conditions. Education, training and skills therefore become a central political focus of egalitarian endeavours, linking together longstanding social goals with pressing economic need. To achieve this vision, however, we also have to reconceptualize the role of the family, and above all the public services and employment policies that allow men and women to strike a new balance between work and family responsibility.

There is, however, a further challenge, which has been skirted for twenty years, and which has sat on the edge of the political mainstream. It goes to the heart of the Left's assumptions about the relationship between economic growth and social change, and challenges its assumptions about the relationship between human beings and nature. It concerns environmental policy, which Stephen Tindale addresses in chapter 9. Tindale argues that social democracy and environmentalism share a number of analytic concepts and policy tools, from commitments to cooperation and collective action to the use of planning and the regulation of markets. However, he argues that there must be a major shift in social democratic thinking if it is to rise to the challenge of sustainable development – the combination of environmental protection and social justice. The search for equity between generations is not the same as equity within generations; in three areas, energy, transport and trade, he discusses the challenges and opportunities of a commitment to combine equity, sustainability and democracy. Political ecology does demand sacrifice, but it is not only an altruistic credo, and should therefore be a new intellectual as well as electoral asset for the Left.

The injunction of environmental politics to 'think global, act local' reflects a widespread sense that political action beyond the local scale is very difficult to organize. Any agenda for the repoliticization, in a broad sense, of the economic sphere, never mind one as ambitious as that described in parts of this book, is a big challenge to the capacity of government. Two particular issues are considered in chapters 10 and 11: first, the issue of political organization beyond the nation-state, and second, the role of parties as agencies for the articulation of the interests and concerns of citizens. We thereby come, with almost the last chapters of this book, full circle, to the organizational and ideological renewal of the Left, and therefore the renewal of politics itself.

Reinventing politics

Politics and political institutions are at their weakest at the international level, precisely where capital is at its strongest, and it is the implications of international economic and social interdependence that are addressed by David Marquand. Specifically, he examines the regime of free trade and the single market that has driven the process of European integration for forty years, and its ramifications for the sort of social democratic strategy discussed by Joel Rogers and Wolfgang Streeck. The danger is that while the power of social democracy as a national project is compromised by economic interdependence, international political institutions are too weak for an effective supranational social democratic strategy. In the European Union, institution building and politics have for forty years taken second place to a functionalist economic logic in which the single market was assumed to lead inexorably to a single currency and finally political union. Today, however, the EU faces a political and economic impasse. Political questions of the identity of Europe, its territory, and its purpose are unresolved, and the centripetal tendencies of unregulated markets, tendencies which reinforce economic divergence and division, threaten to make monetary union impossible.

Marquand advances the case for a sharp break from the logic of European development that has prevailed since the Treaty of Rome, and argues that the political 'cart' must now come before the economic 'horse' in the construction of a viable and secure European space. Economic institutions will not solve political questions; this is the weakness of the functionalist rationale for European cooperation and development. Unless political questions are addressed first, and for Marquand they point to a federalist project to counter the dangers of economic and social divergence, '*Europe des patries*' will collapse under the weight of social dumping and cut-throat competition.

Manuel Escudero's chapter takes a different tack; he tackles the question of agency. The traditional source of working-class strength, in the trade union movement, has been under sustained attack, and political parties are subject to cynicism and sometimes opprobrium for their ossification and in some cases corruption. The framework for Escudero's examination of the nature and renewal of party organization is the new cultural context for political debate. All the evidence suggests that the political messenger can corrupt the political message, as well as fail to convey it. In Britain, the values of the Labour Party remain, according to reputable surveys of public opinion, popular (SCPR, 1993; Swift et al., 1992), but the party has had little credibility as a vehicle for the realization of those values. Escudero argues that there is a disjunction between the culture of politics and the culture of society at large. He says that contrary to some interpretations, this culture is not by definition right-wing, but it does require the renovation of traditional politics. The new imperatives are for pluralism, flexibility and above all a commitment to the radical extension of democracy. The organizational forms of the twentieth century are inadequate to what Escudero describes as a world of fragmentation.

Escudero prescribes four key principles for the reinvigoration of political parties. They attack the age-old problems of organizational oligarchy and hierarchy. Escudero argues for the extension of citizen control, through open primaries, the organized circulation of elites, through a system of mandatory re-election, the deepening of a democratic political culture, through financial transparency and scrutiny, and the organization of parties as 'parties of rights', vesting members with substantive power. Political parties remain, for all their limitations, potent vehicles for political change, and their organizational reform as well as ideological renewal is an important aspect of renewal on the Left.

This takes us back to the starting point of this introduction: that the widely diagnosed 'crisis of politics' is not confined to technical problems of organization, but revolves around the ideological question of the identity of the Left, and its renewal. In chapter 12, James Cornford and Patricia Hewitt suggest 'ten commandments' to guide the process; the propositions speak for themselves, but there is a further issue that needs to be addressed in this Introduction. It concerns the very title of this book, and the very notion of 'the Left'.

Reinventing the Left

John Stuart Mill wrote more than a century ago that 'ideas, unless outward circumstances conspire with them, have in general no very rapid or immediate efficacy in human affairs' (Hall, 1989: 390). But ideas do matter in politics, for both analysis and prescription, and there is at the moment a sustained attack on the idea that the Left stands for anything any more, and on the conviction that the terms Left and Right have any meaning in modern politics. These attacks share a common root, namely an insistence that the project of the Left – an emancipating. egalitarian and universalist project – was a product of a particular historical epoch that has in the advanced industrial economies come to an end. This is a very serious charge.

There are broadly two ways of thinking about the definition of the 'Left'. One is relative, where the Left exists in relation to the prevailing political centre of gravity. Ben Pimlott has argued that 'the Left' is an inherently 'positional concept'. 'Leftness is an expression in political geography', he writes (Pimlott, 1988: 80). Various ideologies and positions have over time been identified with the Left, from socialism to citizenship to democracy. Thus, Pimlott points out that as late as 1933, the *Oxford English Dictionary* defined the Left as 'those holding relatively liberal or democratic opinions'. In the positional sense, there will always be a Left, but the term also has a more definitive meaning, in the twentieth century associated with communist, socialist and social democratic movements, some of whose practices, the first most obviously, have been deformations of the values that the Left seeks to uphold. It is in both the positional and definitive sense that people argue for the 'end' of the politics of Left and Right. In this book, it is both positional and definitional reinvention that is attempted. The chapters which follow refute various definitions of the Left – the Left as statists, the Left as economic determinists, the Left as representatives solely of industrial workers. In this sense, the traditional definitions of Left and Right – set by counterpositions of market and state, individual and collective, public and private sphere – are superseded. But the essays in this book all seek to give modern relevance to old values. These values have inherent in them an ambition to change in fundamental ways advanced capitalist societies, whose inequalities of power and opportunity in the name of market rule provide not just the moral but the social and economic reason for the existence of a 'Left'.

None of the authors of the essays in this volume believes that this project can be achieved by revolutionary upheaval, but they do believe in social and economic reform. The Left retains its distinctive place in politics today not because of its utopian vision of the future, but by virtue, first, of its critique of the present,[9] in other words its analysis of advanced industrialized societies, and second its ambition progressively to achieve change. While there is an immediate argument within politics about the sorts of capitalist society – regulated and humanized, or deregulated and Hobbesian – we want to live in, there remain ambitions fundamentally to realign the economic and social order. In this context, to reinvent the Left is to give its practice a cutting edge that the old formulas no longer possess, and to make possible radical changes that are badly needed.

Notes

1 The 'evils of transition', as Keynes put it, place a heavy burden on any proposals for change. See Skidelsky (1992: 62).
2 For an examination of the strains between class and gender-based political strategies in Sweden, see Jenson and Mahon (1993).
3 Peter Drucker's *Post-Capitalist Society* is an exception.
4 Its editorial column (12 September 1992) has made 'the case for central planning', and called for 'an intelligent alliance of state and market . . . governments must take charge . . . never seeking to shirk their responsibility as chief executive'.
5 Robert Heilbroner (1993: 127) recalls Schumpeter's comment that 'Capitalism creates a rational frame of mind which, having destroyed the moral authority of so many other institutions, in the end turns against its own . . . the rationalist attitude does not stop at the credentials of kings and popes, but goes on to attack private property and the whole scheme of bourgeois values.'
6 Bobbio said this of democracy. See Bobbio (1987: 31).
7 It is sobering in this context to read in Nigel Swain's account of the Hungarian attempt at market socialism of economic inefficiency on a grand scale, and monopoly producers subject to neither financial nor democratic restraints (Swain, 1992: 226).
8 I am grateful to Anton Hemerijck for this formulation.
9 Eric Hobsbawm (1992: 63) has argued that 'the difference between liberals and socialists today is not about socialism but about capitalism.'

References

Albert, M. 1992: *Capitalism Against Capitalism*. London: Whurr.
Barry, B. 1993: Justice, freedom and basic income. Unpublished paper presented to Fabian Society Socialist Philosophy Group, 30 October.
Beck, U. 1992: *Risk Society: towards a new modernity*. London: Sage.
Bobbio, N. 1987: *The Future of Democracy*. Cambridge: Polity Press.
Crosland, A. 1956: *The Future of Socialism*. London: Faber.
Drucker, P. 1993: *Post-Capitalist Society*. Oxford: Butterworth-Heinemann.
Dunn, J. 1993: *Western Political Theory in the Face of the Future*. Cambridge: Cambridge University Press.
Eley, G. 1992: Reviewing the socialist tradition. In C. Lemke and G. Marks (eds),*The Crisis of Socialism in Europe*, London: Duke University Press.
Esping-Andersen, G. 1990: *The Three Worlds of Welfare Capitalism*. Cambridge: Polity Press.
Gray, J. 1993: *Beyond the New Right*. London: Routledge.

Green, D. 1993: *Reinventing Civil Society: the rediscovery of welfare without politics*. London: IEA.

Habermas, J. 1990: What does socialism mean today? *New Left Review*, 183 (Sept./Oct.), 3–21.

Hall, P. 1989: Conclusion. In P. Hall (ed.), *The Political Power of Economic Ideas: Keynesianism across nations*, Princeton, NJ: Princeton University Press.

Heilbroner, R. 1993: *21st Century Capitalism*. New York: Norton.

Hitchens, C. 1993: *For the Sake of Argument*. London: Verso.

Hobsbawm, E. 1992: The crisis of today's ideologies'. *New Left Review*, 192 (Mar./Apr.), 55–64.

Jenson, J. and Mahon, R. 1993: Representing solidarity: class, gender and the crisis in social democratic Sweden. *New Left Review*, 201 (Sept./Oct.), 76–100.

Johnson, N. 1992: What will you conserve? *Times Literary Supplement*, 9 October, 10.

Pimlott, B. 1988: The future of the Left. In R. Skidelsky (ed.), *Thatcherism*, London: Chatto and Windus.

Scharpf, F. 1991: *Crisis and Choice in European Social Democracy*. Ithaca, NY: Cornell University Press.

SCPR 1993:*British Social Attitudes: the Cumulative Sourcebook*. Aldershot: Gower.

Skidelsky, R. 1992: *John Maynard Keynes: the economist as saviour 1920–1937*. London: Macmillan.

Swain, N. 1992: *Hungary: the rise and fall of feasible socialism*. London: Verso.

Swift, A., Marshall, G. and Burgoyne, C. 1992: Which road to social justice? *Sociology Review* (November), 28–31.

Part I

The Context: Understanding the Present

1 Brave New World: The New Context of Politics

Anthony Giddens

My theme is a world that has taken us by surprise. The world of the late twentieth century has not turned out in the way the thinkers of the Enlightenment anticipated when they sought to give direction to history by overcoming the influence of tradition and dogma. They believed, reasonably enough, that the more, as collective humanity, we got to know about social and material reality, the more we would be able to control them in our own interests. In the case of social life in particular, human beings could become not just the authors, but the masters, of their own destiny.

Yet events have not borne out this idea. The world in which we live today is not one subject to tight human control – the stuff of the ambitions of the Left and, one could say, the nightmares of the Right. Almost to the contrary, it is one of dislocation and uncertainty, a 'runaway world'. And, disturbingly, what was supposed to create greater and greater certainty – the advance of human knowledge and intervention – is actually deeply involved with this unpredictability. Examples abound. Consider, for instance, the debate about global warming, which concerns the possible effects of human activities upon climatic change. Is global warming happening, or is it not? Probably the majority of scientists agree that it is; but there are others who question either the very existence of the phenomenon or the theory advanced to account for it. If global warming is indeed taking place, its consequences are difficult to assess and problematic – for it is something which has no real precedents.

The uncertainties thus created I shall refer to generically as *manufactured uncertainty*. Life has always been a risky business. The intrusion of manufactured uncertainty into our lives does not mean that our existence, on an individual or collective level, is more risky than it used to be. Rather, the sources, and the scope, of risk have altered (Beck, 1992).

Manufactured risk is a result *of* human intervention into nature and into the conditions of social life. The uncertainties (and opportunities) it creates are largely new. They cannot be dealt with by age-old remedies; but neither do they respond to the Enlightenment prescription: more knowledge, more control. Put more accurately, the sorts of reaction we might make to them today are often as much about 'damage control' and 'repair' as about an endless process of increasing mastery.

The advance of manufactured uncertainty is the outcome of the long-term development of modern institutions; but it has also *accelerated* as the result of a series of changes that have transformed society (and nature) over the past four or five decades. Pinpointing these changes is essential if we are to grasp the altered context of political life today. Three sets of changes are particularly important; these affect especially the industrialized countries, but are also to some degree world-wide in their impact.

Globalization, tradition, uncertainty

First, there is the influence of intensifying *globalization* – a notion much talked about today, but as yet only poorly understood. Globalization is not only, or even primarily, an economic phenomenon; and it should not be equated with the emergence of a 'world system'. Globalization is really about the transformation of space and time. I would define it as *action at distance*, and relate its growth over recent years to the development of means of instantaneous global communication and mass transportation (Giddens, 1990).

Globalization is not just about the creation of large-scale systems, but about the transformation of contexts of social experience. Our day-to-day activities are increasingly influenced by events happening on the other side of the world; and, conversely, local life-style habits become globally consequential. Thus my decision to buy a certain item of clothing has implications not only for the international division of labour but for the earth's ecosystems.

Globalization should be seen not simply as an 'out there' phenomenon but as an 'in here' one also: it affects not only localities but even intimacies of personal existence, since it acts to transform everyday life. It is not a single process, but a complex mixture of processes, which often act in contradictory ways, producing conflicts, disjunctures and new forms of stratification. Thus, for instance, the emergence of local nationalisms, and an accentuating of local identities, are directly bound up with globalizing influences, to which they stand in opposition.

Second, and partly as a direct result of globalization, we can speak today of the emergence of a *post-traditional social order* (Giddens, 1994). A post-traditional order is not one in which tradition disappears – far from it. It is one in which tradition changes its status. Traditions have to *explain themselves*, to become open to interrogation or discourse. At first sight, such a statement might seem odd. For have modernity and traditions not always been in collision? Was the overcoming of tradition not the main impetus of Enlightenment thought in the first place?

In earlier phases of the development of modern societies, however, the refocusing of tradition played a major part in stabilizing the social order. Grand traditions were invented, or reinvented, such as those of nationalism or of religion. No less important were reconstructed traditions of a more down-to-earth kind, to do with, among other areas of social life, the family, gender and sexuality. Rather than being dissolved, these became re-formed in such a way as to plant women firmly in the home, reinforce divisions between the sexes and stabilize certain 'normal' canons of sexual behaviour. Even science itself, seemingly so wholly opposed to traditional modes of thought, became a sort of tradition. Science, that is, became an 'authority' which could be turned to in a relatively unquestioning way to confront dilemmas or cope with problems.

In a globalizing, culturally cosmopolitan society, traditions become forced into open view: reasons or justifications have to be offered for them. Sometimes this is the result of the active struggles of social movements. Feminism, for instance, problematized femininity, propelling questions of gender and sexuality into the public domain. Maleness for a long while remained unarticulated, part of unspoken gender traditions – but now, of course, the issue of 'what it is to be a man' has become a matter of open debate.

The rise of *fundamentalism* has to be seen against the backdrop of the emergence of the post-traditional society. The term 'fundamentalism' has only come into wide currency quite recently – as late as 1950 there was no entry for the word in the *Oxford English Dictionary*. Here, as elsewhere, the appearance of a new concept signals the emergence of new social forces. What is fundamentalism? It is, so I shall argue, nothing other than *tradition defended in the traditional way* – but where that mode of defence has become widely called into question. The point about traditions is that you do not really have to justify them: they contain their own truth, a ritual truth, asserted as correct by the believer. In a globally cosmopolitan order, however, such a defence becomes dangerous, because essentially it is a refusal of dialogue. Fundamentalism tends to accentuate the 'purity' of a given set of doctrines, not because it wishes to set them off from other traditions, but because it is a rejection of a model of truth linked to the dialogic engagement of ideas in a public space. It is dangerous because it is edged with a potential for violence. Fundamentalisms can arise in all domains of social life where tradition becomes something which has to be *decided about* rather than just taken for granted. There arise fundamentalisms not only of religion, but of ethnicity, the family and gender, among others.

The transformation of tradition in the present day is closely linked to the transformation of nature. Tradition and nature used to be, as it were, relatively fixed 'landscapes' structuring social activity. The dissolution of tradition (understood in the traditional way) interlaces with the disappearance of nature – where 'nature' refers to environments and events given independently of human action. Manufactured uncertainty intrudes into all the arenas of life thus opened up to decision making. Consider, for example, reproduction. For many women, life used to be a more or less chronic round of pregnancy, childbirth and childcare. It was changes in tradition that first of all altered this situation. With the coming of small families, having a child became more of a distinct 'decision' than it was before, and 'sexuality' began to become detached from reproduction. The introduction of new reproductive technologies, however, further changed the pre-given 'landscape' – for now it is possible even to reproduce without any sexual contacts at all.

The third basic change affecting contemporary societies is the expansion of *social reflexivity*. In a detraditionalizing society the individual must become used to filtering all sorts of information relevant to his or her life situation, and routinely acts on the basis of that filtering process. Take the decision to get married. Such a decision has to be made in relation to an awareness that the nature of marriage has changed in basic ways over the past few decades, that sexual habits and identities have changed too, and that women demand more autonomy in their lives than ever before. Such knowledge, moreover, is not just knowledge about an independent social reality; as applied in action it influences what that reality actually *is*. The growth of social reflexivity is a major factor introducing a dislocation between knowledge and control – a prime source of manufactured uncertainty.

A world of intensified reflexivity is a world of clever people. I do not mean by this that people are more intelligent than they used to be. In a post-traditional order, individuals more or less have to engage with the wider world if they are to survive in it. Information produced by specialists (including scientific knowledge) can no longer be wholly confined to specific groups, but becomes routinely interpreted and acted upon by lay individuals in the course of their everyday actions.

The development of social reflexivity is the key influence upon a diversity of changes that otherwise seem to have little in common with one another. Thus the emergence of 'post-Fordism' in industrial enterprises is commonly analysed in terms of technological change – particularly the influence of information technology. But a prime reason for the growth of 'flexible production' and 'bottom-up decision making' is that a universe of high reflexivity leads to greater autonomy of action, which the enterprise must recognize and draw upon.

The same applies to bureaucracy and to the sphere of politics. Bureaucratic authority, as Max Weber made clear, used to be the condition of organizational effectiveness. In a more reflexively ordered society, operating in the context of manufactured uncertainty, such is no longer the case. The old bureaucratic systems start to disappear, the dinosaurs of the post-traditional age. In the domain of politics, states can no longer so readily treat their citizens as 'subjects'. Demands for political reconstruction, for the elimination of corruption, as well as widespread disaffection from orthodox political mechanisms, are all in some part expressions of increased social reflexivity.

Socialism, conservatism and neo-liberalism

It is in terms of these changes that we should look to explain why socialism is ailing. In the shape of Soviet communism (in the East) and the Keynesian 'welfare compromise' (in the West), socialism worked tolerably well when most risk was external (rather than manufactured) and where the level of globalization and social reflexivity was relatively low. When these circumstances no longer apply, socialism either collapses or becomes turned onto the defensive – it is certainly not any more in the vanguard of 'history'.

Socialism was based upon what might be called a 'cybernetic model' of social life, one which strongly reflects the Enlightenment outlook mentioned at the beginning. According to the cybernetic model, a system (in the case of socialism, the economy) can best be organized by being subordinated to a directive intelligence (the state, understood in one form or another). But while such a set-up might work reasonably effectively for more coherent systems – in this case a society of low reflexivity, with fairly fixed life-style habits – it does not do so for highly complex ones.

Very complex systems depend upon a large amount of low-level input for their coherence (provided by a multiplicity of local pricing, production and consumption decisions in market situations). The human brain probably also works in such a way. It was once thought that the brain was a cybernetic system, in which the cortex was responsible for integrating the central nervous system as a whole. Current theories, however, emphasize much more the significance of low-level inputs in producing effective neural integration.

The proposition that socialism is in serious difficulties is much less controversial now than it was even a few short years ago. More heterodox, I think, is a second assertion I want to make: that conservatism faces problems of just as profound a kind. How can this be, for has conservatism not triumphed world-wide in the wake of the disintegrating project of socialism? Here, however, we must distinguish conservatism from the Right. What has come to be understood as 'the Right' today is neo-liberalism, whose links with conservatism are at best tenuous. For if conservatism means anything, it means the desire to conserve – and specifically it means the conserving of tradition, as the 'inherited wisdom of the past'. Neo-liberalism is not conservative in this (quite elemental) sense. On the contrary, it sets into play radical processes of change, stimulated by the incessant expansion of markets. Paradoxically, the Right here has turned radical, while the Left seeks mainly to conserve – trying to protect, for example, what remains of the welfare state.

In a post-traditionalist society, the conserving of tradition cannot sustain the sense it once had, as the relatively unreflective preservation of the past. For tradition defended in the traditional way becomes fundamentalism, too dogmatic an outlook on which to base a conservatism which looks to the achievement of social harmony (or 'one nation') as one of its main *raisons d'être*.

Neo-liberalism, on the other hand, becomes internally *contradictory* and this contradiction is increasingly plain to see. On the one hand neo-liberalism is hostile to tradition – and is indeed one of the main forces sweeping away tradition everywhere, as a result of the promotion of market forces and an aggressive individualism. On the other, it *depends upon* the persistence of tradition for its legitimacy and its attachment to conservatism – in the areas of the nation, religion, gender and the family. Having no proper theoretical rationale, its defence of tradition in these areas normally takes the form of fundamentalism. The debate over 'family values' provides a good example. Liberal individualism is supposed to reign in the marketplace – and the purview of markets becomes greatly extended. The wholesale expansion of a market society, however, is a prime force promoting those very disintegrative forces affecting family life which neo-liberalism, wearing its fundamentalist hat, diagnoses and so vigorously opposes. This is an unstable mix indeed (Gray, 1993).

If socialism and conservatism have disintegrated, and neo-liberalism is paradoxical, might one thus turn to 'liberalism' *per se* (capitalism plus liberal democracy, but shorn of New Right fundamentalisms) in the manner, say, of Francis Fukuyama (Fukuyama, 1992)? I do not think so, for reasons which I shall simply state here, but elaborate upon in what follows later. An ever-expanding capitalism runs up not only against environmental limits in terms of the earth's resources, but against the limits of modernity in the shape of manufactured uncertainty; liberal democracy, based upon an electoral party system, operating at the level of the nation-state, is not well equipped to meet the demands of a reflexive citizenry in a globalizing world; and the combination of capitalism and liberal democracy provides only limited means of generating social solidarity.

All this reveals plainly enough the exhaustion of received political ideologies. Should we therefore perhaps accept, as some of the post-modernists say, that Enlightenment has exhausted itself and that we have more or less to take the world as it is, with all its barbarities and limitations? Surely not. Almost the last thing we need now is a sort of 'new medievalism', a confession of impotence in the face of forces larger than ourselves. We live in a radically damaged world, for which radical remedies are needed. There is a very real and difficult issue to be faced, however: the problematic relation between knowledge and control, exemplified by the spread of manufactured risk. Political radicalism can no longer insert itself, as socialism did, in the space between an abandoned past and a humanly made future. But it certainly cannot rest content with neo-liberal radicalism – an abandonment of the past led by the erratic play of market forces. The possibility of, even the necessity for, a radical politics has not died along with all else that has fallen away – but such a politics can only be loosely identified with the usual orientations of the Left. It must cope with a world that has run up against the limits of modernity.

What might be called 'philosophic conservatism' – a philosophy of protection, conservation and solidarity – acquires a new relevance for political radicalism today. The idea of living with imperfection, long a leading emphasis of philosophic conservatism, here might be turned to radical account. A radical political programme – one that takes things by the roots – must recognize that confronting manufactured risk cannot take the form of 'more of the same,' an endless exploration of the future at the cost of the protection of the present or past.

It is surely not accidental that these are exactly the themes of that political force which can lay greatest claim to inherit the mantle of Left radicalism: the green movement. This very claim has helped to obscure the otherwise rather obvious affinities between ecological thinking, including particularly 'deep ecology', and philosophic conservatism. In each case there is an emphasis upon conservation, restoration and repair. Green political theory, however, falls prey to the 'naturalistic fallacy' and is dogged by its own fundamentalisms. In other words, it depends for its proposals upon calling for a reversion to 'nature'. Yet nature no longer exists! We cannot defend nature in the natural way any more than we can defend tradition in the traditional way – yet each quite often *needs* defending.

A framework for radical politics

Our relation to nature – or what is no longer nature – is one among other institutional dimensions of modern society, connected particularly to the impact of industry, science and technology. Although closely bound up with it, the consequences of industrialism can be distinguished from the partly independent influence of capitalism, defined as a competitive market system of economic enterprise, in which goods and labour power are commodities. If the oppositional force of socialism has been blunted, must a capitalistic system reign unchallenged? I do not think so. Unchecked capitalistic markets still have many of the unhappy results to which socialists have long pointed, including the dominance of economic imperatives over all others, universal commodification and the polarization of wealth and income. The critique of these tendencies surely remains as important as it ever was, but today cannot be developed in an effective way from the cybernetic model of socialism.

Political and administrative power does not derive directly from control of the means of production, whatever Marx might have said on the matter. Standing opposed to political authoritarianism is the influence of democracy – the favourite term of the moment, for who is not a democrat now? The question is, however, what exactly we should understand by democracy. For at the very time when liberal democratic systems seem to be spreading everywhere, we find those systems under strain in their very societies of origin.

The problem of democracy, or so I shall argue, is closely bound up with a further dimension of the modern social order: control of the means of violence. The management of violence is not ordinarily part of conventional forms of political theory, whether Left, Right or liberal. Yet where, as in current social conditions, many different cultures are thrust into contact with one another, the clash of fundamentalisms becomes a matter of serious concern.

On the basis of the foregoing comments I want to propose a six-point framework for a reconstituted radical politics, one which draws upon philosophic conservatism but preserves some of the core values hitherto associated with socialist thought. I do not pretend to develop any of these in the detail that would be required either to justify them fully or to flesh out their policy implications.

1 There should be a concern to repair *damaged solidarities*, which may sometimes imply the selective preservation, or even perhaps reinvention, of tradition. This theorem applies at all the levels which link individual actions not just to groups or even to states, but to more globalized systems. It is important not to understand by it the idea of a revival of civil society, now so popular among some sections of the Left. The concept of a 'civil society', lying between the individual and state, for reasons I should not go into here, is a suspect one when applied to current social conditions. Today we should speak more of reordered conditions of individual and collective life, producing forms of social disintegration to be sure, but also offering new bases for generating solidarities.

A starting point here is a proper assessment of the nature of individualism in present-day society. Neo-liberalism places great stress upon the importance of individualism, contrasting this to the discredited 'collectivism' of socialist theory. By 'individualism', however, neo-liberals understand the self-seeking, profit-maximizing behaviour of the marketplace. This is a mistaken way, in my view, of interpreting what should more appropriately be conceived of as the expansion of social reflexivity.

In a world of high reflexivity, an individual must achieve a certain degree of autonomy of action as a condition of being able to survive and forge a life; but autonomy is not the same as egoism and moreover implies reciprocity and interdependence. The issue of reconstructing social solidarities should therefore not be seen as one of protecting social cohesion around the edges of an egoistic marketplace. It should be understood as one of *reconciling autonomy and interdependence* in the various spheres of social life, including the economic domain.

Consider as an illustration the sphere of the family – one of the main arenas in which detraditionalization has proceeded apace. Neo-liberals have quite properly expressed concern about disintegrative tendencies affecting the family, but the notion that there can be a straightforward reversion to 'traditional family values' is a non-starter. For one thing, in the light of recent research we know that family life in early modern times often had a quite pronounced dark side – including the physical and sexual abuse of children, and physical violence by husbands against wives. For another, neither women nor children are likely to renounce the rights that they have won, and which in the case of women also go along with widespread involvement in the paid labour force (Hewitt, 1993).

Since once again there are no real historical precedents, we do not know how far family life can effectively be reconstructed in such a way as to balance autonomy and solidarity. Yet some of the means whereby such an aim might be achieved have become fairly clear. Enhanced solidarity in a detraditionalizing society depends upon what might be termed *active trust*, coupled with a renewal of personal and social *responsibility* for others. Active trust is trust which has to be won, rather than coming from the tenure of pre-established social positions or gender roles. Active trust *presumes* autonomy rather than standing counter to it, and it is a powerful source of social solidarity, since compliance is freely given rather than enforced by traditional constraints.

In the context of family life, active trust involves *commitment* to another or others, that commitment implying also the recognition of obligations to them stretching across time. Strengthening family commitments and obligations, so long as these are based upon active trust, does not seem at all incompatible with the diversity of family forms now being pioneered in all the industrialized societies. High rates of separation and divorce are probably here to stay, but one can see many ways in which these could enrich, rather than destroy, social solidarity. Recognition of the prime importance of the rights of children, together with responsibilities towards them, for instance, could provide the very means of consolidating the new kinship ties we see around us – between, say, two sets of parents who are also step-parents and the children they share. Recombinant families may bring in their train a rich nexus of new kin ties, almost like pre-modern extended kin groups.

2   We should recognize the increasing centrality of what I shall call *life politics* to both formal and less orthodox domains of the political order. The political outlook of the Left has always been closely bound up with the idea of emancipation. Emancipation means freedom, or rather freedoms of various kinds: freedom from the arbitrary hold of tradition, from arbitrary power and from the constraints of material deprivation. Emancipatory politics is a politics of life-chances and hence is central to the creation of autonomy of action. As such it obviously remains vital to a radical political programme. It is joined today, however, by a series of concerns coming from the changes analysed earlier – the transformation of tradition and nature, in the context of a globalizing, cosmopolitan order. Life politics is a politics not of life-chances but of life-style. It concerns disputes and struggles about how (as individuals and as collective humanity) we should live in a world where what used to be fixed by either nature or tradition is now subject to human decisions.

Life politics includes ecological problems and dilemmas, but understands these as linked to wider questions of identity and life-style choice – including some of the key issues raised by feminism. It would be a basic error to see life politics as only a preoccupation of the more affluent. In some respects, in fact, the opposite is true. Some of the poorest groups come up against problems of detraditionalization most sharply. Thus women are leaving marriages in large numbers and seeking to recast their lives – the large majority of marriages in most western countries are now actively broken up by women, a sea change of great significance. Many, however, become part of the 'new poor', especially if they are lone parent heads of households. Cast down economically, they are also called upon to pilot new forms of domestic life and kin relations.

The emergence of life politics helps explain why some types of issue – such as abortion – come to appear so prominently on the political agenda, but life politics also impinges on more 'standard' areas such as work, employment and unemployment. Like so many other areas of social life, work was until quite recently experienced by many as fate. Most men could expect to go out to work at a relatively early stage of their lives and continue to do so until retirement age. For many women, the complementary prospect was confinement to the domestic milieu. Protest against such 'fate' was first of all mostly emancipatory in impulse. This was true of the union movement, dominated by men, which developed most strongly among manual workers, who more than anyone else experienced work as a given set of conditions, offering little autonomy of action. It was also true of earlier forms of feminism.

In current times, even among more deprived groups, neither paid work nor domesticity is usually approached as fate (unemployment, perversely, more often is). There is a wide reflexive awareness that what counts as 'work' is much more broadly defined than it used to be, and that work is a problematic and contested notion. Given changes in the class structure, few people now automatically follow the occupations of their parents or those typical of homogeneous working communities. Even – or perhaps one should say especially – against the background of a shrinking labour market, it becomes clear that there are decisions to be made, and priorities located, not just about trying to get one job rather than another, but about what place work should have as compared to other life values.

3   In conjunction with the generalizing of social reflexivity, active trust implies a conception of *generative politics* which comes to the fore today. Generative politics exists in the space that links the state to reflexive mobilization in the society at large. For reasons already discussed, the state can only to a limited degree function as a cybernetic intelligence. Yet the limitations of neo-liberalism, with its idea of the minimal state, have become very apparent. Generative politics is a politics which seeks to allow individuals and groups to make things happen, rather than have

things happen to them, in the context of overall social concerns and goals.

Generative politics implies:

(a)   seeking to achieve desired outcomes (a phrase that, however, covers a nest of difficult problems) through providing conditions for social mobilization or engagement;

(b)   creating circumstances in which active trust can be built and sustained, whether in the institutions of government as such or in other related agencies;

(c)   according autonomy to those affected by specific programmes or policies, and in fact aiming to develop such autonomy in many contexts;

(d)   encouraging the development of ethical principles of action, rejecting the indifference of (some versions of) socialism to ethics, but also the unhappy neo-liberal marriage of market principles and authoritarianism;

(e)   decentralizing political power: decentralization is the condition of political effectiveness because of the requirement for bottom-up information flow and recognition of autonomy. The push and pull between decentralized power and the political centre, however, is not a zero-sum game. Decentralization can enhance the authority of the centre, either because of political trade-offs or because of the creation of greater legitimacy.

Generative politics is a defence of the politics of the *political domain*, but does not situate itself in the old opposition between state and market. It works through providing material conditions, and organizational frameworks, for the life-political decisions taken by individuals and groups in the wider social order. Such a politics depends upon building active trust both in the institutions of government and in connected agencies. Appearances perhaps to the contrary, generative politics is in the present day the main means of effectively approaching problems of poverty and social exclusion.

Generative politics is not a panacea. The shifting character of the state, and the fact that more or less the whole population lives in the same 'discursive space' as state and government agencies, produce major new political dilemmas and contradictions. For example, where the national polity has become only one among other points of reference for an individual's life, many people might not often 'listen' to what is going on in the political domain, even though they may keep mentally 'in touch' on a more consistent basis than before. 'Tuning out' may express a distaste for the antics of politicians, but may also go along with a specific alertness to questions the person deems consequential. Trust here might mingle with cynicism in an uneasy combination.

4   The shortcomings of liberal democracy, in a globalizing, reflexive social order, suggest the need to further more radical forms of democratization. Here I wish to stress the importance of *dialogic democracy*. Among the many forms and aspects of democracy debated in the literature today, two main dimensions of a democratic order can be distinguished. On the one hand, democracy is a vehicle for the representation of interests. On the other, it is a way of creating a public arena in which controversial issues – in principle – can be resolved, or at least handled, through dialogue rather than through pre-established forms of power. While the first aspect has probably received most attention, the second is at least equally significant.

The extension of dialogic democracy would form one part (although not the only one) of a process of what might be referred to as the *democratizing of democracy*. Where the level of social reflexivity remains quite low, political legitimacy continues to depend in some substantial part upon traditional symbolism and pre-existing ways of doing things. All sorts of patronage and corruption can not only survive but, within the political leadership, become accepted procedure. In a more reflexive order, however – where people are also free to ignore more or less the formal political arena if they so wish – such practices are liable to be called into question.

Greater transparency of government would help the democratizing of democracy, but this is also a phenomenon which extends into areas other than that of the formal political sphere. Outside the arena of the state, it may be suggested, dialogic democracy can be promoted in three main contexts. In the area of personal life – parent-child relations, sexual relations, friendship relations – dialogic democracy advances to the degree to which such relationships are ordered through dialogue rather than through embedded power. What I have elsewhere called a 'democracy of the emotions' (Giddens, 1993) depends upon the integrating of autonomy and solidarity mentioned earlier. It presumes the development of personal relationships in which active trust is mobilized and sustained through discussion and the interchange of views, rather than by arbitrary power of one sort or another.

Thus parents' authority would no longer be a 'given', a fact of life for them and their children alike; it would become more actively negotiated on both sides. To the extent to which it comes into being, a democracy of the emotions would have major implications for the furtherance of formal, public democracy. Individuals who have a good understanding of their own emotional make-up, and who are able to communicate effectively with others on a personal basis, are likely to be well prepared for the wider tasks and responsibilities of citizenship.

Dialogic democracy can also be mobilized through the activities of self-help groups and social movements. Such movements and groups express, but also contribute to, the heightened reflexivity of local and global social activity today. In contemporary societies, far more people belong to self-help groups than are members of political parties. The democratic qualities of social movements and self-help groups come in large part from the fact that they open up spaces for public dialogue in respect of the issues with which they are concerned. They can force into the discursive domain aspects of social conduct that previously went undiscussed, or were 'settled' by traditional practices. They may help contest 'official' definitions of things; feminist, ecological and peace movements have all achieved this outcome, as have a multiplicity of self-help groups.

Some such movements and groups are intrinsically global in scope, and thus might contribute to the wider spread of forms of dialogic democracy. Given that the ideal of a world government is implausible, mechanisms of dialogic democracy operating not just through states and international agencies, but also through a diversity of other groupings, become of central importance. For a long while democratizing influences on a global level were seen in the conventional terms of international relations theory. The international arena was considered as 'above' the level of nation-states. In this conception, democratization would mean the construction of the institutions of liberal democracy writ large. The 'empty' or 'anarchic' areas connecting states, in other words, would have to be filled in. Such an idea has not of course become irrelevant, but looks to be of more restricted importance where globalization and reflexivity are so deeply intertwined. For many globalizing connections do not flow through the nation-state, but in large part bypass it.

5 We should be prepared to *rethink the welfare state* in a fundamental way. In many countries what remains of socialist ideology has become concentrated upon protecting the welfare state against the attacks of the neo-liberals. At least one book has been written invoking philosophic conservatism to defend welfare institutions – as institutions that have a proven track record and have withstood the 'test of time' (Tannsjo, 1990). And indeed there may very well be basic features of the welfare state which should be preserved against the potential ravages of cut-backs or of privatization. In terms of trust and solidarity, for example, welfare provisions or services quite often embody commitments that would

simply be eroded if a more market-led, 'business' orientation were introduced.

Yet the welfare state was formed as a 'class compromise' or 'settlement' in social conditions that have now altered very markedly; and its systems of security were designed to cope more with external than with manufactured risk (Ewald, 1986). Some of the major problematic aspects of the welfare state have by now been identified clearly enough, partly as the result of neo-liberal critiques. The welfare state has been less than wholly effective either in countering poverty or in effecting large-scale income or wealth redistribution. It was tied to an implicit model of traditional gender roles, presuming male participation in the paid labour force, with a 'second tier' of programmes directed towards families without a male breadwinner. Welfare state bureaucracies, like bureaucracies everywhere, have tended to become inflexible and impersonal; and welfare dependency is probably in some part a real phenomenon, not just an invention of neo-liberalism. Finally, the welfare state was consolidated in the post-war period at a point where chronically high levels of unemployment seemed unlikely to return.

The reconstruction of welfare institutions is a complex matter, which I could not pretend to discuss adequately in the space available here. A radical rethink of the welfare state, however, would probably involve disentangling its key components. A new 'settlement' is urgently required today; but this can no longer take the form of a 'top-down' dispensation of benefits. Rather, welfare measures aimed at countering the polarizing effects of what, after all, remains a class society must be empowering rather than merely 'dispensed'. They must be concerned with just that reconstruction of social solidarity mentioned earlier, on the level of the family and that of the wider civic culture. And such a settlement has to be one that gives due attention to gender, not only to class.

Coping with manufactured uncertainty creates a whole new spectrum of problems – and, as always, opportunities – for the reform of welfare. Here one should think of reconstruction along the lines of models of *positive welfare*. The welfare state grew up as a mode of protecting against misfortunes that 'happen' to people – certainly so far as social security is concerned, it essentially picks up the pieces after mishaps have occurred. Positive welfare, by contrast, places much greater emphasis upon the mobilizing of life-political measures, aimed once more at connecting autonomy with personal and collective responsibilities.

An example would be the area of health care, now so deeply caught up in the fiscal dilemmas of the state. Health-care systems are still mostly based upon treating illnesses once they have been contracted. A common reaction of critics of such systems is to advocate giving a greater role to preventative medicine, and no doubt this is right and proper. More far-reaching, however, is the suggestion that we must abandon what has been called the 'biomedical' model of health and illness, in favour of one which places a greater stress upon holism and, more particularly, which connects health to environmental conservation and protection (Hall, 1990). Such an approach would involve a new appreciation of the inter-relation of positive health with the transformation of local and global life-styles. Reducing ecotoxicity, which demands collective action as well as the assumption of new personal responsibilities, would be a health-care measure more profound in its implications than anything attempted in current systems of health provision.

6   A programme of radical politics, for reasons already given, must be prepared to confront *the role of violence* in human affairs. The fact that I have left this question until last does not mean at all that it is the least important. It is, however, one of the most difficult of issues to deal with in terms of received political theory. Neither socialist thought nor liberalism have established perspectives or concepts relevant to producing a normative political theory of violence; while Rightist thought has tended to think of violence as a necessary and endemic feature of human life.

The topic is a big one. The influence of violence, after all, stretches all the way from male violence against women through casual street violence to large-scale war. Are there any threads that connect these various situations and that therefore might be relevant to a theory of pacification? I think there are, and they bring us back to the themes of fundamentalism and dialogic democracy.

In any social circumstances, there are only a limited number of ways in which a clash of values can be dealt with. One is through geographical segregation; individuals of conflicting dispositions, or cultures hostile to one another, can of course coexist if they have little or no direct contact. Another, more active, way is through exit. An individual who, or group which, does not get along with another can simply disengage or move away, as might happen in a divorce.

A third way of coping with individual or cultural difference is through dialogue. Here a clash of values can in principle operate under a positive sign – it can be a means of increased communication and self-understand-ing. Understanding the other better leads to greater understanding of oneself, or one's own culture, leading to further understanding and mutu-ality. Finally, a clash of values can be resolved through the use of force or violence.

In the globalizing society in which we now live, the first two of these four options become drastically reduced. No culture, state or large group can with much success isolate itself from the global cosmopolitan order; and while exit may be possible, in some situations, for individuals, it is not available to larger social entities.

The relation between dialogue and violence, strung out along the edge of possible fundamentalisms, thus becomes particularly acute and tense for us today. This reduction of options is dangerous, but it also offers sources of hope. For we know that dialogue can sometimes replace violence, and we know that this can happen both in situations of personal life and in much larger social settings. The 'gender fundamentalism' that violent men sustain towards their partners, and perhaps towards women in general, can at least in individual cases be transformed through greater self-understanding and communication. Dialogue between cultural groups and states is both a force acting directly against fundamentalist doctrines and a means of substituting talk for the use of military power.

The dark side is obvious. Violence plainly often stems from clashes of interest, and joustings for power; hence there are many quite strictly material conditions which would have to be altered to contest and reduce it. Moreover, the centrifugal forces of dispersal within and between societies in the present day might prove too great to manage without explosions of violence, on the small and larger scale. Yet the connections I have explored between autonomy, solidarity and dialogue are real; and they correspond to observable changes in local settings of interaction as well as in the global order.

Coda: the question of agency

What of the question of agency? If it be agreed that there is still an agenda for radical politics, who is to implement it? Does 'radical politics' still mean the same as 'Left politics'?

The answer to the second of these questions is surely 'no'. Since the Right, however, has largely thrown in its lot with neo-liberalism, the future success of Leftist parties is likely to depend upon how far they can colonize the terrain I have sought to identify. Left parties will have to work in tandem with many other groups and movements if they are to stake out this territory and hold it. And they will have to mix repair and restoration with a cautionary acceptance of the imperfectibility of things.

References

Beck, U. 1992: *Risk Society: towards a new modernity.* London: Sage.

Ewald, F. 1986: *L'Etat providence.* Paris: Grasset.

Fukuyama, F. 1992: *The End of History and the Last Man.* London: Hamish Hamilton.

Giddens, A. 1990: *The Consequences of Modernity.* Cambridge: Polity Press.

Giddens, A. 1993: *The Transformation of Intimacy.* Cambridge: Polity Press.

Giddens, A. 1994: Living in a post-traditional order. In U. Beck, A. Giddens and S. Lash: *Reflexive Modernization,* Cambridge: Polity Press.

Gray, J. 1993: *Beyond the New Right.* London: Routledge.

Hall, R. H. 1990: *Health and the Global Environment.* Cambridge: Polity Press.

Hewitt, P. 1993: Reinventing families. (The Mishcon Lecture.) University College, London.

Tannsjo, T. 1990: *Conservatism for Our Time.* London: Routledge.

Comment: Power, Politics and the Enlightenment

Perry Anderson

In a culture that typically confines political discussion to electoral agendas – the immediate programmes and constituencies of familiar commentary – it is all too rare for deeper sociological reflections to connect with partisan divisions. T. H. Marshall's theory of citizenship had remarkably little impact on post-war Labour thinking; Raymond Williams's writing on culture and communication virtually none at all. It will be interesting to see whether 'the new context of politics' of which Anthony Giddens writes includes an alteration of this pattern. His own work on modernity would be a test case. It is a pleasure to comment on its sequels here.

Giddens frames his argument as a criticism of the legacy of the Enlightenment. Its claim to emancipate humanity from the shackles of custom and dogma, he maintains, was based on the assumption that increase of knowledge – the advance of science, natural and social – would enable an increase of control by men and women over their own fate. In fact, what the arrival of modernity has brought is new kinds of uncertainty, manufactured by human development itself – a risky and 'runaway' world, which is inherently unamenable to 'the Enlightenment prescription'. For more knowledge, in greater technological capacities, may often generate less control, in more unstable ecological or social environments. Enlightenment optimism was misplaced. Any radical politics today cannot be triumphalist: it must be reparative and cautionary.

Knowledge and control

How valid is this contrast? Two objections can be made to it. In contemporary discussions, the Enlightenment is all too often stylized into an overpowering confidence in cognitive mastery of the world, as the key to a beneficent progress. In fact, the very first classic of the Enlightenment, Montesquieu's *Persian Letters*, questioned just this belief in terms whose starkness yields nothing to late twentieth-century anxieties.

> You wrote at some length, in one of your letters, about the development of the arts, sciences and technology in the West. You will think me a barbarian, but I do not know whether the utility that we derive from them compensates mankind for the abuse that is constantly made of them... I am always afraid that they will eventually succeed in discovering some secret which will provide a quicker way of making men die, of exterminating whole countries and nations. (Montesquieu, 1973: 192)

The Enlightenment, in all its complexity and depth, needs to be defended and developed, rather than discarded, by the Left today. That its central ideals, of whose necessary limits and hazards few of its leading thinkers were unaware, remain perfectly actual, Giddens's argument itself goes on to make clear. For the whole thrust of his subsequent account of a 'post-traditional order' is to emphasize the growth of social reflexivity at large – in other words, the increasing number of situations in which people now make conscious choices, between alternatives, on the basis of new forms of knowledge available to them, where once they merely adhered to precedent or custom. What *philosophe* would have demurred at that? Somewhat cryptically, Giddens suggests that such reflexivity nevertheless 'introduces a dislocation between knowledge and control'. But how does modern knowledge of contraception, to take an example he cites a few lines earlier, dislocate birth control? Is it not obvious that it rather – paradigmatically – enables it?

Compression has no doubt created the slippage here. What Giddens no doubt has in mind is not 'control' as such, but *centralized* control. It is any cybernetic model of social process, totalizing information into planned overall outputs, that the emergence of a multitude of clever individuals disrupts. Tacitly, in other words, it is less the increase of knowledge itself that spreads uncertainty than the multiplication of knowers. It is clear from the examples he gives that Giddens regards the economic and political consequences of this growth of reflexivity – say, new methods of production or protests against corruption – as on the whole hopeful. They condemn without appeal, he argues, both any nostalgia for bureaucratic socialism and efforts to cling to traditional conservatism. What then of liberalism? The question is an acute one for his argument, since the multiplicity of cognitive agents is the founding thesis of Hayek's critique of social constructivism, the most powerful theoretical version of contemporary liberalism – that which forecast the world-wide sway of the market, as a spontaneous economic order generated by a multitude of rational maximizers, acting without coordination. Does the logic of Giddens's case not lead to the conclusion that this must be the only ideology that captures the conditions of decentralized reflexivity – hence its predictable triumph today over its rivals?

Giddens resists this move. 'Neo-liberalism' proper, he contends, is self-contradictory, since it exalts the values of the market at large, yet seeks to preserve traditions it must erode – inherited attachments to nation, religion, gender, family. The element of truth in this is plain. But the history of political thought is a warning against any assumption that discrepant values cannot be coherently upheld by an effective ideology. It was not Filmer's attempt to model the state on the patriarchal family that proved influential, but Locke's denial of any similarity between political and parental authority. Today, the doctrine of separate 'spheres of justice', each with its distinct set of values, devised for the Left, belongs to the everyday common sense of the Right. Neither Reagan nor Thatcher ever suffered from combining appeals to free trade and the nuclear family. Giddens concedes that his objection applies less to a liberalism that can dispense with moral anachronisms, but argues that as a doctrine it still lacks answers for many global issues. That is uncontroversial enough. But to say that 'all this reveals the exhaustion of received political ideologies' is a large jump. The reality is that the liberalism which claims victory over socialism today is at the zenith of its self-confidence; it numbers more adherents across the world than any time in this century. It is a mistake for the Left to comfort itself by thinking otherwise. It was Gramsci who said that a major ideology can only be successfully engaged if it is confronted in its strongest expressions – never by underestimating it, or picking off its weaker forms. There is a reigning view of the world today, and it is not an accident that it claims descent from the Enlightenment: Smith in one hand, Madison in the other. That is the terrain that the Left must contest, not evacuate.

Dialogue and conflict

Giddens offers an original vision of some of the ways in which it could, in practice, do so. His six-sided framework for a new radical politics could, perhaps, be reformulated into four central themes in a more familiar – if less searching – idiom. The issues he highlights are those of welfare (points 1 and 5), work (point 2), democracy (points 3 and 4), and peace (point 6). He makes thoughtful suggestions about all of them, in a modest compass. For the wider horizon behind his proposals, sketching what a true 'post-modernity' might be like, the concluding scenario of *The Consequences of Modernity* (Giddens, 1990) should be borne in mind. For present purposes, one can only register sympathy with the objectives Giddens sets out – but a reservation about the means he seems to be recommending to achieve them, which touch on one of the ends themselves. The repair of damaged solidarities, in the fabric of families and communities, requiring the invention of freer and more enabling forms of social security; the equitable distribution of work, as choice rather than destiny, or loss of it; the deepening of democratic self-determination, generating new possibilities of voluntary action and broadening their scope; the diminution of civic and international violence – all of these should mobilize the energies of the Left.

But is the idea of a 'dialogue' the appropriate conception for pursuing them? The notion of democracy as a field of discourse rather than an arena of interests is usually identified with the work of Habermas, in which it takes its most systematic form. Its germination lies in his study of the new 'public sphere' of the leading European states of the eighteenth century, composed of the periodicals, clubs, coffee-houses and circulating libraries of an emergent civic culture, within the husk of a still aristocratic society. Here was the seed-bed of disinterested dialogue about matters of common concern, which Habermas later developed into a more general theory of 'communicative' – as opposed to 'instrumental' or 'strategic' – reason, modelled on dialogue. Giddens has often been a shrewd critic of Habermas, but here he seems to follow him very closely. There is a difficulty in doing so, however. The public sphere of Addison or Voltaire or Lessing might on occasion approach the conditions of an 'ideal speech situation', in which arguments were exchanged in perfect equality and goodwill, the less cogent ungrudgingly yielding to the more persuasive. But if it could do so, this was because the dialogue unfolded within a more or less uniform – and necessarily restricted – social group, and because it did not trench directly on politics. The *ancien régime*, in France or Germany or elsewhere, did not yield to the force of the better argument: it fell under the hard blows of social conflict. One of the witnesses of its fall was Hegel. In the thirties, Kojève summarized the lesson he drew from the spectacle like this: 'To be sure, history is, if you like, a long "discussion" between men. But this *real* historical "discussion" is something quite different from a philosophic dialogue or discussion. The "discussion" is carried not with verbal arguments, but clubs and swords or cannons on one side, and with sickles and hammers or machines on the other' (Kojève, 1969: 185). The imagery remains a trifle old-fashioned, as befitted a Hegelian. Marx was more modern: it was 'the artillery of commodities' that would convince the world of the truth of capital.

Are such simple observations outdated today? The framework of constitutional democracy in the West excludes violence as a means of persuasion – but has it thereby entrenched dialogue? If it had, the very distinction between friend and foe – which defined the realm of the political for Carl Schmitt – would have disappeared, in a consensual quest for ultimate agreement. Who imagines this is the reality of partisan struggle in our societies? Politics remains eminently strategic: not an exchange of opinion, but a contest for power. If its rhetoric tends to avoid reference to divisions within the social body – parties nominally appealing to the whole nation – its calculus, as any campaign manager knows, does not. The proper connotation of 'dialogue' in contemporary democracies is not that of the *Symposium*, but that of the fictions of stage or studio: theatre rather than philosophy, closer to Mamet than to Plato. So long as the social conditions of politial communication and expression continue to be so vastly unequal, in our class-divided societies, it could scarcely be otherwise.

The danger of conceiving democratic life as dialogue is that we may forget that its primary reality remains strife. All the issues Giddens rightly poses for a radical agenda divide, since they call on material resources that are limited and over which adversary forces maintain a privileged hold. Gender equality cannot be realized without lifting the economic handicap from maternity; work cannot be assured to all who seek it without infringing the prerogatives of corporate investment; electoral democracy cannot be deepened without treading on the interests of established parties; peace cannot be assured without altering the hierarchy of nuclear security. It is a mistake to imagine that there is a quick route to universal goals, to which all can rally without loss. The short cut usually leads back only too soon to particular interests. The hyprocrisies of the 'international community' as a code word for the dominant powers are plain enough. 'Social citizenship' universalized welfare benefits, ostensibly to avoid stigmatization of the poor, actually to purchase the consent of the better-off – in a typical figure of democratic 'dialogue' understood in the rhetorical sense. Is the result really to the advantage of the worse-off today? These are the kinds of hard question the Left needs to ask itself. Here the model of dialogue is a lure. Ironically, the notion that reason will answer to reason is indeed a legacy of the Enlightenment. But it remains its most utopian.

44 Perry Anderson

References

Giddens, A. 1990: *The Consequences of Modernity.* Cambridge: Polity Press.
Kojève, A. 1969: *Introduction to the Reading of Hegel.* New York: Basic Books.
Montesquieu, C.-L. 1973: *Persian Letters.* London: Penguin.

Part II

Citizenship, Equality and Democracy

2 Inequalities of Power, Problems of Democracy

David Held

This essay argues for a politics of empowerment – a politics which aims to create the possibility of a free and equal citizenry.[1] Such a politics takes as its *raison d'être* the creation of 'equal autonomy' for all citizens – what I call 'a common structure of action'. Paradoxically, a common structure of action requires that groups of citizens – systematically disadvantaged citizens – be treated unequally in order that they might become equally free. A politics of empowerment, therefore, is a politics that obliges us to address illegitimate asymmetries of power and opportunity. It is a political project defined by both democracy and justice. In order to grasp the nature of this project in outline, it is useful to begin by reflecting on the ideas of the modern state and of democracy.

The modern state and democracy

The importance and appeal of the idea of the modern state lies in the notion of a common structure of authority, a circumscribed system of power, which provides a regulatory mechanism and check on rulers and ruled alike (see Skinner, 1978: 349ff). Governments are entrusted with the capacities of the state to the extent that they uphold the rule of law. The equal treatment of all before the law, and the protection of subjects from the arbitrary use of political authority and coercive power, are *sine qua non*. While the state is the burden individuals have to bear to secure their own objectives, it is also the basis upon which it is possible to safeguard their claim to equal rights and liberties. The appeal of the state lies, in short, in the promise of a political community which is governed by a fair framework – a framework which is, in principle, equally constraining and enabling for all its members.

The idea of democracy derives its power and significance, by contrast, from the idea of self-determination or autonomy; that is, the notion that members of a political community should be able to choose freely the conditions of their own association, and their choices should provide the ultimate legitimation of the form and direction of their polity. A 'fair framework' for the regulation of a community is one that is freely chosen. If democracy means 'rule by the people', the determination of public decision making by equally free members of a political community, then the basis of its justification lies in the promotion and enhancement of autonomy, for both individuals and the collectivity. And such a justification assumes that people are the best judges of their own ends, that they are able to respect each other's capabilities, and that they can accept the authentic and reasoned character of others' judgements (see Held, 1987: 269–71; cf. Dunn, 1992: v–vii, 239ff).

The relation between the ideas of 'the state' as a fair framework and of 'the people' as deliberatively determining agent(s) requires further specification. What is at issue is the relation between the state and democracy – a fraught and highly contested terrain in political thought, to say the least. But some illumination can be gained by reflecting on what I call the 'principle of autonomy' – a principle that finds resonances in all those traditions of political theory preoccupied with ascertaining the circumstances under which people can enjoy free and equal relations.

The principle of autonomy

The principle of autonomy can be stated as follows:

> persons should enjoy equal rights (and, accordingly, equal obligations) in the framework which generates and limits the opportunities available to them; that is, they should be free and equal in the determination of the conditions of their own lives, so long as they do not deploy this framework to negate the rights of others.

Two notions require elucidation:

1   The notion that persons should enjoy equal rights and obligations in the framework which shapes their lives and opportunities means that they should enjoy equal autonomy – a 'common structure of action' – in order that they may be able to pursue their projects, both

individual and collective, as free and equal agents (cf. Rawls, 1985: 245ff). Such a condition is inconsistent with, and would need to filter out, those ends and goods, whether public or private, which erode or undermine the structure itself (see Miller, 1989: 72–81).

2 The concept of 'rights' connotes entitlement capacities, that is, capacities to pursue action and activities without the risk of arbitrary or unjust interference. Rights define legitimate spheres of independent action (or inaction). They are entitlements within the constraints of community, enabling – that is, creating spaces for action – and constraining – that is, specifying limits on independent action so that the latter does not curtail and infringe the liberty of others. Hence, rights have a structural dimension, bestowing both opportunities and duties; they are an entitlement to claim and be claimed upon (cf. Rawls, 1971: 544–5; Barry, 1989: 200).

The question I wish to pose is this: is a system of political, economic and social power which generates systematic asymmetries of opportunity compatible with the principle of autonomy?

Power and nautonomy

Where relations of power systematically generate asymmetries of life-chances they may create a situation which can be called 'nautonomic'. Nautonomy refers to *the asymmetrical production and distribution of life-chances which limits and erodes the possibilities of political participation*. By life-chances I mean the chances a person has of sharing in the socially generated economic, cultural or political goods, rewards and opportunities typically found in their community (see Giddens, 1973: 130–1). Nautonomy refers to any socially conditioned pattern of asymmetrical life-chances which places artificial limits on the creation of a common structure of action.

Nautonomic structures are shaped by the availability of a diverse range of socially patterned resources from the material (wealth and income) and the coercive (organized might and the deployment of force) to the cultural – the stock of concepts and discourses which mould interpretative frameworks, tastes and abilities. The availability of such resources in a community depends evidently enough on the capability of groups to exclude 'outsiders' and to control resources denied to others. The attempt to control, if not monopolize, any range of resources according to particular social criteria, such as class, race, ethnicity or gender, can be denoted a form of social exclusion or 'social closure' (see Parkin,

1979). Any system of power in which particular life-chances and opportunities are subject to closure can create nautonomic outcomes and, thereby, undermine or erode the principle of autonomy. Thus, those who do not have access to, for instance, an adequate income, educational opportunities or the organized media are unlikely, in societies like our own, to be able to exercise their potential as active citizens.

When power generates nautonomic outcomes, participation is involuntarily restricted or artificially delimited. To the extent that nautonomy exists, a common structure of action is not possible, and democracy becomes a privileged domain operating in favour of citizens with significant resources. In such circumstances, people can be formally free and equal, but they will not enjoy rights which shape and facilitate a common structure of action and which safeguard their capacities. People's equal interest in the principle of autonomy will not be protected; and the claims which they might legitimately make, and which might legitimately be made upon them, will not be adequately entrenched.

Liberalism and Marxism

Traditionally, liberals have conceived of the state as the key site of power in the community. On the one hand, the state must have a monopoly of coercive power in order to provide a secure basis upon which trade, commerce and family life can prosper. On the other hand, by granting the state a regulatory and coercive capability, liberals recognized that they had accepted a force which could and frequently did deprive citizens of political and social freedoms. While liberals affirmed the necessity of the state to govern and regulate society, they also came to conceive of civil and political rights as essential for the regulation of this regulator.

In contrast to this view, Marxists and socialists have typically placed emphasis upon the centrality of economic and productive relations in public and private life. The key source of contemporary power – private ownership of the means of production – is, they hold, ostensibly *depoliticized* by liberalism; that is, it is arbitrarily treated as if it were not a proper subject of politics. The economy is, as a result, regarded as nonpolitical, in that the massive division between those who own and control the means of production, and those who must live by wage-labour, is conceived as the outcome of free private contracts, and not a matter for the state. But it is the liberal claim that there is and ought to be a clear distinction between the world of civil society and that of the political which Marxists and socialists, of course, reject. For them, one of the key consequences of the capitalist relations of production is the creation of inequality of such magnitude that it corrodes liberty. The challenge to liberty derives from inequality, or liberty of a distinctive kind: liberty to accumulate unlimited wealth, to organize economic activity into hierarchically ordered enterprises, and to make the exigencies of capital the imperatives of society as a whole (cf. Dahl, 1985).

The Marxist critique of liberalism raises important questions – above all, about whether markets can be characterized as 'powerless' mechanisms of coordination and, thus, about whether the interconnections between economic power and the state are a central matter in the analysis of power and politics. But it also raises difficulties by postulating (even in its subtler versions) a direct connection between the political and the economic. By seeking to understand the political by reference to economic and class power, by rejecting the notion of politics as a form of activity *sui generis*, and by championing the 'end of politics' in a post-capitalist order (for politics will be redundant when class is abolished in this interpretation), Marxism itself tends to marginalize or exclude from politics certain types of issue: essentially, all those issues which cannot be reduced to class-related matters. It is no accident that Marxism does not offer systematic accounts of the dangers of centralized political power or of the problem of political accountability, accounts which represent the very strengths of liberal analysis.

The accounts of power in both liberal and Marxist political theory are too narrow to encompass adequately the range of conditions necessary for the possibility of a common structure of action. Generally, these two political traditions have failed to explore the impediments to participation in democratic life other than those imposed, however important these may be, by the axes of state and economic power. The roots of the difficulty lie in narrow conceptions of power itself.

In the liberal tradition, power has often been equated with the world of government and the citizen's relation to it. Where this equation is made and where power is regarded as a sphere apart from economy or culture, a vast terrain of power is excluded from view, including the spheres of productive and reproductive relations. The Marxist conception raises related difficulties through its exclusion or underestimation of forms of power – and of forms of social structure, collective organization, agency, identity and knowledge – other than those rooted squarely in production. In order to grasp the conditions necessary for the entrenchment of the principle of autonomy a broader conception of sites of power is required than can be found in either of these traditions.

Sites of power

Any domain of action which disrupts systematically people's equal interest in autonomy requires critical examination. The compatibility of autonomy has to be explored with respect to any organization of life-chances and participative opportunities which systematically stratifies collectivities or groups in relation to a wide array of phenomena, including: security of personhood; physical and psychological well-being; opportunities to become active members of the community; security of cultural identity; ability to join civic associations; capacity to influence the economic agenda; ability to participate in political debate and electoral politics, and ability to act without becoming vulnerable to physical force and violence. Disadvantage in any of these domains could weaken or demobilize the capacities of individuals and groups. A diverse set of sites of power needs, accordingly, to be considered – encompassing realms which can be referred to as the body, welfare, culture, civic associations, the economy, regulatory and legal institutions, and organized violence and coercive relations. To anticipate the main argument I want to make: people's equal interest in the principle of autonomy requires protection across each of these sites; and unless it is so protected, a common structure of action cannot be fully entrenched. Democracy demands the just allocation of power and authority in and across all key sites of power. Given the restrictions on the length of this chapter, I can only offer one illustration of these arguments now (see Held, forthcoming: ch. 6).

'The body' as a site of power refers to the way in which physical and emotional well-being is organized through distinctive networks and institutional milieus, informal and formal, across intersecting social spaces from the local to the international. Relations of power operate in this domain to produce and reproduce a pattern of well-being which is structured asymmetrically within nations and across them. Although I will not document this latter claim here at any length, it is not difficult to illustrate it. Life- or survival chances (measured by life expectancy and age-specific mortality rates), physical ill-health (assessed by the prevalence of serious diseases, disabilities and developmental deficiencies) and mental illness all tend to be correlated directly with geography, class, gender and race and, accordingly, with particular clusters of deprivation found – most dramatically – among countries of the South, among non-whites, among the poor and working classes and among women. These correlations and clusters are not, however, restricted to countries of the South, and can be found widely in the North as well. The patterns of social closure and opportunity among men and women, working, middle and upper classes, blacks and whites, and various ethnic communities profoundly affect their well-being across all categories of health in both Europe and the United States.

In this context, groups of people find themselves in nautonomic circumstances if they do not have access to the conditions – that is, appropriate food and nutritional levels, adequate health amenities and resources, and sufficient health services – which allow them 'to play the roles, participate in the relationships and follow the customary behaviour which is expected of them by virtue of their membership of society' (Townsend, 1987: 130, 140; and see Doyal and Gough, 1991: chs 8–10). In the domain of the body, nautonomy can be defined as a lack of resources (typically nutritional, housing and financial) and a lack of opportunities (typically educational and health-related) which prevent people from obtaining the conditions necessary for participating fully in public and private life. A stark example of such nautonomy is revealed in the continuing pervasiveness of the institutions of 'male sex-right', which ensure male domination within the family and violence against women (from routine sexual harassment to rape) in public and private spaces – with devastating consequences for the potential autonomy of women (see Kelly, 1988; Pateman, 1988; Giddens, 1992).

Nautonomy can be embedded in any of the key sites of power but is likely to be embedded in and across many of them. While sources of nautonomy vary over time, and can be found in shifting clusters of power relations, they are most often locked into a number of such sites, creating self-reinforcing mechanisms (cf. Mann, 1986: ch. 1). Social stratification is one of the key means in and through which sites of power can be articulated and rearticulated to produce nautonomic outcomes. Class, race, gender and ethnicity are among the key categories of group formation which singly or in combination shape the form and dynamics of the key sites of power. The dynamics and interrelations of such sites have direct implications for the degree to which autonomy can be enjoyed. Autonomy is, in essence, structured through power.

Democracy and democratic public law

It follows that a democracy would be fully worth its name if citizens had the actual power to be active as citizens; that is to say, if citizens were able to enjoy a bundle of rights which allowed them to command democratic participation and to treat it as an entitlement (cf. Sen, 1983: ch. 1). Such a bundle of rights should not be thought of as merely an extension of the sphere of accumulated private demands for rights and privileges over and against the state, as many liberal thinkers have conceived rights; nor should it be thought of as simply redistributive welfare measures to alleviate inequalities of opportunity, as many theorists of welfare have interpreted rights. Rather, it should be seen as entailed by, and integral to, the very notion of democratic rule itself. If one chooses democracy, one must choose to operationalize a structural system of empowering rights and obligations, for such a system constitutes the interrelated space in which the principle of autonomy can be pursued – and enacted. Accordingly, to argue for democracy is also to argue for distributive justice. Democracy and distributive justice are inseparable, although how exactly they interrelate and delimit each other remains to be specified.

It is usually accepted that democracy entails certain substantive goods in the form of primary civil and political rights. By primary civil and political rights is typically meant all those rights – from freedom of speech, press and assembly to the right to vote in a free and fair election and form opposition political parties – that are necessary in order for citizens to be able to govern themselves. They are the packages of rights which follow from the right to self-government through democratic rule. However, civil and political rights alone cannot create a common structure of action – a fair framework of social, economic and political autonomy – which is necessary for democracy. Bundles of rights which are pertinent to each of the spheres of power must be regarded as integral to the democratic process. If any one of these bundles is absent, the democratic process will be one-sided, incomplete and distorted. If any one of these categories of rights and obligations is missing or unenforced, people's equal interest in the principle of autonomy will not be fully protected. It does not follow, it should be stressed, that democracy is an all-or-nothing affair. The entrenchment of civil and political rights alone is, of course, of great moment. None the less, democracy must be understood as a continuum across which rights *within* clusters will be more or less enforced, and *different* rights clusters will be more or less entrenched.

Seven clusters of rights, corresponding to the key sites of power, are necessary to enable people to participate on free and equal terms in the regulation of their own associations: health, social, cultural, civil, economic, pacific and political rights.[2] (See Table 2.1.) Primary political rights might be robust in a political community, but unless other rights clusters are recognized there will be significant areas in which large numbers of citizens will not be 'free and equal' and areas in which, although citizens may well enjoy equal rights in principle, they will not be able to take advantage of these equally in practice. If citizens, for example, enjoy tough social, civil and political rights and yet suffer marked disparities in physical security and/or control over their bodies due, for instance,

Table 2.1 Sites of power, types of right

Sites of power	Categories of rights	Examples of rights	Particular domain of action which right helps empower
1 Body	Health	Physical and emotional well-being	Pursuit of bodily needs and pleasures
		Control over fertility	Biological reproduction; freedom to be or not be a parent
2 Welfare	Social	Social security	Development of abilities and talents
		Universal and free childcare and education	
3 Culture	Cultural	Freedom of thought and faith	Pursuit of symbolic orders and modes of discourse
		Freedom of expression and criticism	
4 Civic associations	Civil	Ability to form or join autonomous associations	Individual and group projects
5 Economy	Economic	Guaranteed minimum income	Ability to pursue economic activity (without immediate financial vulnerability)
		Access avenues to productive resources	
6 Coercive relations and organized violence	Pacific	Peaceful coexistence	Physical security and non-coercive relations
		Lawful foreign policy	
		Due process and equal treatment before the law	
7 Regulatory and legal institutions	Political	Adequate and equal opportunities for deliberation	Participation in public agenda setting, debate and electoral politics
		Universal and secret ballot	

to little or no control over fertility and reproduction, a strong case can be made that for large numbers of citizens – in this case, women – the efficacy of their rights will fall far short of that of men. In brief, people's equal interest in the principle of autonomy can only be protected if they enjoy a common structure of action across each of the sites of power.

Taken together, the seven bundles of rights constitute the interrelated spaces in and through which the principle of autonomy can be entrenched. Each bundle of rights represents a fundamental enabling condition for political participation and, therefore, for legitimate rule. Unless people enjoy liberty in these seven spheres, they cannot participate fully in the 'government' of state and civil affairs. The seven categories of rights do *not* articulate an endless list of goods; rather, they articulate necessary conditions for free and equal participation. The condition for the possibility of democracy is a constitutional structure which entrenches rights and duties across the seven spheres. Such a structure would help constitute an empowering legal order, circumscribing a common structure of action. A legal structure, moreover, which recognized citizens in their capacity as citizens in and across the seven domains of power could be regarded justifiably as a democratic public law.

The rights and obligations that are entrenched in a democratic public law must be defined fairly broadly, without regard to specific interests, in order that they can be used to resolve disputes among such interests in particular arenas of interaction (see Miller, 1989: 308). In addition, they must be framed in sufficiently abstract and general terms so that the exact way in which they are met can reflect the diverse material and cultural circumstances of distinct political communities. The universality of democratic rights should be distinguished from specific 'institutional' or 'organizational' prerogatives, often themselves incorporated as rights in law in individual communities (see Bellamy, 1993: 43–76). Thus, while democratic public law must entrench rights of a general type, such as physical security, control over fertility, liberty of expression and criticism, access avenues to or accountability of productive resources, these require institutional and organizational specification if they are to be successfully embedded in political communities. Democratic public law lays down an *agenda* for democratic politics, but necessarily leaves open the exact interpretation of each of the items on the agenda.

For example, democratic public law would stipulate that the physical security of men and women be guaranteed, but would leave components of this to be determined locally: different communities would need to decide whether physical security could be achieved via increased policing, community 'watch schemes', a curfew on those with violent records, increased street lighting and so forth. Likewise, democratic public law requires that women and men enjoy control over fertility, but the enactment of this right depends on decisions about such matters as free abortion on demand, the availability of contraception, sex education, etc., which must involve local considerations and community deliberation. The general issue of principle specified by each democratic right can be distinguished from the particular conditions of its enactment, although the latter must constitute arrangements which are not open to arbitrary abuse and alteration.[3]

The obligation to nurture self-determination

If people's equal interest in autonomy is to be protected, it will mean giving very particular attention to those groups of people who are either disabled by social institutions and structures from participating in the determination of their own lives, or who are disadvantaged, within existing institutions and structures, by virtue of some physical or mental characteristic. If people's equal interest in the principle of autonomy is to be protected, extensive redistribution of goods and services may be required in order to ensure that people who have been handicapped, through nautonomic circumstances and/or unequal endowment, receive those resources needed to further their status as equally free within the process of self-determination (cf. Miller, 1989: 72–3; Dworkin, 1978).

A commitment follows both to the creation of a common structure of action and to the unequal treatment of members of a political community in order to ensure that they can all enjoy a common structure of action. The principle of autonomy, thus, lays down an *obligation* to ensure that those who cannot fully enjoy autonomy under existing circumstances – whether for social and/or physical reasons – are enabled so to do in the long term. A common structure of action can only be created by policies premised on the recognition of *unacceptable structures of difference* which they seek to overcome. Elsewhere, I have referred to this commitment as entailing a 'double-sided' policy process aimed at 'alleviating the conditions of the least well-off while restricting the scope and circumstances of the most powerful' (Held, 1987: 295).

In sum, I have tried to argue that:

1   democracy requires citizens to be free and equal in the determination of the conditions of their own association;

2   a free and equal citizenry requires not just formal rights and duties in the realm of politics and civil society – although it does require

these – but also access to the skills, resources and opportunities to make these formal stipulations count in practice;

3   asymmetries of power, arising from diverse sites of domination, can erode the project of democratic autonomy, the empowerment of citizens within and across all key sites of power; hence, only a common structure of action will do as an ultimate objective of democratic politics;

4   the establishment of democratic autonomy is not to be confused with establishment of equality *per se*; rather, its preoccupation is with the creation of equal participative opportunities, the basis of a substantive and enduring settlement between freedom and equality.

Democracy, thus, entails a commitment to a set of empowering rights and duties. To deny entitlement capacities in any significant domain of action is to deny human beings the ability to flourish as human beings and it is to deny the identity of the political system as a potentially democratic system. A democratic legal state, a state which entrenched and enforced democratic public law, would set down an axial principle of public policy – a principle which stipulated the basis of self-determination and equal justice for all and, accordingly, created a guiding framework to shape and delimit public policy.

Notes

1   The ideas in this chapter are substantially developed in my forthcoming volume, *The Principle of Autonomy and the Global Order: foundations of democracy* (Cambridge: Polity Press).

2   The concept of the 'political' denotes, in this context, the realm traditionally associated with the form, organization and operations of 'the state' or 'apparatus of government', and the latter's relation with its citizens. This 'narrow' usage should be distinguished from the 'broader' use of the concept which treats the political as coextensive with the whole range of sites and sources of power. Politics, in this account, is about power in general; that is, about the *capacity* of social agents, agencies and institutions to maintain or transform their social or physical environment. It is about the resources which underpin this capacity and about the forces that shape and determine its exercise. As a result, politics is characterized as a universal dimension of human life, independent of any specific 'site' or set of institutions. I use the notion of the political in both senses. The context in which the different conceptions of politics are used will, I hope, leave no ambiguity as to their meaning.

3   The separation of democratic public law from the particular conditions of its enactment generates a guiding framework for political activity which can remain sensitive to the traditions, values and levels of development of particular societies. It allows space for the mutual delimitation of democratic principle and practice, on the one hand, while recognizing that the former must

provide a non-negotiable set of orientation points for the latter, on the other. For without this recognition, democratic rights would be no more than rhetorical, and democratic politics would be without a *constitutive core* which precisely permits its characterization as democratic. Cf. Parekh (1992: 169–73).

References

Barry, B. 1989: *Theories of Justice*. London: Harvester Wheatsheaf.
Bellamy, R. 1993: Citizenship and rights. In R. Bellamy (ed.), *Theories and Concepts of Political Analysis: an introduction*. Manchester: Manchester University Press.
Dahl, R. 1985: *A Preface to Economic Democracy*. Cambridge: Polity Press.
Doyal, L. and Gough, I. 1991: *A Theory of Human Needs*. London: Macmillan.
Dunn, J. (ed.) 1992: *Democracy*. Oxford: Oxford University Press.
Dworkin, R. 1978: Liberalism. In S. Hampshire (ed.), *Public and Private Morality*. Cambridge: Cambridge University Press.
Giddens, A. 1973: *Class Structure of the Advanced Societies*. London: Hutchinson.
Giddens, A. 1992: *The Transformation of Intimacy*. Cambridge: Polity Press.
Held, D. 1987: *Models of Democracy*. Cambridge: Polity Press.
Held, D. forthcoming: *The Principle of Autonomy and the Global Order: foundations of democracy*. Cambridge: Polity Press.
Kelly, L. 1988: *Surviving Sexual Violence*. Cambridge: Polity Press.
Mann, M. 1986: *The Sources of Social Power*. Vol. 1. Cambridge: Cambridge University Press.
Miller, D. 1989: *Market, State and Community*. Oxford: Clarendon Press.
Parekh, B. 1992: The cultural particularity of liberal democracy. *Political Studies*, XL, Special Issue on Prospects for Democracy, 160–75.
Parkin, F. 1979: *Marxism and Class Theory*. London: Tavistock.
Pateman, C. 1988: *The Sexual Contract*. Cambridge: Polity Press.
Rawls, J. 1971: *A Theory of Justice*. Cambridge, MA: Harvard University Press.
Rawls, J. 1985: Justice as fairness; political not metaphysical. *Philosophy and Public Affairs*, 14 (3), 223–51.
Sen, A. 1983: *Poverty and Famine*. Oxford: Oxford University Press.
Skinner, Q. 1978: *The Foundations of Modern Political Thought*. Vol. 2. Cambridge: Cambridge University Press.
Townsend, P. 1987: Deprivation. *Journal of Social Policy*, 16 (2), 125–44.

Comment: Deciding about Rights

Anna Coote

An essential feature of a democratic state is that it can create the conditions for all citizens to enjoy autonomy in equal measure. This proposition is central to David Held's argument. In order to promote autonomy, it is necessary to understand where power lies and how it is distributed between individuals and groups. Held argues that power is located in a number of sites, and citizens who lack power in one of these may have less chance of enjoying power in others. Opportunities tend to drain away from the relatively powerless and flow towards the relatively powerful. To create the conditions for equal autonomy, the flow of power and opportunity must be checked and redirected. Held suggests that one way of tackling this formidable task is to introduce citizens' rights, designed and organized around the different sites of power.

In this commentary, I focus on the practical implications of Held's analysis, addressing two questions among many which arise from his argument.[1] What kinds of rights can be introduced at local and national levels? And how are the details to be agreed upon? Rights are not a substitute for democratic processes, but depend absolutely upon them for their legitimacy and their effectiveness. At the same time, rights can help to ensure effective and legitimate democratic decision making. Rights and 'voice' are interdependent. If both are at their best, they can sustain and strengthen each other. If either one is weak, the other will suffer.

What kinds of rights?

We cannot begin to consider the effect of rights on democracy unless we understand their diverse forms and functions, and the range of possibilities and problems which rights can present. Different kinds of rights have different resource implications. While it costs money to uphold civil liberties (by means of police, courts, lawyers, judges, prisons), these costs are more modest, more controllable and more predictable than the costs of enforcing substantive social and economic rights. If all citizens had equal and enforceable rights to health care, education and housing, for example, then the state would have a duty to provide extensive – and expensive – services. It would be hard to control the costs of providing such services, or to predict the volume of demand.

In addition, there is the problem of political viability. The idea that citizens should have civil and political rights is well established in judicial and political circles, even though many of these rights are in practice fragile or illusory. But the idea that they should also have social and economic rights remains controversial in political terms, and unrealized in practice. The case for introducing such rights would need, at the very least, to be built upon some positive experience of codified human rights. In some countries, notably the UK, there is no such experience.

There are pragmatic, if not principled, grounds for treating social and economic rights differently from civil and political ones. Political and civil rights can be a route to social and economic rights, but not vice versa. If all individuals in a society were comfortably housed and enjoyed reasonable standards of health care, education and social insurance, but had no civil or political rights, they would have no constitutional means of winning the rights they lacked. By contrast, a society in which individuals enjoyed the right to vote and freedom of speech, assembly, movement and so forth would hold out the possibility of winning social rights through the democratic process. Social rights may be necessary for the just enforcement of existing civil rights, but on their own they cannot be a means of achieving them. And indeed, without civil rights, social rights are almost certainly unenforceable and therefore meaningless.

Rights can be expressed either as duties imposed on authorities or as entitlements held by individuals. Individual entitlements are unenforceable without corresponding duties, but duties do not always imply specific entitlements. Most national legislation under which health care and education are provided do not allow for individual enforcement. There are also diverse ways in which new rights may be established and enforced. They can be introduced by statute, with or without entrenchment, or by means of ministerial regulation; they can be set out in statutory or non-statutory codes; they can be issued unilaterally by the authority, or negotiated with groups of citizens or service users. Rights may be enforced through the courts by means of judicial review, through courts or tribunals by individual claims, or through designated complaints and appeals procedures, which may or may not involve a final appeal to the courts. Where there are no means of enforcement, rights can be expressed as a declaration of purpose: in this case, they may be implemented by administrative procedures, such as the setting of goals and timetables, with designated strategies for achieving targets. Where there are no means of implementation, the language of rights is purely aspirational: a right is not what *is*, but what *ought to be*.

In practice, the elasticity of the idea of rights may be a blessing. We should not assume a scale of worthiness, stretching from 'good/real' enforceable individual entitlements at the top to 'bad/unreal' aspirational rights at the bottom. At best, enforceable entitlements can bring tangible benefits to individuals and help to promote the fair distribution of power and autonomy. At worst, they can clog up the courts, make hay for the lawyers, favour better-off litigants and play havoc with public finances. At worst, aspirational rights can act as a cynical camouflage for government inaction, and deceive and alienate the public. At best, they can play a useful role in raising public expectations, creating a climate of opinion favourable to equal citizenship and providing a focus for campaigns. What is probably needed is a strategic mix of different kinds of rights, serving different purposes in and around the sites of power identified by Held.

Basic civil and political liberties are in many countries enshrined in a Bill of Rights as part of a written and entrenched constitution. Social and economic liberties are often added in, but rarely carry anything like the same weight. If they are to be constructively applied, a more complex approach is required. To start with, it is useful to distinguish between substantive and procedural rights. The former are rights to actual benefits, facilities and services. The latter are rights to fair treatment for those who have dealings with providers of benefits, facilities and services.

One proposal published by the Institute for Public Policy Research is for a national 'Social Charter' based on international agreements such as the European Social Charter, which would embody substantive rights to such things as medical care, social security and housing. It would be introduced by an ordinary statute and expressed in terms of duties imposed upon national and local government departments and agencies. It would not be directly enforceable by individuals, thus reducing the problem of public spending commitments. But it would act as an important expression of shared aims and values. It would function as a guide for interpreting existing laws and for formulating new ones, it could be implemented by means of goals and timetables, and it could provide a set of criteria for measuring the performance of public bodies.

This would provide a strong framework, within which procedural rights could operate. Procedural rights should be based on principles of judicial fairness already well established in UK law: rights to a fair hearing; to equal and consistent treatment; to unbiased decisions; to structured discretion; to reasons for decisions; and to appeal and complaint. Appropriately expressed and effectively applied, procedural rights could help to ensure equal access to social and economic goods, and facilitate their fair distribution. They could also ensure that individuals were treated with dignity and respect. But they would stop short of guaranteeing to individuals specific benefits, facilities or services. The effect would be to extend civil liberties to the administration of public services – and to provide individuals with enforceable entitlements to fair treatment. Although procedures do cost money, it is easier to predict and control the volume of public funds they would absorb. There is no single formula for putting the principles of judicial fairness into practice. Procedures would have to be custom-made for each area of social and economic provision.

There are tensions which must be addressed between the desire to confer genuine and empowering rights on individuals, and the desire to avoid rigidity and proliferation of rules and regulations, to keep open the channels of democratic debate and to keep lawyers at bay. It would probably help to maximize the use of non-statutory codes and procedures, to extend the jurisdiction of tribunals and to strengthen advice and advocacy systems so that lawyers are brought in only as a last resort. In the UK, any attempt to increase rights – political, civil, economic or social – should in any case be part of a broader effort to modernize the legal system and reform the judiciary.

Forms of decision making

A strategic mix of rights, of the kind outlined above, would require a considerable amount of devolved decision making, particularly in developing social and economic rights. The matter of how decisions are made and by whom, as well as how decisions are reviewed and their impact assessed, therefore becomes crucial. If decisions about rights are to check and redirect the flow of power and opportunity, they cannot be left to those who already have more than their fair share of both. Yet it is neither possible nor desirable for everyone to participate in all decisions: so the ideal of maximal participation is tempered by the practical requirements of modern government.

Working out how the public should participate in decisions about rights is not just a technical matter: it is highly political. The 'public interest' is multidimensional and often inharmonious. It is not just that different communities and groups have different and conflicting interests;

individuals can have more than one set of interests, reflecting different relations with state and society. We are 'customers' when we use public services, and as such we are concerned with how we ourselves and our immediate family are affected by various forms of provision at the point of use. We are 'citizens' not by virtue of our use of services but because we are part of a community. As citizens, we have wider concerns – not just about ourselves, but about our neighbours and other members of the community, both now and in the future. The interests of customers and citizens may conflict, within and between individuals and groups. Citizens' rights and customers' rights are different, but related instruments. Customers and citizens exert power, and experience powerlessness, in different ways and with different consequences. The distinction is particularly salient when it comes to social and economic goods.

With this in mind, how are decisions about rights to be taken and by whom? Representative democracy with universal suffrage and regular elections is of course the best-known form of collective decision making. In theory, at least, it addresses the diverse and shared interests of the population as a whole. But in a large and complex society, the distances between the decision and the elector are so great that the amount of power actually exercised by the individual citizen is negligible. How else may the public participate? One option is for members of the public to vote on a specific question or series of questions, in local or national referenda. There are examples (in the US) of 'people's referenda' where an issue is raised in the community and, if sufficient support is demonstrated, must then be put to the vote. A referendum may prompt an extensive and well-informed public debate, or railroad public opinion into oversimplified decisions about complex questions. A great deal depends on how much the public knows and understands about the issue in question, on how the question is worded, and on how power is distributed between those who campaign for and against.

Another possibility is to apply the jury principle to some local decisions. Individuals would be selected at random from the electoral register to form a citizen's jury for a finite period, to deliberate upon matters of local concern. There are various ways in which the juries might be used – for example, to monitor performance following decisions taken by elected representatives or government agencies, to assess and review decisions before they are implemented, to advise on decisions yet to be taken, or to take decisions on behalf of the community, which would then be implemented by the elected authority. A selected jury could perform a local function similar to that of either a select or a standing parliamentary committee. How well this worked would depend on how the juries received evidence, on what resources they had at their disposal, and on procedures for deliberation.

The idea of public consultation overlaps with that of citizens' juries, but offers further possibilities. Its effectiveness, from the public's point of view, depends on what questions are asked, by whom, of whom, by what means and on the basis of what information; on whether any dialogue takes place and, if so, with whom; on how the answers are processed and conclusions drawn, and on what action is taken as a result. All these decisions remain in the hands of those who consult – as is the decision whether or not to consult in the first place. At worst, it can be a highly manipulative process, benefiting no one but the consulting body. At best, it can be a route towards more open and appropriate decisions, more enlightened decision makers and a better-informed public.

The critical difference between consultation and negotiation is that the latter culminates in some form of shared decision making. One model is provided by the local service agreements pioneered by a handful of local authorities in the UK. Well-publicized open meetings are called at which members of the public are invited to discuss in detail the planning of a local service. These neighbourhood forums are asked to suggest improvements. Officers respond and a dialogue takes place, leading to a negotiated agreement which embodies changes to the service. This is published and distributed in each neighbourhood as a form of guarantee, with a procedure for complaining if the terms are breached.

Negotiated agreements represent an approach to decision making which addresses members of the public both as citizens and as customers. Assuming that this approach operates smoothly and achieves its full potential (a big assumption), it can go a long way towards bridging the gap between the individual citizen/customer and the decision. It calls for clear and thorough communication of relevant information, sets high standards of participative democracy and can be expected to raise the expectations of the public about the quality of service. The success of this approach depends upon a supportive political culture, not just on the part of the local authority, but within the local community. This can be nurtured but cannot be sustained unless the formula is applied sparingly. Negotiation takes time and energy, which are scarce and precious resources – especially among women. If every service were subjected to local negotiation, the likely result would be increasing apathy and disbelief, leading to anger and resentment.

There is no perfect way of deciding about local rights. But the process of making such decisions is a vital one which must be seen to be fair and which could itself be subject to a rights-based approach. If the principles of judicial fairness were applied, decision making would have to be open and to follow explicit guidelines, to be unbiased and to treat individuals equally and consistently. Reasons for decisions would have to be given, with rights of appeal. Procedures for decision making could be established nationally or locally, and could be set out in statutory or voluntary codes. The rights of appropriate associations to be consulted in policy formation, to participate in decisions and to pursue complaints and appeals could be promoted through similar means. The best hope is to match forms of decision making to types of decision, in such a way as to generate public understanding and support as well as effective outcomes.

Conclusion

Talking about rights in abstract terms can be an important consciousness-raising exercise. Putting rights into practice, so that people can feel the difference, is a daunting and complicated task. The strength of the rights-based approach lies in its flexibility, if we understand more fully how it can be applied in different ways to different sites of power, and to different dimensions within those sites of power. The approach must be gradual and experimental, so that lessons can be learned along the way, and public support encouraged and sustained. But if the goal of a democratic state is to create the conditions for all citizens to enjoy autonomy in equal measure, then citizens need rights. They must have a fair say in how they are developed, and they must know what to expect from whatever rights are produced by that process.

Notes

1   My commentary draws extensively upon Coote (1992), particularly the contributions from Denis Galligan, Norman Lewis and Mary Severinatne, Wendy Thomson, and Nina Biehal, M. Fisher, P. Marsh and E. Sainsbury.

Reference

Coote, A. (ed.) 1992: *The Welfare of Citizens: developing new social rights*. London: Institute for Public Policy Research/Rivers Oram Press.

3 Equality, Difference and Democracy

Elizabeth Meehan

This chapter deals with three issues. The first of these is that the meaning of equality is contested; yet it still has a powerful appeal and has to remain a core value of the Left. One of the controversies about equality is that it seems to embody a contradiction in its meaning; that is, equality demands the same legal and political treatment of everyone, when in reality people are in different situations (often related to people's group memberships) which need to be acknowledged by different treatment so that they can enjoy equal levels of well-being. Thus, the second issue of the chapter is whether the Left can overcome this problem when meeting socioeconomic needs. Another controversy about equality is whether thought and action should concentrate primarily on economics or on politics. The third part of the chapter, then, examines the claim that the Left has focused too exclusively on the socioeconomic sources of political inequality at the expense of the non-material needs of human beings, for example political participation.

The argument of this chapter is that, though there are disagreements over the legitimacy of policies that take account of people's differences stemming from class, gender or ethnicity, it is possible to make a case for combining specific and equal treatment in the socioeconomic sphere. But, in accepting that the pursuit of equality should extend into the political realm, I argue that to use an idea of justice based on group difference in this context carries risks as well as opportunities. The very basis of new versions of radical democracy is an insistence on moral reasoning and deliberation. This means that policies and procedures can

In addition to thanking conference participants for their contributions, I would like to thank Michael Drolet, Edward Horesh, David Miliband and Fiona Williams for their helpful comments on various drafts.

result only from a collective endeavour; yet, as will be shown, these endeavours may not always produce congenial outcomes.

Equality

Political equality has inspired the mobilization of groups excluded from the alleged universalism of liberal societies; for example, all women and working-class men in the eighteenth and nineteenth centuries and racial and religious minorities in the civil rights movements of the 1960s (for example, Mitchell, 1987; Forbes, 1991; Parvikko, 1991). The idea had this effect because 'at its best... [it] is ... a profound egalitarianism that offers all citizens the same legal and political rights, regardless of their wealth, status, race or sex' (Phillips, 1992:77). On the other hand, it is an idea that is exasperatingly hard to pinpoint. '[I]t may denote a moral belief, a rationalist precept, an *a priori* principle, a right, a means to an end or an end in itself' (Forbes, 1991). Moreover, appeals to equality as a belief, a right, a means or an end may have in mind either the procedures of equal treatment or concerns about egalitarian material outcomes – and sometimes, even though they may conflict in particular choices, both.

More fundamental a problem for socialists is that liberal political equality is based on what they see as a false idea of the individual and social relations. '[L]iberalism... abstracts the person from all his or her "contingent" and "external" relations with other people and nature' (Parekh, 1992: 161–2). This contrasts with other outlooks in which individuals are constituted by their community membership: for example, in the solidaristic moral orders envisaged in Idealism at the turn of the nineteenth and twentieth centuries (Vincent and Plant, 1984), in socialism and among some modern, social rights advocates (Jordan, 1989).[1]

Whereas the socialist critique of liberalism regards it as illusory to celebrate equal legal and political rights when there is a more fundamental inequality in socioeconomic relations between classes, radical feminists locate another illusion in a hidden, subordinating sexual contract that underlies the social contract (for example, Pateman, 1988). Here, it is argued, the basic concepts of both liberalism and social democracy are irremediably gendered – and something analogous is argued by Black Power critics of civil rights goals (Brah, 1992).

In Athenian democracy, public decision making about justice required rational disinterestedness – a quality that was believed to reside only in men. To fit them for public life, men needed sustenance in the private sphere from the 'natural' dispositions of women to give them affection and care. Such beliefs about the different natures and roles of men and women continued into the modern world. The liberal democratic revolution against patriarchy[2] was, in Pateman's view, only half a revolution. Sons and brothers threw off rule by fathers, but women continued to be incorporated into society not as individuals but as legal dependants – as wives, daughters and sisters. This remained the case even when liberal democracy, influenced by socialists, acquired its welfare dimensions. It is well documented now how deeply imbued social security, social assistance, education and taxation systems have been with sexism. Consequently, social rights advocates are wrong, Pateman (1989) suggests, not to realize that 'fraternity' means what it says and is not a synonym for 'communality'.

For socialist feminists, both socialism and radical feminism have been much-needed correctives to liberalism because of the way such critiques have highlighted the adverse consequences for women of the division between the private and public realms. By emphasizing that the proper concern about equality is its public manifestation, and believing, therefore, that 'all legitimate democratic aspirations' have been met, liberals often overlook the fact that continuing differences in the private sphere effectively undermine women's formal civil and political status (Phillips, 1992:77). And this is compounded by New Right endeavours to return responsibility for need from the public sector to the private realm (Pixley, 1993).

However, both democrats and socialist feminists have been re-examining the liberal idea of political equality – for similar reasons. Radical democrats have begun to emphasize that the materialist focus on socio-economic relations has not brought about justice and political autonomy (Mouffe, 1992). Material inequalities remain and deprived groups are less able than others to ensure that their interests, as defined by themselves, have a place on the political agenda. But this does not isolate them from the effects of public policy designed by others. Even if the actions of others are well intentioned, it is argued, we ought to reformulate political practice in order to find ways of empowering people to say for themselves what their needs are and to contribute to a collective view as to the proper political priorities (for example, Mouffe, 1992; Pixley, 1993).[3] Socialist feminists also argue that too exclusive a focus on the material bases of political inequality cannot foster the 'autonomy and self-respect that feminism seeks to develop' (Phillips, 1992:77). What is necessary is 'for women to shake off their status as dependants, and ... this happens only through the activity of women themselves' (Phillips, 1992:77).

In arguing in her various works for the right of political autonomy, Phillips emphasizes the need to avoid the liberal fallacy of slipping from the liberating position that differences should not count in determining who has rights into a constraining one where all differences can safely be ignored. This brings us to the apparent contradiction that equality demands both the same and different treatment.

Equal and specific treatment

The effects of the principle of equal treatment are problematic in two main ways. On the one hand, if people are in different situations because of their group memberships, laws which ignore these differences and treat individuals *as if they were the same* are unlikely to redistribute social justice to groups as a whole, though they may be used successfully to remedy instances of personal inequity. This kind of criticism of the equal-treatment basis of anti-discrimination legislation is well known. On the other hand, it may sometimes be the case that group differences are taken into account but with disadvantageous consequences – when, for example, a defence based upon generalizations about a group is accepted as a reasonable ground for treating an individual detrimentally, regardless of personal attributes. When considering whether and how differences amongst people should be taken into account, arguments vary according to the way in which individuals are defined by their group membership. Race and sex inequality can be seen as fundamentally different from at least the individual instances of disadvantage that arise from class inequality.

The idea of social citizenship developed by T. H. Marshall combines the abstract principle of the sameness of status and the recognition that the practical experience of justice varies between classes. Despite the libertarian criticism that taxation and redistribution are coercive, social citizenship is compatible with the idea of equal treatment. This is because, in principle, any individual may find himself or herself in a position where it becomes necessary to activate entitlements (Parker, 1975). This is not to say that there are not better ways of taking individual circumstances into account than current practice, and I shall return to this. For the moment the point is that there is a different situation if we argue that inequality exists by virtue of membership of some group identifiable by different, innate characteristics. The fact that biological categories, though not the social construction put upon them (see next section), may be fixed can lead to two contrary positions; eschewing the identification of groups on the basis of their difference or espousing separatism in order to circumvent what is seen as illegitimately enforced assimilation. But advocates of the politics of accommodation can find ways of avoiding the disadvantageous suppression of difference and, what is more, they can frame most legislation in ways which need not worry universalists.

There is a body of liberal and social democratic thought that accepts the need to minimize the adverse impact of group membership and past discrimination against a group. The idea of indirect discrimination, for example, acknowledges the fact that the removal of discrimination is not merely a matter of ensuring equity between two individuals but that, statistically speaking, one group in society may be more likely than another to suffer arbitrary disadvantage. Other liberals, closer to the libertarians noted above, may reject such steps because of the potential harm they see in identifying groups for specific treatment[4] and because the principles of individual equity and group justice sometimes conflict in particular situations (for instance, in disputed American affirmative action schemes).

One example of confusion about what to do is the controversial division among American feminists about whether or not women should try to ensure that pregnancy leave from work is treated as analogous to rights relating to sickness that men, too, might claim, or whether it should be taken into account in public policy as a normal event of life, which is necessary to society but specific to women (Bacchi, 1991). English courts have ruled similarly to the first of these positions – that women had to find some way of making pregnancy comparable to a male experience leading to absence from work.

The liberal problem with specific treatment for groups identified by difference is misplaced, according to Bacchi (1991) and Bussemaker (1991). They argue that what genuine advocates of universalism and equal treatment are really worried about is not differentiation in itself but the purposes for which it is intended; that is, they are worried about the detriment that can follow, and often does, from racial or sex-based classification schemes. Avoidance of capricious detriment is the philosophy of the US Supreme Court's 'strict standard' scrutiny, which rules out racial classifications that have adverse effects unless there is an overriding public purpose, such as the security of the state, *and* it can be shown that there was no other means of meeting that purpose.[5] The corollary of the argument of Bacchi and Bussemaker is that, if a piece of specific treatment is intended to improve access to or protection by something that is valued in society, its specificity should not worry liberals. This would justify a ruling in the European Court of Justice that, since pregnancy is unique to women, discrimination on grounds of pregnancy is direct discrimination (Collins and Meehan, forthcoming).

The Bacchi and Bussemaker argument can also be made about the positive steps or 'affirmative action' to enable disadvantaged groups to qualify in the same way as others. Though both liberal and social democrats sometimes describe such steps as patronizing, judgements must depend on content. Well-constructed schemes do not 'give people a job merely because of their sex or colour' but may include the provision of information, appropriate education and training, proper childcare facilities, reconsideration of the times of meetings, transport and so on. When such measures attempt to circumvent the adverse consequences of the domestic division of labour, women are intended as the main beneficiaries. But, in these kinds of measure – unlike specific provisions relating to births – provisions can be framed in ways that enable particular people in the dominant groups to use them too; for example, male workers who share domestic responsibilities can also place their children in workplace crèches for all employees.

There is evidence that specific and universal treatment can be combined acceptably. For individuals who have particular needs but whose 'difference' is not necessarily associated with innate group identities, some Scandinavian countries provide exemplars of treatment with equal dignity in the administration of general benefit systems. These methods include information about eligibility, easily accessible in public libraries and community centres, and computer technology in social security offices, which enable officials and claimants to see simultaneously how their circumstances might or might not be covered by legislation. The existence, too, of policies aimed at specific groups, such as the young and elderly and their carers, helps them to avoid disadvantage in the labour market and public life. Though introduced with class cohesion in mind, Scandinavian welfare systems have particularly benefited women more than in other countries (Siim, 1991).

There are, of course, pitfalls in devising welfare systems that take account of group differences in order to promote similar levels of autonomy. This is evident both in how member states are responding to the European Union requirement for equality in national social security schemes and in criticisms of those responses. Most countries are eliminating direct discrimination by relabelling insurance-based entitlements as payable, not to fathers, but to 'heads of household' or 'breadwinners'. Yet, women's different career opportunities and lower earnings mean that it is rarely economically rational for a two-adult household to decide that the woman should be designated as its head. Thus, attempts to eliminate direct discrimination can increase indirect discrimination. Mangen (1990) proposes a solution in which insurance credits could be given for work, such as caring for families, that is socially valued but unpaid. But his solution assumes that, in practice, credits would be awarded to women and, therefore, raises in a new form the leitmotif of feminists arguments about the welfare state. Did family allowances, and would Mangen's proposal, institutionalize sexism or grant women a modicum of independence from their partners?

The answers to these and related questions, according to several writers about sex equality, welfare and democracy (for example, Siim, 1991; Phillips, 1991; Pixley, 1993), should take account of the views of the people affected by public policy. Their work suggests the need for something more than a vision of the 'good society' imposed from the top. Equal citizenship, it is argued, means that people should not be passive recipients of policies in which they have had no part but which they know to be unlikely to confer greater freedom. To ensure equal citizenship there must be a polity that respects the outlooks of marginalized people sufficiently strongly to create opportunities for them to put across their views. This is the final part of my argument.

Political equality and group difference

Radical thinking of the post-modern kind might be thought to make the pursuit of reform futile. Crudely put, the post-modern position is that none of our categories is fixed but all always have to be understood in terms of context. Post-modernism can be read as meaning that, if everything is contextual, there can be no truth; that it is totalitarian to behave as if there were; and, hence, totalitarian even to look for it. McClure (1992) draws attention to a poignant coincidence of timing. This is that, just as minorities have thought they were on the brink of winning tangible benefits for their group, academic discourse seems to tell them that their definitions of themselves and the rights for which they struggle are dissolvable. Nevertheless, she points out, recognizing that identities are constructed does not amount to saying that people cannot be agents. And, as Phillips (1992) suggests, the original meanings of statuses and rights do not necessarily restrict the ability of people to be the agents of change. This is illustrated by Brah (1992: 126–30) when she argues that the Black Power movement in America mobilized 'the term black ... [in order to reclaim] ... an African heritage that had been denied to black Americans by racism. [T]he Black power ideology did not simply reclaim a pre-given ancestral past. In that very process, it also constructed a particular version of this heritage.'

New radical and feminist theories of democracy emphasize four components of politics; civil associations, political authority, challenges to that authority from civil society, and the methods of defining legitimate public priorities. Civil associations are linked with identities by Phillips

(1991) when she argues against the politics of separatism. Identities arising from womanhood are relevant to citizenship, in her view, since participation by any agent tends to take place in organizations that are based on social roles. But the practice of equal citizenship must involve interacting with others in the public space to decide upon proper public policies. Walzer (1992) makes the general case that civil society gives rise to various roles and associations; we are acting as citizens when, through those associations with which we choose to identify, we interact with other communities or associations of interest.

The proper nature of the political authority is equally critical to both feminist and democratic theory. It is important that the system avoids a defect that has been identified in conventional pluralist theory. Pluralist theory often assumes that the state is a neutral arbitrator amongst groups and that groups have equal access to the authorities. Though formal rules may imply that this is so, social structures mean that some interests are more influential than others. Thus, the political authority in a radically democratic polity has a special responsibility to ensure that all voices are heard and all legitimate interests are on the agenda. As in the socio-economic sphere, this means being aware of those differences between groups which contribute to exclusion and which need to be accommodated in order to bring about inclusion. It may be difficult to devise an authority that is not neutral but, nevertheless, is regarded as fair. This can be seen in controversies over the closeness of the European Commission's contacts with the employee wing of the 'social partners', objected to by powerful employers in representations to their governments (Meehan, 1993). Another example in what, on the face of it, is a more hospitable body is the controversy over 'black sections' in the British Labour Party. However, given the right circumstances, it may be possible to find consensus. For example, various writers have pointed out that, in the last years of the American New Deal, there was agreement that it was right to bring civil rights groups into the heart of decision making in Washington and for administrators to counterbalance the power of employers by taking special steps to inform vulnerable workers of their rights (Meehan, 1984).

While rejecting compulsory participation in the tradition of Rousseau as unrealistic or even desirable, modern reformers propose that civil society must always be prepared to challenge political decisions about who and which agendas are included. Though practical politicians sometimes despair of people's willingness to participate, Siim's (1991) work on Scandinavia[6] shows that challenges have been possible. Made more autonomous as a result of welfare legislation, women, she argues, have been able to modify the original motivations of public policy with a more feminist dimension. Hart (1993), too, shows how black farm-workers (mainly male) and domestic servants (black and white females) were able to challenge the way in which the 1936 American Fair Labor Standards Act was being interpreted. Through legal and political action, they were able to overturn the idea that 'work' and 'worker' were confined to the conventional model of male manufacturing, excluding agricultural and domestic work on the ground that these were governed not by employment contracts but by familial relationships.

In considering the proper methods of defining public priorities, new theories of democracy embody the old Commonwealth or Republican idea that decisions should be the outcome of reasoned discussion based upon good information (Sevenhuijsen, 1991; Beer, 1993; Miller, 1992). Decisions are not to be judged as just or legitimate because they have been arrived at by an overarching principle such as majoritarianism or equal treatment. Instead, fair and legitimate outcomes are those that seem reasonable to all concerned after various interests have been articulated, reconsidered and adapted in the light of other interests that are learned about. This means that we have to accept, without succumbing to the most extreme forms of post-modernism, that there can be no solutions, such as either liberal democratic versions of political equality or a socialist transformation of economic relations, that are correct for all people at all times. If this, in itself, is uncomfortable, there are also other difficulties that we have to try to deal with. These include: dealing with repugnant opinions; fundamental clashes of core values between groups, not amenable to reasoned discussion; treating groups as though their identities were immutable; failing to recognize emergent groups; and the fact that we have cross-cutting group identities.

Even among people who are more similar than different in their origins, there is the perennial question of what to do about opinions that might be repugnant to the majority, whether or not they have a legitimate public place and how such matters should be decided upon. We have not so far been able to find agreement about 'platforms' for revisionist historians of the Holocaust or about pornography. One possibility lies in the absence of legal censorship and reliance on human beings' ability to exercise John Stuart Mill's 'moral suasion' – with certain safeguards which aim, such as those in race relations legislation, to prevent and punish harm. But toleration, even if reluctant and restricted, can be construed as denying equal respect to vulnerable groups. So, if Miller's (1992) 'deliberative democracy' is persuasive, the best that people from broadly similar traditions can hope for is some freely reached agreement about what freedoms and restrictions will best suit us all for the time being. The *fatwah* against Salman Rushdie makes it seem unlikely that deliberation would always resolve contradictory core values between different cultures, though, as noted below, it may be possible in some situations.

One problem in identifying groups to promote equal political access is that the defining features of a group may, inappropriately, become fixed for all time (Phillips, 1992). Another is that group identity may be latent. Presumably, in a democratic polity groups must have opportunities to redefine themselves. There are signs of this even in societies which are not as democratic as reformers would wish. Different ethnic minorities already increasingly reject the dominant tendency to label them all 'black', as though they were a single set of interests (Brah, 1992: 126–30). There is also the emergence of new groups, even among those who have had no voice of their own before. Most notable among recent emergent groups are children, who may 'divorce' or hang on to one set of parents or another.

A more difficult problem in ensuring that identities and interests are not overlooked arises from the existence of cross-cutting identities which mean that we do not all fit readily into an obvious group. Detriment can follow from failure to recognize the existence of intra-group differences that arise from cross-cutting identities, one of which subordinates us both to the leaders of what others decide is our main group and to society at large. This is an issue for women's groups in Northern Ireland, who say that their interests cannot be defined solely by whether they belong to Catholic or Protestant, Nationalist or Unionist communities. But, it is also said, the dominance of group identities defined by religion and/or constitutional interests means that some of the things women want do not get on to the political agenda.

A similar example from Great Britain, where the 'democratic deficit' is less than it is in Northern Ireland, is illustrated in a dispute between a male leader of the British Muslim community and a Muslim woman speaking of her experience of Muslim education.[7]. The former advocated respect for different group traditions within the same polity through the public funding of Muslim girls' schools. The latter was convinced that combining cultural and sex segregation subordinated female pupils to the patriarchs of their own community, and was intended to do so. In her view, vulnerable pupils needed a secular polity that recognized their femaleness more than their religion. This dilemma is familiar and challenging enough. But there is another, more extreme version of it for people who support feminist demands for women to control their own bodies *and* equal treatment of cultural difference. Can the forbidding of female infibulation, which rejects arguments about how girls of east African origin come to feel that they belong to their own community, constitute a form of cultural imperialism? Many of the critics of outright prohibition of infibulation are opposed, themselves, to the practice. But, they argue, change in practice must stem from discussion which includes those for whom the practice is traditional. Some clashes of core values non-negotiable, other, apparently defining differences may be amenable, albeit with difficulty, to solutions arrived at through deliberation.

Conclusion

Though consensus over equal and specific treatment may be possible in the socioeconomic sphere, and though political arrangements can be made hospitable to groups whose difference has made them marginal, the problems discussed in the last section show, I think, that we are unlikely to be able to eliminate entirely an age-old question. This is the puzzle of why people should accept the modification of their demands when confronted by the interests and values of others. The traditional answer is that they do so when they believe that the rules are fair or reasonable. For example, no one has ever said that there was a perfect electoral system, but it is agreed that there are systems which are fairer or more reasonable in light of the different purposes of elections and the priorities attached to those purposes.

The most urgent task of reformers is to construct institutions and procedures that are accessible to those whose situations have given rise to the most trenchant criticisms of liberal democracy – so that people can agree upon what mixture of policies appropriately acknowledges their sameness and differences for the time being. To take account of the vulnerable, emergent and cross-cutting groups mentioned above, we might have to say now that the price of equality, not liberty, is eternal vigilance. This might help us to face what seems inevitable; that not all of the people will get what they need all of the time, though, in a radical democracy, they might at least know it would be worth trying again.

Notes

1 And in other bodies of thought; for example, in the Athenian idea that individuals are human beings only in communities where their essentially political natures can be expressed (Jordan, 1989); in Hindu and Chinese societies where individual identities are functions of past incarnations or of ancestral and descendant families (Parekh, 1992: 161); and in pre-liberal societies in which a craftsman's tools constituted his 'inorganic body' and could not be alienated (Parekh, 1992: 161).

2   This was Robert Filmer's concept of patriarchy; rule by status and family headship, culminating in the 'highest' – the royal – family.
3   Social democrats point to the danger of naive prioritization of non-material human needs, and to the possible subversion of 'post-industrial' theories of need by New Right governments to make more palatable the breaking of commitments to welfare and full employment (Pixley, 1993; Coenen and Leisink, 1993).
4   For example, Americans with Japanese surnames were interned during World War II. This was upheld in the Supreme Court, though later constitutional specialists have argued about the legitimacy of the ruling on the ground that some method other than 'blanket' internments might have been used to meet the public interest objective.
5   See note 4 again. In contrast, UK judges presiding over some race and sex discrimination cases have been criticized for too readily accepting defences by employers based on what the latter see as 'reasonable' assumptions. And it is often noted that they defer, without probing, to government assertions that the national interest, undefined, justifies some course of action or other.
6   I am grateful to Fiona Williams for pointing out to me that the administration of general welfare in Sweden is sometimes dominated by paternalistic values and that its immigration policy does not encourage difference but is assimilationist.
7   This is taken from an unpublished source (a university seminar), but comparable disputes appear from time to time in the newspapers.

References

Bacchi, C. 1991: Pregnancy, the law and the meaning of equality. In E. Meehan and S. Sevenhuijsen (eds), *Equality Politics and Gender*, London: Sage.
Beer, S. H. 1993: *To Make a Nation: the rediscovery of American republicanism.* Cambridge, MA: Belknap Press of Harvard University Press.
Brah, A. 1992: Difference, diversity, differentiation. In J. Donald and A. Rattani, (eds), *Race, Culture and Identity*, London: Sage.
Bussemaker, J. 1991: Equality, autonomy and feminist politics. In E. Meehan and S. Sevenhuijsen (eds), *Equality Politics and Gender*, London: Sage.
Coenen, H. and Leisink, P. (eds) 1993: *Work and Citizenship in the New Europe.* Edward Elgar: Aldershot.
Collins, E. and Meehan, E. forthcoming: Women's rights in employment and related areas. In G. Chambers and C. McCrudden (eds), *Human Rights in the UK* (provisional title), Oxford and London: Oxford University Press/Law Society.
Forbes, I. 1991: Equal opportunity: radical, liberal and conservative critiques. In E. Meehan and S. Sevenhuijsen (eds), *Equality Politics and Gender*, London: Sage.
Hart, V. 1993: The right to a fair wage: American experience and the European Community Charter of Fundamental Social Rights of Workers. In V. Hart and S. Stimpson (eds), *Writing a National Identity: political, economic and cultural perspectives on the written constitution*, Manchester: Manchester University Press.

Jordan, B. 1989: *The Common Good: citizenship, morality and self-interest.* Oxford: Blackwell.

Mangen, S. 1990: The implications of 1992 for social policy; social insurance. In S. Mangen, L. Hantrais and M. O'Brien (eds), *1. The Implications of 1992 for Social Insurance.* Aston University: Cross-National Research Group, Cross-National Research Papers. New Series: The Implications of 1992 for Social Policy.

McClure, K. 1992: On the subject of rights: pluralism, plurality and political identity. In C. Mouffe (ed.), *Dimensions of Radical Democracy: pluralism, citizenship, community.* London: Verso.

Meehan, E. 1984: *Women's Rights at Work: campaigns and policy in Britain and the United States.* London and Basingstoke: Macmillan.

Meehan, E. 1993: *Citizenship and the European Community.* London: Sage.

Miller, D. 1992: Deliberative democracy and social choice. *Political Studies,* XL, Special Issue on *Prospects for Democracy,* 54–67.

Mitchell, J. 1987: Women and equality. In A. Phillips (ed), *Feminism and Equality,* Oxford: Blackwell.

Mouffe, C. (ed.) 1992: *Dimensions of Radical Democracy: pluralism, citizenship, community.* London: Verso.

Parekh, B. 1992: The cultural particularity of liberal democracy. *Political Studies,* XL, Special Issue on *Prospects for Democracy,* 160–75.

Parker, J. 1975: *Social Policy and Citizenship.* London: Macmillan.

Parvikko, T. 1991: Conceptions of gender equality: similarity and difference. In E. Meehan and S. Sevenhuijsen (eds), *Equality Politics and Gender,* London: Sage.

Pateman, C. 1988: *The Sexual Contract.* Cambridge: Polity Press.

Pateman, C. 1989: *The Disorder of Women.* Oxford: Blackwell and Polity Press.

Phillips, A. 1991: Citizenship and feminist politics. In G. Andrews (ed.), *Citizenship,* London: Lawrence and Wishart.

Phillips, A. 1992: Must feminists give up on liberal democracy? *Political Studies* XL, Special Issue on *Prospects for Democracy,* 68–81.

Pixley, J. 1993: *Citizenship and Employment: investigating post-industrial options.* Cambridge: Cambridge University Press.

Sevenhuijsen, S. 1991: Justice, moral reasoning and the politics of child custody. In E. Meehan and S. Sevenhuijsen (eds), *Equality Politics and Gender,* London: Sage.

Siim, B. 1991: Welfare state, gender politics and equality policies: women's citizenship in the Scandinavian welfare states. In E. Meehan and S. Sevenhuijsen (eds), *Equality Politics and Gender,* London: Sage.

Vincent, A. and Plant, R. 1984: *Philosophy, Politics and Citizenship.* Oxford: Blackwell.

Walzer, M. 1992: The civil society. In C. Mouffe (ed.), *Dimensions of Radical Democracy: pluralism, citizenship, community,* London: Verso.

Comment: Citizenship and Political Change

Raymond Plant

Elizabeth Meehan's paper raises some important questions in political philosophy and in the space available to me I can do no more than reflect on them. The central issue at stake is the contrast and tension between on the one hand a conception of the project of the Left in terms of the idea of citizenship, which seems to imply some sense of common identity underpinning a set of rights and entitlements in the political, civil and economic sphere, and on the other hand a recognition of the importance of difference in society – in other words the ways in which people conceive of their identities and what is important to them in terms of their attachments to particular groups and communities, whether these attachments are chosen or inherited. Citizenship seems to embody a sense of common identity, common good and possibly common purpose, although individuals conceive of their identities in richer, more detailed and more differentiated ways. This raises key questions about the role of equality in terms of public policy.

If one takes the citizenship approach then it is arguable that the concern with equality should be directed towards those goods which are part of the common identity of citizens; that is to say, towards securing equality in terms of the exercise of political, civil and social rights. What equality might mean here could be quite complex – sometimes it will be concerned with procedures designed to secure equality before the law in the sense of due process; sometimes it will be concerned with access and the demand that everyone should have free and equal access to health care at the point of delivery; sometimes it will be substantive and directed towards a minimum wage or basic income, guaranteed by citizenship rather than the market. The main point, however, is that there would be a clear set of goods towards which egalitarian considerations should be directed, namely that bundle of goods which defines the common basis of citizenship. Critics of this view, however, argue that this approach is deficient in a number of respects.

First of all, its concern with the public and political value of citizenship as a source of common identity is likely to mean that policy will neglect areas which are perceived to fall outside of this arena – for example, gender inequality as it is manifested in family life, which may on citizenship assumptions be regarded as part of the private sphere. In addition a politics of common citizenship is rather abstract and universalizing and neglects the importance of difference in terms of community and group membership, which is central not only to how people conceive of their identity, but also, crucially, to how they are motivated in politics. People act out of close and felt attachments rather than from loyalty to abstract principles. This is a point which communitarians of both Left and Right have made against liberal rights-based approaches to politics since the time of Burke. Finally, it is argued that the common identity which it is assumed underlies the citizenship approach is one which may exclude some groups in society just because they do not conceive their lives according to the assumptions of this identity. If there is a common good and a common purpose assumed within the citizenship approach, it is that of individual autonomy. But if this is so then critics might well argue that this is not a neutral value compatible with all group and community attachments in our society. Take, for example, Islam and its adherents in Britain. As I understand it they would not see individual autonomy as being some kind of neutral and overriding value, but rather one which compels them to construe their religion and its intrinsic social demands and habits in a liberal manner which is in conflict with a conscientious attachment to those beliefs. So a public philosophy of citizenship and the common identity on which it is based is not in fact a common value, but one which already assumes that individuals and groups are committed to liberal values, which they may not be.

These are the dilemmas as I see them, and I want to spend the rest of this commentary dwelling on them rather than attempting to resolve them. It is, however, worth remarking at the beginning that this debate on the Left is quite far removed from the preoccupations of traditional Marxism, whether one takes the citizenship approach or for that matter the critical stance which I have outlined. The Marxist critique of the citizenship approach is set out essentially in Marx's essay *On the Jewish Question* and in his *Critique of Hegel's Philosophy of Right*. In these two works he criticizes the idea that autonomy and liberation can come through political reform and particularly political rights. Such rights, achieved through liberal constitutional reforms, would neglect the infrastructure of exploitation and the extraction of surplus value. The constitutional reform approach also makes a mistake in believing that, as Hegel thought, the state could be a universal or the bearer and securer of a sense of common identity. Such a sense of identity secured through politics neglects the divisive class basis of politics in liberal societies. At the same time Marx also rejected the idea that the facts of economic exploitation could be changed by measures of social justice and the social democratic pursuit of equality within mixed economy societies. The source of this critique is to be found in *The Critique of the Gotha Programme*. In Marx's view the social democratic assumption that there could be a politics of just distribution – to secure to citizens outside of the market and through politics resources which they would not get in an equal and secure way through the market – was a delusion. It was concerned with treating symptoms rather than causes. The maldistribution of resources which is the concern of the social democrat is a consequence of the maldistribution of the ownership of the means of production in society. It does seem clear, therefore, that an approach to the project of the Left in terms of citizenship and a politics of common identity marks a pretty decisive break with Marxism, and this should be fully understood in a revaluation of the Left's future.

It is also true, however, that the critics' approach as outlined earlier embodies a substantial break with Marxian assumptions. The critic of the common-identity approach wants to appeal to autonomous group and community membership as being important factors in the constitution both of individual identity and of appropriate political demands. However, those who take these views as a criticism of citizenship do not assume, as would traditional Marxism, that such group and community identities are rooted in economic and ultimately class interests. This reductionism is rejected and the sources of identity are taken to be legitimate and autonomous in their own right. Hence the citizenship debate on each side seems to me to be quite removed from many of the class-based assumptions of left-wing projects inspired by Marxism.

It is, I think, important to try to explain why what I have called the politics of common identity underlying citizenship approaches has taken the form that it has. First of all, it is, I think, a reaction to Marxism and its rejection of the possibility of common purpose and common identity within a society such as ours. It has also grown out of a concern that there should be a real focus for the non-Marxian Left's concern with social justice, equality and distributive politics. It has been a common argument from the Right, and one to which the Left has been vulnerable, that if the government is in the business of distributing resources in the interests of greater equality, then unless there is some focus to this, about the appropriate areas in which we should be trying to secure greater social justice, groups and coalitions of groups will attempt to use their power to extract resources from government to improve their own position. This might mean that in the absence of an antecedently clear idea about the focus for social justice – on the rights of citizenship, for example – then government could fall victim to coalitions of interest groups and that, far from achieving social justice, securing the equal rights and resources of citizenship would in fact become a fig leaf for an unprincipled distributive struggle between coalitions of interest groups. On this view it is important to have a focus and a set of associated criteria for citizenship and the rights and goods that go with it, rather than public policy being shaped by the demands of particular sorts of powerful groups in society. What the critics see as important groups which mediate a sense of personal identity, the citizenship theorist might see as essentially predatory groups seeking to extract resources from government. The idea of a common identity and a set of common goods to go with it could on the other hand act as a filter through which the claims of groups could be assessed. Without some such antecedent set of principles, governments of the Left will fall victim to powerful interest group coalitions.

The other strength of the citizenship approach as seen by its defenders is that it does provide a sense (albeit thin) of common purpose within a society which is otherwise pluralistic to a very high degree. We have very little experience, it is argued, of societies which lack a reasonably high degree of homogeneity. To collapse modern western European societies into a politics of pluralism, with different groups seeking a voice and resources, is highly dangerous. We do need a sense of common values in society. These can no longer be substantial values, for example those drawn from religion or from a shared sense of history and tradition; rather they have to be thinner values. As Rawls argues, we have to put right before the good. We differ over our conceptions of the good both as individuals and as groups, and we need to identify behind those differences a thin common identity of common citizenship which will be concerned with equal civil and political rights and fair and equal access to the bundle of social and economic goods, such as income, education, health care and social security. These are so-called primary goods, that is to say necessary conditions of pursuing our own conception of the good, whatever it may turn out to be. On this view, therefore, we should see the common identity of citizenship as a way of tying a pluralistic society together, while preserving the richness of group life within that set of constitutional and social rights and entitlements.

There are, I think, three basic objections to this view. The first, which I have mentioned already and will not repeat, is that such an approach is not in fact a neutral one, but basically implies a commitment to a liberal ideology, and is one which then requires individuals and groups to conceive of their political identity in liberal ways. The second in a sense relates to this and involves reference to the sort of post-modern critique indicated by Elizabeth Meehan. On this view the citizenship approach assumes that there are certain kinds of universal goods, both procedural such as rights and substantive such as entitlements to various goods, which all individuals are thought to need irrespective of their particular attachments and identities. This assumes a kind of unencumbered, enduring, thin, abstract conception of political personality lying behind individual attachments and sentiments. It is central to the post-modern critique to reject any such assumption. The citizenship approach replaces individuals and their particularity with an abstract kind of peg on which to hang a set of political goods and associated concerns. This abstraction is not and cannot be a foundation for politics in a situation of pluralism. This kind of concern goes along with a general philosophical critique of searching for a foundation for political action which is in some sense neutral and lies behind people's explicit sense of identity. We have to cope on the surface of politics with the identities which people have constructed for themselves, not to construct an abstract identity lying behind all of that. The final criticism which relates to the points made by Meehan about democracy is that in a sense the politics of citizenship and common identity is anti-democratic. This might sound paradoxical, since those who favour the citizenship approach see citizenship as the key to democracy, so let me explain.

If we refer back to the critique of group influence on politics mentioned earlier, are not the attempt by the citizenship theorist to lay down in advance what should be the rights and entitlements of citizenship, and the assumption about common identity which underpins these as a way of filtering and providing an antecedent benchmark for judging the claims of groups, anti-democratic? It implies that there is a set of goods associated with citizenship which stand above politics and democratic negotiation, particularly if these are seen to be embodied in, for example, a Bill of Rights. Such an approach ties political and democratic debate in advance, and this may at some point do violence to individual and group identities and attachments. On this view it would be far better, for example, to accept the post-modern critique of the citizenship approach, accept that there can be no philosophical foundation for political action which can, as it were, be set up as a prior foundation to constant democratic negotiation and renegotiation. What might be thought to matter most on this basis is not an antecedent politics of citizenship but rather ensuring that political parties are themselves broad coalitions of groups, so that all voices can be represented via the main parties under the electoral system, or by ensuring that there is constant negotiation and renegotiation of political demands through a change in the electoral system to one of pure proportionality, so that Parliament becomes as exact a replica of the balance of group voices in society as can be managed. On this basis, if there is a common identity, it will emerge from negotiation and bargaining; it will not be some kind of antecedent moral framework for politics, such as the citizenship approach might imply.

Overall, therefore, the debate started in this chapter by Elizabeth Meehan is an important one for the future of the Left, and for judging the extent to which the reinvention of the Left should be seen in terms of trying to establish a set of principles antecedent to politics, and how far as an alternative it should adopt a much more radical approach to democracy, or at least that form of democracy. A radical view of proportional representation, which in a sense corresponds to the postmodern critique of political principles by seeking to replace foundational principles of political action by a recognition of the constant need to negotiate and renegotiate political identities and the policies which flow from them, would be a genuine departure, but one not without problems.

4 Ethnic Difference and Racial Equality: New Challenges for the Left

Tariq Modood

There are now over 10 million non-white people, or people of non-European origin, in the European Union (EU). While only about a third have citizenship in the EU member states (more than half of whom are in the UK), the majority were born or are effectively settled in the relevant EU state. Three-quarters of them are in just three states: over 2 million in Germany, 3 million in Britain, and more than 3 million in France. Indeed, they are highly concentrated, constituting typically about 15 per cent or 20 per cent of the population in and around major conurbations.

Their concerns represent major challenges for public policy, and for the Left, whose traditional preoccupation with class politics too often overlooked other sources of social solidarity and injustice, like gender or race. This point has been well made by feminists who have played a major role in ushering in a new concern with the politics of 'difference' (Phillips, 1993). In the United States, the politics of difference has been the basis of a 'rainbow coalition' political strategy (I. M. Young, 1990). In Europe, people of non-European origin need explicitly to feature in a pluralistic vision that should be the basis of any reinvention of the Left.

Post-war Europe needed cheap labour to perform unskilled and unwanted jobs in an expanding economy, and the bulk of the migrations occurred in response to this need. The new ethnic minorities therefore

I am grateful to David Miliband for his editorial guidance on this chapter. It is a development of my argument in *Racial Equality: colour, culture and justice*, an 'issue paper' published by the Commission on Social Justice (Modood, 1994a).

entered European society at the bottom. That situation has more or less persisted for four decades. While some groups have an educational and economic profile similar to or perhaps better than the average of the European country in question (for example, Indonesians in the Netherlands; east African Asians, Indians and Chinese in Britain; and perhaps some black Caribbean and African groups in France), on the whole migrants and their descendants suffer much higher levels of unemployment than white people (sometimes three or more times higher). The majority of those in employment are in unskilled and semi-skilled work.

Most groups have a historical relationship with the receiving society based on racism, slavery or conquest, colonial rule and economic dependence, a relationship evident in their experience of racial discrimination, social exclusion, racial harassment and racial attacks, not to mention cultural contempt and the pressures of assimilation. In short, the new ethnic minorities of western Europe are a natural constituency of concern for a Left concerned with inequalities of power and opportunity. Racial equality and minority rights are issues which should be integral to a European politics of social justice. But how should this concern be understood and expressed?

The context

The view across the Channel from the UK is sobering. On the one hand, institutional anti-racism is weak in most of the EU countries. The policies and laws of *de facto* exclusion and inequality are often not even balanced by policies and laws of inclusion and equality. The emptiness of various constitutional declarations is evident in the fact that very few cases have reached the courts and that the Netherlands alone comes close to Britain in terms of legislation and implementation, in particular in having an unambiguous concept of indirect discrimination and a racial equality agency (Forbes and Mead, 1992). On the other hand, violent, militant and electoral racisms are present at alarming levels in all the member states with significant non-white populations and are growing. Taken together these two factors mean that Europe may be moving from a comparatively bad situation to a worse one.

A recent report on measures to combat racial discrimination in employment in the member countries of the EU concluded that 'the rights and freedoms of Asian and Black people and members of other visible minority groups in Britain are not secure in other member states' (Forbes and Mead, 1992: iii). The researchers found that there was *overt* discrimination (eliminated in Britain through legislation in the 1960s and

1970s) in many countries. In Belgium and Denmark, for instance, 'racial discrimination is frequently practised openly, and is viewed as quite normal behaviour' (pp. 30–1). It was found that in France 'there has been a widespread disposition to discriminate in accordance with the belief that unemployment among French nationals should be reduced even at the expense of better-qualified non-French individuals in the labour market' (p. 34). Elsewhere it has been reported that 'Germany has seen massive ousting of Turks from employment, to be replaced by East Germans – their labour market's new second tier' (Baldwin-Edwards, 1991: 209). That this 'ethnic cleansing' has been at all possible is itself the result of a racist definition of German nationality, which readily grants German citizenship to newly arrived ethnic Germans from eastern Europe while withholding it from socially integrated Turks with two or three decades of residence, as well as from their children and grandchildren.

The electoral successes of the far-Right and racist parties across Europe have so far been greatest in France, where it has been argued that the electoral strength of the Front National 'has pushed much of the mainstream political right to a final abandonment of any pretence towards civic integration of the country's immigrant population' (Husbands, 1992: 273–4). A result has been that while the Germans have been waking up to the challenge of moving from a nationality based exclusively on *jus sanguinis* (parental nationality) to *jus soli* (birthplace), Prime Minister Balladur's centre-Right government has shifted in the opposite direction so as to deprive its large Maghrebian population of French citizenship in the future. The essential element of this French debate has perhaps been best captured by Etienne Balibar, who wrote that if 'Islam is now the second religion of France ... fear of Islam must be the premier religion' (*Liberation*, 3 November 1989). It is estimated that there have been over two hundred racist killings of Arabs ('Arabicides') in France since 1970, and yet the subject is taboo (Giudice, 1992; Woodall, 1993). Much of the recent violence has been caused or exacerbated by the panic about refugees and asylum seekers, and has led to restrictive measures and the removal of rights, including in Britain.

In Britain, where one can argue that the legal framework for enhancing racial equality is most developed, there are none the less points of comparison with the rest of Europe. It is now apparent that racially motivated violence and harassment have been more persistent and widespread than ever admitted. There were an estimated 140,000 such incidents in 1992 (according to the Home Office), but the issue has been neglected, even on the Left. Partly out of a general suspicion of the police, antagonism and mutual distrust between the police and especially young Afro-Caribbean men were theorized as the essential relationship between the British criminal justice system and the non-white population (Hall et al., 1978; Keith, 1993). If racial attacks constitute the area of greatest failure and urgency, the other central failure is a lack of engagement with ethnicity and the challenges of the insertion of new cultural communities into a society. There has been some support for the idea of multiculturalism and celebration of diversity, but little thought has been given to how this is compatible with civic integration and social solidarity. Hence important questions about the rights of minorities, the 'costs' of cultural diversity, and to what extent the state should protect or promote cultural practices have hardly been discussed.

By uniting all those who suffer from white racism into a single category of *blackness* the race egalitarians of the 1980s did provide a sharper political focus and achieved a partial mobilization of the oppressed groups. But they failed to appreciate that the ethnic pride of various groups, necessary for a confident and assertive participation in a society from which the groups had been excluded and held as inferior, could not be built out of the mere fact of common inequality. Excluded groups seek respect for themselves as they are or aspire to be, not simply a solidarity on the basis of a recognition of themselves as victims; they resist being defined by their *mode of oppression* and seek space and dignity for their *mode of being* (Modood, 1992). Hence, however disappointing it has been to the Left, it is not all that surprising that most Asians have not positively embraced the idea of themselves as 'black' (Modood, 1988, 1994b) and that many Muslims have mobilized around a Muslim rather than a 'black' identity (Modood, 1990, 1992). The narrow focus on colour-racism and the development of a unitary, non-white political identity has not only been politically short-sighted but, as will be argued below, obscured important dimensions of racism.

While there is continuing evidence of racial discrimination against all non-white groups (as well as to some extent against Travellers, and Irish and Jewish communities), and of racial inequalities, in particular the severely disadvantaged position of Bangladeshis, Afro-Caribbeans and Pakistanis (Jones, 1993; Modood, 1993a), what is at work is a plurality of factors, interacting in a complex way. Increasingly, race relations, discrimination and disadvantage cannot be satisfactorily analysed in terms of a simple black–white divide. The situation of non-whites now is so varied that aggregate statistics about 'black' unemployment, or, say, under-representation in a particular occupation or economic sector, or rate of homelessness, are blunt tools for the analysis of comparative deprivation or need. They are sometimes worse than meaningless because, by aggregating together groups whose condition is dissimilar, they mask the true extent of the disadvantaged condition of some ethnic groups. Compound statistics about Asians too ought to be met with suspicion, because the differences between, for example, east African Asians and Bangladeshis are much greater than between Asians and non-Asians. Where data are not available or not made available except in terms of 'black' and 'white' populations, or in terms of black, Asian and white, serious mapping of racial inequality is impossible.

Discrimination, disadvantage and difference

Discrimination can be based on colour-racism in the direct form of discriminatory behaviour, or in the indirect form of policies and practices which have a disproportionate, even if unintended, unfavourable impact upon some or all non-white groups. The cumulative effects of this discrimination, especially when intergenerational, is what is meant by 'racial disadvantage', namely a socioeconomic gap between white and (some) non-white groups which would persist even if discrimination were to disappear tomorrow. Racial discrimination, however, is not a discrete form of disadvantage (it is connected to other disadvantages); it is not a unitary form of disadvantage (it takes various forms); and it is not necessarily linked to racial disadvantage (despite discrimination, some groups can achieve significant socioeconomic mobility).

Racial discrimination is not a discrete form of disadvantage because many forms of indirect discrimination ('institutional discrimination') and racial disadvantage are closely related to structural inequalities better understood in terms of class. Ostensibly colour-blind recruitment policies – for example, those that give first preference to people from elite universities – will none the less have a racially exclusionary effect, but through the conditions of disadvantage and their effect on educational attainment, rather than through racism itself. It perpetuates racial disadvantage, but the discrimination is effected through what the disadvantaged have in common across racial boundaries, rather than what separates them. In this case, to attack the class bias of the policy is in effect to attack the racial bias and vice versa; a policy aimed at removing the conditions of racial disadvantage would make little headway if it did not challenge the existing structure of opportunities created by class divisions. Hence, an attack on certain kinds of racial inequality is only possible within a much more extensive commitment to equality and social justice. In so far as race-specific policies can provide opportunities for education, training, employment and social mobility, restrictions upon which can all be forms of indirect racial discrimination, they can only be wholly effective as refinements of broad social programmes to improve the relevant opportunity structures for all racial groups. The race dimension of such programmes would be designed to ensure that those most disadvantaged were not overlooked by the programme and got the particular kind of assistance they needed in a culturally appropriate way; it could not be a substitute for a social equality programme – even in respect of disadvantaged racial groups (Wilson, 1987).

Racial discrimination is not, secondly, a unitary form of disadvantage because not all non-white groups are discriminated against in the same way or to the same extent. Colour-racism may be a constant, but there are other kinds of racism at work in Britain. Colour-racism is the foundation of racism rather than the whole edifice. Direct discrimination depends upon stereotypes, and there are no stereotypes about 'blackness' as such: the stereotypes are always about specific groups or quasi-groups ('Jamaicans are lazy', 'Asians don't mix', 'Muslims are fanatical', etc.). Hence, different groups will be affected differently, and some groups can become or cease to be more 'acceptable' than others (white people have in surveys always stated more prejudice against Asians than against Afro-Caribbeans, and this is now rising, especially amongst the young; see K. Young, 1992). Moreover, stereotypes, like all social generalizations, allow for counter-examples, so that individuals of any group who are able to demonstrate, for example, in an interview, that they are a counter-example to the stereotype, will receive less unfavourable treatment. Indirect discrimination depends on policies and practices which (unintentionally) disproportionately disadvantage one group compared to others. Groups whose language, religion, customs, family structures, and so on are most different from the white majority norm will experience the most disadvantage and exclusion. So, just as colour-blind class discrimination can be a form of indirect racial discrimination, so membership of a minority community can render one less employable on the grounds of one's dress, dietary habits, or desire to take leave from work on one's holy days rather than those prescribed by the custom and practice of the majority community.

This direct and indirect discrimination, taken together, constitutes 'cultural-racism' (in contrast to colour-racism) and is targeted at groups perceived to be assertively 'different' and not trying to 'fit in'. It is racism which uses cultural difference to vilify or marginalize or demand cultural assimilation from groups that also suffer colour-racism. Racial groups which have distinctive cultural identities or community life will suffer this additional dimension of discrimination and prejudice. This form of racism is least acknowledged, debated or repudiated, and is not properly outlawed (the courts have deemed discrimination against Muslims to be lawful), and yet is the racism that is on the increase, has the greater impact upon Asians and is an important cause of the rising levels of racial violence in Britain and Europe. Contemporary attacks upon Muslims are not a case of straightforward religious bigotry or of colour-racism but of the phenomenon I am calling 'cultural-racism'. It is because of its complex character that it cannot be properly defeated by the politics of religious harmony or by opposing colour-racism, but only by a movement that understands the pluralistic phenomenon of cultural-racism. This approach can also explain some of the contradictions in contemporary racism, such as the observation that white working-class youth culture is incorporating, indeed emulating, young black men and women while hardening against groups like south Asians and Vietnamese (Cohen, 1988: 83; Back, 1993).

One way to understand the emergence and growth of cultural-racism is to see it as a backlash against the emergence of 'public ethnicity'. Minority ethnicity, albeit white ethnicity like that of the Jewish community, has traditionally been regarded in Britain as acceptable if confined to the privacy of family and community, and if it does not make any political demands. However, in association with other sociopolitical movements (feminism, gay rights, etc.) which challenge the public–private distinction or demand a share of the public space, claims are increasingly made today that ethnic difference is something that needs not just 'mere' toleration but to be publicly acknowledged, resourced and represented. Thus there is a vague multiculturalism as a policy ideology, and it has perhaps contributed to a new ethnic assertiveness, so that many of the race relations conflicts today arise out of a demand for public space, public respect and public resources for minority cultures, and for the transmission of such cultures to the young. Yet, because the British racial equality legal and policy framework is premised on colour-racism, rather than cultural-racism, there is no clear view from any part of the political spectrum (except perhaps from the nationalist Right) about to what extent these political demands are justifiable, especially in relation to religious communalism, and how cultural racism should be tackled.

Prejudice and antipathy against ethno-religious groups pose a challenge the seriousness of which has yet to be appreciated. While a secular framework need not necessarily be insensitively hegemonic, I think that contemporary secular multiculturalists are unaware of the contradictory signals that they are sending out. Multiculturalists who state that public recognition of minority cultures is essential to equal citizenship, while combining this with a denial of an equivalent public recognition of religion, can only convey the message that religious identity has and ought to have less status than other forms of group identity (Modood,

1994c). Why should it be the case that groups proclaiming themselves to be 'black' are to be empowered and given distinctive forms of political representation, but equally disadvantaged groups that mobilize around a religious rather than a colour identity are to be discouraged? While such questions are not answered, non-white religious groups may rightly complain of double standards.

Discrimination and outcomes

Racial discrimination is, thirdly, not necessarily linked to racial disadvantage because some groups migrate with skills and capital, and because some discriminated groups put in extra time and energy, work and study harder, develop self-help and/or other networks to compensate and, therefore, avoid the socioeconomic disadvantages that would otherwise result from discrimination. There is now growing evidence that some Asian groups experience discrimination in selection processes *and* are over-represented (in the sense of appearing in greater proportion than their share of the overall population) in higher education admissions and in entry to prestigious professions such as medicine, accountancy and law (Modood, 1992: ch. 6; Modood, 1993a). This may be a confusing development, even though it is not unique to Britain, and the signs of it happening have been there for some years. In considering the implications of such developments for rethinking racial equality, the following in particular need to be borne in mind.

First, it is not necessarily the case that the upwardly mobile groups experience less discrimination than the less mobile groups; on the contrary, Asians suffer as much prejudice as any group, and it is not obvious that the successful Asian groups experience less discrimination or hostility than the others. Moreover, it is not the case that as a group is perceived to be successful and separated out from other minorities, it will attract less prejudice and discrimination: as the Jews know, those considered to be 'too successful' can suffer more prejudice than those thought to be inferior. Secondly, if measures to eliminate discrimination are successful, it will mean that groups like Indians or Chinese may increase their 'over-representation' in higher education, the professions, and management, for some of those presently kept out will get in. At whose expense should this be? Is it clear that it should be at the expense of whites rather than, say, Pakistanis? As ethnic monitoring becomes more extensive, this argument about overrepresentation will force itself into debates. It has already done so at prestigious US universities, at a number of which Chinese and other Asians have complained that making entry easier for some minorities has the effect of imposing a ceiling upon them. The universities do not deny the charge but say it has to be offset against the wider goal of 'proportional representation'.

An alternative egalitarian defence might be that equality of opportunity is about process, not outcome, about fairness in selection, not numbers in outcome. If so, this would mean a major shift or retreat, as most equality statements (sex as well as race) currently say the opposite. It is therefore important to see why egalitarians currently think of equality in terms of outcomes as well as fairness. Ethnic origin data collection was first introduced on the basis of the reasonable assumption that differential statistics would be *prima facie* evidence of discrimination, of practices that needed to be investigated and justified. Where justification was not possible, the practices were to be eliminated. Yet even where this was done, further monitoring revealed that there was still an inequality in outcomes. Moreover, arguments about the fairness of procedures were proving to be time-consuming and intractable and were perceived as too academic or formalistic by egalitarians and recruiters alike. The simple goal of 'mirroring' the population or achieving proportionality in outcomes as the definition of absence of discrimination, cut through this knot, and made possible the setting of numerical targets or quotas. While this has now become the understanding of equal opportunities at policy level (for gender even more so than for race), Bhikhu Parekh has argued that to commit policy to proportionality is 'to ignore [the disadvantaged groups'] diversity of talents and aptitudes, to control and curtail their right of self-determination, and to mould them in the image of the dominant world' (Parekh, 1992: 270).

If one accepts that different groups legitimately have different norms, priorities and cultural commitments, it *is* difficult to see why the measure of equality should assume that all groups equally pursue the same experiences, education, occupational and other personal goals and make the same compromises between work, family and recreation. Without such an assumption, equality has to be interpreted in a more complex way, as outcomes that are the product of free choices. Yet this surely, especially on a macro-societal level, is even more difficult to measure than fairness in procedures at an institutional level. Hence it is difficult to see how we can altogether give up on equal opportunities as proportionality in outcomes. It must at least figure at the start of equality debates, even if it does not tell the full story. In talking of racial disadvantage we must necessarily be talking about comparative outcomes, about socioeconomic profiles. What we cannot assume is that racial discrimination is the effective cause of racial disadvantage or that the elimination of discrimination will of itself eliminate the conditions of disadvantage, let alone produce freely chosen outcomes. Conversely, the commitment to the elimination of discrimination cannot be put aside just because the discriminated group has managed to avoid relative disadvantages. The right not to be discriminated against by public institutions and in civil society is fundamental.

It is worth spelling out one important corollary of this. To pursue a more vigorous, US-style affirmative action approach to achieve equality of outcomes (inevitably based on soft or hard quotas) will create *prima facie* cases of injustice to individuals (for example, individuals denied entry onto a university course because of a policy which prefers others with lesser qualifications) not just against whites but also against some minorities. Such a policy is not likely to be considered just or necessary unless it can be demonstrated that it is the only way to overcome racial disadvantage, but this would be difficult to sustain at a time when some minorities were being visibly successful. A broad, class-based attack on socioeconomic disadvantage is more likely to win public support and avoid racial and ethnic conflict.

Policy dilemmas

Racial equality thinking, where it reduces racial discrimination to colour-discrimination, and/or fails to think through the implications of public ethnicity, and/or assumes too close a linkage between discrimination and disadvantage, fails to keep up with the sociocultural developments that are taking place. At the very least, these changes challenge the assumptions of political 'blackness': the view that colour-racism is the most important determinant in the outcomes of non-white people who, therefore, form a quasi-class with a common socioeconomic position and interests. They should also challenge the view that the only remedy for their disadvantage is through political power. For the reality is that those groups that evidence social mobility (Indians and Chinese) have no special access to state power and have assiduously kept a low political profile (in so far as they seek political power, it is to consolidate rather than to initiate social mobility). This should encourage sober reflection on the nature and extent of state intervention in this area. Yet the first conclusions one may come to are hardly unproblematic.

Ethnicity – that is, norms, group solidarities and patterns of behaviour which are not merely the products of majority exclusion and may be valued by the community in question, which may inculcate them in its young – can clearly be a resource. It can provide the strength to cope with racism and majority contempt, to instil group pride, to organize

forms of welfare and cultural needs satisfaction, to create business opportunities and enclaves, to maintain across the generations the discipline of
deferred gratification needed to climb educational, business and career
ladders, and so on. It may, therefore, be thought that sound policy should
endorse ethnicity and encourage communities to use their own traditions
to develop themselves. Not only would this be in keeping with multiculturalism but it would mean less direct state intervention and state
management of services, and would therefore be one extension of the
idea of the 'enabling state'.

Two problems, however, immediately suggest themselves. First, some
communities may be too fragmented or too resourceless to benefit from
this approach. It does not follow, however, that this approach is not
appropriate for any group. Secondly, the legitimizing of 'difference' that
this approach involves might increase group consciousness and therefore
encourage the potential for group competitiveness rather than intergroup
social solidarity. Perhaps we need an open recognition that multiculturalism is a legitimate limit on individualism. This, however, is not as simple
an idea as it might sound, or easy to use as the basis for political
consensus. Consider equal opportunities recruitment policies. The principle often enunciated is of overcoming stereotypical bias by treating
everyone the same: but how can one do that if people have different
norms, sensibilities and needs? It is not possible to treat someone as an
individual if one is ignorant about his or her cultural background and
the things that matter to him or her, for the greater the ignorance about
a group of people by an outsider or observer, the greater the reliance
on a stereotype. To decrease the use of unfavourable stereotypes, one
has to increase the level of knowledge about the groups, and to make
sure that the knowledge used is not only of the outsider's generalizing
type but includes some understanding of how the group understands
itself, of what it believes to be some of its distinctive qualities or virtues.

An abstract, culture-blind individualism will necessarily impose
majority norms and expectations. On the other hand, to treat minority
individuals differently can be very difficult to justify in any particular
case, let alone to institutionalize through policies and procedures and to
support by building the necessary consensus amongst managers, staff,
etc. Where active multiculturalism contradicts such a basic (if partial)
intuition of fairness as uniformity of treatment, it will be very difficult
to get public support for differential policies that not merely are about
tolerating difference but involve large-scale resource commitments. A
debate about the implications of cultural difference for equality is therefore unavoidable if multiculturalism is to mean more than tokenistic
recognition of minority culture.

Not only is there a clash between some of our intuitions about fairness and equality, but well-meaning policies may well collide. Some have expressed concern that policies of multiculturalism which, say, allow Asian girls to be withdrawn from certain activities at school (for example, sex education, sport, dance) or not to be entered for certain subjects, collude with traditional views on gender difference and sex roles. Similarly, though less noticed as an example of how tackling some forms of discrimination actually reinforces others, is how many racial equality policies currently act as a barrier to recognizing the needs of, say, Muslims. An example is the same-race adoption and fostering policies which place black Muslims with black Christians, and Asian Muslims with Hindus and Sikhs.

A consideration of the position of Muslims within an egalitarian perspective is urgent. By the usual socioeconomic measures of disadvantage Muslims are among the very worst-off groups, and yet, unlike religious groups like Sikhs and Jews, they are not deemed to be an ethnic group and so are outside the terms of existing anti-discrimination legislation (UKACIA, 1993). Their low level of representation in mainstream institutions and fora in Britain is chronic: no Muslim has ever sat in either House of Parliament or even been chosen by a political party to fight a winnable seat. Given that they form nearly half the non-white population in Britain and over 60 per cent in the EU (Anwar, 1993), it is difficult to see how there could be a race relations settlement without the Muslim communities. Combining as they do the facets of being a socioeconomic underclass, targets of colour-racism and victims of cultural racism, they join in their person the three 'Cs' of race: colour, class and culture. Muslims are an important test of whether racial equality policies can be extended to meet the new challenges of the 1990s.

Conclusions

Despite these various tensions and dilemmas, some of which cannot be resolved without considerably more thought and debate than they have received so far, I offer the following six conclusions as the basis for rethinking racial disadvantage in the context of the new pluralism.

The first principle of racial equality should be anti-discrimination; that is to say, the right of individuals to full participation in all the major aspects of the common social life without being penalized for their racial, ethnic or religious identity, regardless of the socioeconomic standing of the group to which the individuals may belong. In failing to protect groups such as Muslims, existing anti-discrimination law in Britain is in need of urgent extension; in many other European countries, anti-discrimination law of any kind is in need of creation. A new offence of racial-religious violence and harassment will assist the urgent task of pushing these matters up the political agenda. The Northern Irish 'incitement to religious hatred' law also has potential for application in Britain and elsewhere (Modood, 1993b).

Second, colour is a factor in the total analysis of social disadvantage and inability to achieve full citizenship, but it is a weak indicator of need over and beyond the elimination of discrimination, for while some non-white groups may have more members in need of assistance, others may have fewer, and the needs in question will not always be based on race but will sometimes be identical to those of white people.

Third, some aspects of racial disadvantage can only be tackled within wide-ranging needs-based or class-based programmes, though the knowledge that non-white groups have been overlooked or discriminated against in the past, and as a result may be sceptical about provisions of new opportunities and benefits, may mean that explicit monitoring and outreach are required to ensure take-up by all individuals with the relevant needs.

Fourth, because racism is wider than colour-racism, we need to be far more informed and sensitive to cultural and religious differences both in identifying 'racial' discrimination and in strategies for its elimination. This will include training for relevant professionals in the complex character of racial inequality and difference, and in the appropriate cultural backgrounds; and also the recruitment, training and promotion of individuals who can positively relate to one or more of the marginalized minority groups and can infuse their understanding into the policy-making and implementation processes.

Fifth, we need to allow communities to use their traditions and values to meet their problems and disadvantages. Communities should be involved as partners at the level of strategic planning (for example, of an urban development programme) as well as in the provision of services (for instance, housing associations, community centres, social and health services). This has to some extent been happening in the development of black and Asian housing associations; it is time that non-European traditions of medicine and therapy were taken more seriously and that social work was able to incorporate the kinds of family-oriented counselling service that are developing in the Asian voluntary and private sector.

Sixth, where supporting ethnic community structures is not a viable approach, effective ethnic monitoring should ensure that action is *targeted* to those who are actually disadvantaged (for example, in the labour market) and not simply to those who are not white. To this end it is essential that racial equality monitoring goes beyond the use of a black-white analysis or even a black-Asian-white analysis. It would be a step backwards to reduce the plural findings of the census into a frame of just two or three categories. Above all, it would be to let down those who are 'the truly disadvantaged' and to whom policy must be targeted.

These measures are of course only possible where there is a broad consensus for racial equality. In building such a consensus, a concern beyond colour-racism may be an asset. In the battle for hearts and minds, it must be of value to re-emphasize the connections between issues of race and class inequality, social deprivation and exclusion. Moreover, given the nature of the most prominent forms of racism in Europe, where hostility to lighter-skinned Maghrebians and Turks can be greater than to culturally integrated and darker-skinned Africans and Caribbeans, some notion like cultural racism must be a precondition of effective anti-racism. Of course, to emphasize any 'difference' may seem to make social justice and social cohesion more difficult, yet these multiple factors of inequality are integral to the challenge of achieving social justice. Multiculturalism is not just about the appearance of society; it is about refashioning concepts of equality to take account of the ethnic mix that exists in most European cities today. Ethnic and religious diversity has the potential to make society more interesting, more dynamic and more enriching for all its members, but will only do so when its complexities are understood and made integral to radical politics.

References

Anwar, M. 1993: *Muslims in Britain: 1991 census and other statistical sources.* Birmingham Centre for the Study of Islam and Christian–Muslim Relations Papers.

Back, L. 1993: Race, identity and nation within an adolescent community in south London. *New Community,* 19(2), 217–33.

Baldwin-Edwards, M. 1991: Immigration after 1992. *Policy and Politics,* 19(3), 119–211.

Cohen, P. 1988: The perversions of inheritance: studies in the making of multi-racist Britain. In P. Cohen and H. S. Bains (eds), *Multi-Racist Britain,* London: Macmillan.

Forbes, I. and Mead, G. 1992: *Measure for Measure: a comparative analysis of measures to combat racial discrimination in the member countries of the European community.* London: Employment Department.

Giudice, F. 1992: *Arabicides: une chronique française 1970–1991.* Paris: La Découverte.

Hall, S., Critchen, C., Jefferson, T., Clark, J. and Roberts, B. 1978: *Policing the Crisis.* London: Macmillan.

Husbands, C.T. 1992: The other face of 1992: the extreme–right explosion in Western Europe. *Journal of Comparative Politics*, 45(3), 267–84.

Jones, T. 1993: *Britain's Ethnic Minorities*: London. Policy Studies Institute.

Keith, M. 1993: *Race, Riots and Policing: lore and disorder in a multi-racist society*. London: UCL Press.

Modood, T. 1988: 'Black', racial equality and Asian identity. *New Community*, 14(3), 397–404.

Modood, T. 1990: British Asian Muslims and the Rushdie affair. *Political Quarterly*, 61(2), 143–60; also in J. Donald and A. Rattansi (eds) 1992, *Race, Culture and Difference*, London: Sage.

Modood, T. 1992: *Not Easy Being British: colour, culture and citizenship*. Stoke-on-Trent: Runnymede Trust and Trentham Books.

Modood, T. 1993a: The number of ethnic minority students in British higher education: some grounds for optimism. *Oxford Review of Education*, 19(2), 167–82.

Modood, T. 1993b: Muslims, incitement to hatred and the law. In J. Horton (ed.), *Liberalism, Multiculturalism and Toleration*, London: Macmillan.

Modood, T. 1994a: *Racial Equality: colour, culture and justice*. London: Institute for Public Policy Research/Commission on Social Justice.

Modood, T. 1994b, Political blackness and British Asians. *Sociology* (November).

Modood, T. 1994c: Establishment, multiculturalism and British citizenship. *Political Quarterly*, 65 (1), 53–73.

Parekh, B. 1992: A case for positive discrimination: In B. Hepple and E. Szyszczak (eds), *Discrimination: the limits of law*, London: Macmillan.

Phillips, A. 1993: *Democracy and Difference*. Cambridge: Polity Press.

UKACIA (UK Action Committee on Islamic Affairs) 1993: *Muslims and the Law in Multi-Faith Britain: need for reform*: A Memorandum to the Home Secretary. London: UKACIA.

Wilson, W.J. 1987: *The Truly Disadvantaged: the inner city, the underclass and public policy*. Chicago: University of Chicago Press.

Woodall, C. 1993: '*Arabicide* in France: an interview with Fausto Giudice. *Race and Class*, 35(2), 21–33.

Young, I.M. 1990: *Justice and the Politics of Difference*. Princeton, NJ: Princeton University Press.

Young, K. 1992: Class, race and opportunity in R. Jowell, L. Brook, G. Prior and B. Taylor, *British Social Attitudes* (the 9th Report), Aldershot: SCPR.

Comment: Minority Rights, Majority Values

Bhikhu Parekh

Tariq Modood has admirably mapped out the complex terrain of racial discrimination. He persuasively argues that racial discrimination takes many forms, of which that based on colour is but one and not always the most objectionable, that it impacts differently on its victims, and that the success of some members of discriminated groups does not disprove the existence of racism. Indeed one could even argue that by leading some communities or individuals to seek in their achievements both a cushion against racism and a way of humiliating their tormentors, and making them aggressively ambitious, racial discrimination distorts their psyche and stunts their all-round development. Their success has a dark shadow and demonstrates the depth and power of racism rather than the opposite. Modood is also right to maintain that race and class stand in a highly complex relationship, that racial disadvantage is built up over generations, and that combating it requires nuanced and target-specific strategies. Since I agree with a good deal of what he says, I shall begin by referring to three small points of disagreement between us, and then go on to develop themes hinted at but not fully explored by him.

First, although Modood rightly argues that people can be discriminated against on cultural grounds, I am not happy with his use of the term 'cultural-racism'. It detracts from the historical specificity of racism, promiscuously reduces all forms of discrimination to so many varieties of racism, and implies that cultural-racism is substantially like and has the same basis and logic as its more familiar biological counterpart.

Second, Modood's tendency to use the term 'race' and its derivatives in a highly general sense leads him to draw questionable comparisons between Britain and the rest of Europe. Racism arises and is legitimized differently in different cultural traditions, with the result that its incidence in different countries cannot be compared in arbitrarily selected and allegedly neutral terms. French racism, for example, is ethnically more tolerant but culturally more oppressive than its British counterpart. If one masters the French language and culture, one is likely to be accepted as an equal and one's colour matters little. The equivalent is not the case in Britain. This may perhaps explain why, although France has during the last two decades witnessed four times as many racial killings as Britain and has a weaker anti-discrimination law, it has also seen Arabs and blacks occupy far higher positions in universities, public life, civil service and government than their counterparts in Britain. The Netherlands is different from both, and operates its own distinct system of exclusion. Racism there is less pervasive and intense than in Britain and France and does not masquerade under the meretricious guise of national identity, yet far fewer immigrants rise to high positions than in either. If we are to counter racial discrimination in Britain, we need to identify its specificity, uncover its distinct cultural and historical roots, and tease out its unique mechanism of operation.

Thirdly, I agree with Modood that the term 'black' was and is too indeterminate to capture the differences of culture and interest between the various groups subsumed under it, and that its subsequent questioning was fully justified and only to be expected. Unlike him, however, I think that it served and can still serve valuable purposes. It stresses the common experiences of discrimination between the various groups, counters and contains their historical legacy of mutual antagonism, and sharply posits an unmistakable other. It also draws upon a rich and evocative historical vocabulary, and captures one of the central roots of racism. Once it was rejected in the name of ethnicity, not only did our political vocabulary become impoverished but also each community went its own way and became vulnerable to a further break-up along national and religious lines. The painful results of this are too obvious to need elaboration, and cannot be countered by a rainbow coalition. Blackness as defined in the 1960s and 1970s was an abstract universal, but rather than reject it in the name of uncoordinated ethnic and religious particularities, we need to redefine it as a concrete universal, capable of both accommodating and integrating these particularities.

Liberation and diversity

I would now like to turn to some of the themes raised by Modood's interesting chapter. He eloquently highlights the pervasive hostility to ethnic differences in almost all European countries. Unlike their counterparts outside and in pre-modern Europe, contemporary European societies find it extremely difficult to live with difference. They do, of course, welcome differences, but only if these are based on individual choice and do not step out of the permissible range of diversity. As a result they have acquired a deep assimilationist thrust, shared alike by conservatives, liberals and socialists. They insist on the centrality of such values as personal autonomy, freedom of choice, independent thought, equality of treatment and common citizenship. Equality of treatment is equated with uniformity of treatment, a departure from it being construed as a privilege. And common citizenship is taken to imply a direct and unmediated relationship between the citizen and the state. This way of thinking encourages a deep suspicion of the communally centred minority ways of life, and is inhospitable to minority demands for the recognition of their cultural differences. Such demands are seen as violations of common citizenship and pleas for privileges. Not surprisingly, a sustained attempt is made in most European countries to dismantle the minority communities and to assimilate their de-ethnicized individual members into the mainstream society.

While assimilationist liberalism rightly stresses the importance of common citizenship, social cohesion, a shared system of meanings, limits to a society's ability to tolerate cultural diversity, and the dangers of overindulging cultural differences,[1] it takes an exceedingly narrow view of these values and additionally violates some of the central principles of liberalism.[2] The liberal is committed to equal respect for persons. Since human beings are culturally embedded, respect for them entails respect for their ways of life. One's sense of personal identity is closely bound up with one's language, characteristic modes of thought, customs, collective memories, and so on, in a word with one's culture. To ignore the latter is to denude the individual of what constitutes him or her as a particular kind of person and matters most to him or her, and that is hardly a way of showing respect.

The assimilationist liberal mistakenly equates equality with uniformity, and fails to appreciate that otherwise different individuals are treated *unequally* if subjected to uniform treatment.[3] Jews are not treated equally if they are required by the law to close their shops on Sundays. For Christians Sunday is a holiday, but not for Jews, who are therefore reduced to opening their shops only five days a week. Muslim women are not treated equally if required to wear trousers at work. Since they are culturally forbidden to expose their bodies in public, the requirement virtually renders them jobless. To exempt them from this requirement is not to privilege them but to ensure them equality of treatment. It is true that differential treatment can become a basis for unfair discrimination, but so can uniform treatment. What is needed is to find ways of being discriminating without becoming discriminatory, and of guarding against the misuse of differences.

Assimilationist liberalism sometimes has the opposite consequences to those intended by it. When it declines to accommodate the demands of cultural minorities, the determined minorities refuse to give in, and exploit such spaces as liberalism itself provides to legitimize their demands. For reasons which we cannot here examine, liberalism is extremely sensitive to religion and anxious not to appear intolerant of deeply held religious beliefs and practices. Minorities are naturally tempted to take advantage of this, and demand recognition of their differences on the ground that these are an integral part of their religion. The Sikh's turban no longer remains a cultural symbol, which is what it largely is, and becomes a religious requirement. The Hindu's refusal to eat beef, the Muslim's use of loudspeakers to call the faithful to prayer, the Rastafarian's dreadlocks and so on come to be presented in similar terms. The morally embarrassed liberal more often than not concedes these demands.

The long-term consequences of this are unfortunate for all concerned. Minorities are increasingly led to define their identity in religious terms, and their religion monopolizes their culture. Lacking the restraining influence of the non-religious elements of their culture, the religion becomes narrow and dogmatic. Contingent cultural practices acquire the status of mandatory religious requirements, and pressures are mounted for their rigorous enforcement. With the religionization of the culture, religious leaders become its sole authentic spokesmen and acquire undue religious and cultural authority. Assimilationist liberalism unwittingly not only arrests the natural growth of community but also paves the way for some form of fundamentalism. It is not often appreciated that fundamentalism is frequently provoked by liberal intolerance, and that once it arises, liberalism feels mortally threatened and unwittingly takes over many of the characteristics of its enemy.

Sometimes when the religionization of their demands does not work, minorities legitimize them as part of their ethnic identity, and insist that the liberal refusal to concede them amounts to a violation of the latter. Cultural practices get ethnicized and are given a pseudo-natural grounding. The same process that occurs in the case of the religionization of culture is repeated here with appropriate modifications, and with similar results. If cultural differences were accepted as legitimate, and if the demands based on them not dismissed out of hand, those involved would not need to ground them in something as intractable and non-negotiable as religion and ethnicity. Religious and ethnic differences would still remain, but there is no need to add to their number.

Discrimination, difference and community

Respecting and promoting cultural diversity requires action at several levels. It requires that cultural minorities should be protected against conscious or unconscious discrimination in socially significant areas of life. It was recently discovered, for example, that ethnic minority candidates for jobs and examinations were systematically underscored by their white interviewers, because their habit of not looking the latter in the eye led the interviewers to conclude that the candidates were shifty and unreliable.

An orthodox Jew contesting police evidence was disbelieved by the magistrate because, though religious, he refused to take the oath. The man was convicted on the basis of false police evidence. It was too late when the judges realized that some devout Jews do not take the oath for fear that they might inadvertently say something wholly or partially untrue and offend God.

In these and similar cases, the parties involved suffered discrimination and disadvantage because of the failure to take account of cultural differences. Those in authority abstracted their acts from the systems of meaning in which they were embedded, and uncritically interpreted them in terms of conventional categories and norms. Not surprisingly, they wholly misunderstood the acts and ended up treating their agents both unequally and unjustly. Individuals are unlikely to be treated equally if their relevant differences are not taken into account. Two examples will indicate how justice can be done against a background of cultural difference. In Holland a Turkish woman's unemployment benefit was discontinued by a government officer because she refused to accept a job in which she would have been the only woman in a group of male workers. On appeal the Dutch Central Court of Appeal ruled that the discontinuation of benefit was unjust, as the woman's refusal to accept the job under culturally and religiously unacceptable conditions was fully justified. A white woman's appeal in a similar situation would have received a different treatment. The two women are treated differently but equally, the equality consisting in the fact that they are judged *impartially* on the basis of the *same* criterion of what constitutes reasonable or acceptable working conditions for each.

Difficult situations do of course arise. In Britain a Nigerian woman scarred the cheeks of her 14- and 9-year-old sons in accordance with her tribal customs. This went against the norms of British society and she was convicted. However, since the woman was following her cultural practice, and since the cuts had been made in a ceremonial atmosphere and were unlikely to inflict permanent damage on the children, she was granted an absolute discharge. The judgement reconciled the demands of the two cultures, and avoided the dangers of both abstract universalism and naive relativism. The Nigerian woman was first judged on the basis of the universally acceptable principle of not causing harm to others. Her culture was then brought in to elucidate the context, reinterpret the nature of the harm and annul the consequences of the application of the universal principle. On the abstract universalist view, she should have been convicted and punished. On the relativist view, she should not have been convicted at all. On the culturally mediated universalist view, which the court took, she was convicted but not punished. The court's judgement indicated to the woman and to the minorities in general that while the British courts respected cultural diversity, they would only do so within certain limits and subject to certain conditions.

Racial disadvantages cannot be eliminated by state action alone. While such action can break the cycle of cumulative handicaps, it can stifle the initiative and resourcefulness of its beneficiaries and even damage them by developing a culture of dependency. The state needs to encourage and, when necessary, help them build up their own communities in order that they may acquire confidence and capacity for concerted action and evolve programmes of action sensitive to their needs.

Decentralization has many virtues, and there is no obvious reason why it should be based only on territorial and occupational and not on communal grounds as well. Similarly there is no reason why active participation in communal life should be considered less valuable than in the conduct of local affairs. Theorists of participation make the mistake of concentrating only on the territorial units and ignoring the increasing importance of communal life. In a society in which neighbours have only limited contacts with each other and are bonded by limited common interests, it is unwise to put all our hopes in neighbourhood communities.

In Britain the state grants considerable autonomy to the Jewish community and does much to reinforce the authority of its representative institutions. Jews may open their shops on Sundays without being in breach of the Sunday trading laws provided they obtain an appropriate certificate from the Board of Deputies of Jews. The Rabbinical courts, to which Jews may take their disputes if they so wish, are recognized by the state and their verdicts are binding on the parties involved. On matters relating to their community, the Board of Deputies is invariably consulted and its views are treated with respect. Thanks to all this, the Jewish community has a collective presence in British public life. While Jews remain free to leave their community and to disagree with its collective pronouncements, those who remain attached to the community respect its democratic structure of authority and are subject to its moral and social pressure. When the crime or divorce rate rises within the community or when the family unit declines, it is widely discussed in synagogues and community newspapers, and appropriate actions are demanded and often taken.

Similar tendencies are also evident among other minorities in Britain, France, Germany and the Netherlands. The French, who for long frowned on and refused to recognize ethnic and religious organizations, are now beginning to stress their value as 'vital social tissues'. Since they are relatively new, the minority organizations lack the cohesion and the democratic structure of their Jewish counterparts. However, they are beginning to develop them. There is no obvious reason why the state should not encourage and sustain this process. To be sure, its job is not to *protect* minority cultures, for if they lacked the required will and capacity they would not survive and the state's protectionist measures would only arrest their natural evolution. Nor is it the state's job to *institutionalize* the relevant communities into bureaucratic corporations and throw its authority behind them. That is the way to social fascism, in which communal corporations, enjoying the patronage and subject to the manipulation of the state, oppress their members, build up vested interests and freeze the inescapable process of cultural change.

What I am proposing has very different implications. Communities that are cohesive, have democratically accountable self-governing institutions, and allow their members a right of exit play a vital role in giving their members a sense of rootedness, harnessing their moral energies for common purposes, and sustaining the spirit of cultural pluralism. Rather than seek to dismantle them in the name of abstractly and narrowly defined goals of social cohesion, integration and national unity, the state should acknowledge their cultural and political value and grant them such support as they need and ask for. They do not threaten its cohesion and unity; on the contrary they give it a moral and cultural depth. There is nothing inviolable about the traditional liberal separation between the state and society. Conducting the affairs of a society as complex as ours is too important a task to be left to the state alone. It requires partnership between the two, and encouraging cohesive communities to run their affairs themselves under the overall authority of the state is an important dimension of that partnership.

Modood rightly points to the growing Islamophobia in Europe, and to the fact that Muslims are subjected to considerable discrimination. The rise of the phobia cannot be explained in terms of the historical memories of the Crusades or of the Muslim rule over parts of Europe. The hostility is often *greater* in those countries that were free from Muslim rule and not extensively involved in the Crusades. What is more, the Muslims have been a significant presence in Europe since the 1960s, but the hostility to them did not develop until nearly two decades later. It would seem that the fear of Islam arose as a result of the increasing militancy of Islam in several North African and Middle Eastern countries, the Islamic revolution in Iran, the Rushdie affair, and the European Muslims' legitimate demands for a greater public recognition of their religious identity. All this frightened the Left, which was alarmed at the rise of forces it had fondly imagined to be on the decline, as well as the secularists and liberals, who had hoped that the post-Enlightenment privatization of religion was a settled feature of European life. It is hardly surprising that these groups have been at the forefront of the crusade against what they misleadingly call Islamic fundamentalism.

If the fear of Islam is to be effectively countered and if Muslims are to enjoy equality of treatment, deeper cultural changes need to occur on both sides. Muslims need to reinterpret their religious tradition, especially as it applies to the *dar-ul-hurb* (non-Muslim world), and create an autonomous space for the state and secular values. For their part Europeans, especially the secularists and the Left, need to appreciate that religious values and sensibilities can give a much-needed moral and spiritual depth to our increasingly instrumentalist social and political life, reaffirm the dimension of sacredness and make a valuable contribution to the conduct of public affairs. Now that the Left is beginning to talk about ethical socialism, it should be more prepared then ever before to abandon its hostility to religion, including Islam. It is only when *both* sides appropriately redefine their respective traditions that they can hope to come together in a spirit of mutual appreciation and complementarity.

Notes

1 Many post-modernist celebrations of cultural diversity fail to appreciate these vital values. As a result they cannot explain how cultural differences can coexist within a single polity, why they are *valuable*, and why racial inequalities are *bad*. This failure mars Homi Bhabha's otherwise perceptive *The Location of Culture* (1994).
2 For a further discussion see my 'Decolonizing liberalism' (1994b).
3 For a full discussion, see my 'Cultural diversity and liberal democracy' (1994a) and 'British citizenship and cultural difference' (1991).

References

Bhabha, H. 1994: *The Location of Culture*. London: Routledge.
Parekh, B. 1991: British citizenship and cultural difference. In G. Andrews (ed.), *Citizenship*, London: Lawrence and Wishart.
Parekh, B. 1994a: Cultural diversity and liberal democracy. In D. Beetham (ed.), *Defining and Measuring Democracy*, London: Sage.
Parekh, B. 1994b: Decolonizing liberalism. In A. Shtromas (ed.), *The End of Isms?*, Oxford: Blackwell.

Part III

Social Solidarity and Economic Prosperity

5 The Politics of Potential: A New Agenda for Labour

Gordon Brown

I want to suggest in this chapter not only how enduring socialist values can be applied in the new circumstances of the 1990s, but also that they must be if we are to address problems of economic decline and unemployment, poverty and social disintegration. There are some who argue that the historic tasks of the Left in Europe have been completed, that free market ideology is triumphant, and that the basic aims of the early socialists – above all of emancipation – can be achieved without a radical transformation of society; in other words that we have now reached the end of ideology, or – as some put it – the end of history.

I believe that this is not only wrong but it is to misunderstand socialism's task. Socialism has always been much more ambitious in its aspirations than the removal of poverty, unemployment and squalor, tasks that remain to be completed, and which it should be said themselves cannot be accomplished without a major reordering of society. At root, our objective is that individuals should have the opportunity to realize their potential to the full – that individuals should be enabled to bridge the gap between what they are and what they have it in themselves to become. Our distinctive argument is that the strength of society is essential not only to tackle all entrenched interests and accumulations of power that hold people back, but also positively to intervene to promote the realization of potential.

One hundred years ago this objective made action against poverty, slums and unemployment the first priority. No one could begin to realize his or her potential as long as she or he went without food, was badly housed or was denied work or income. Fifty years ago the route to achieving this objective involved setting a floor of rights to social security, employment, health care and educational opportunities. Now in a global economy, where in industry, labour and skill are increasingly more important than capital, where in society, individual aspirations are rightly greater than ever, and where, as Anthony Giddens points out in this volume, just about everyone has become a decision maker in his or her own right, our view of what it means to realize potential has to be much more ambitious than ever before, and I would argue thus truer to the original vision of pioneering socialists.

I want to suggest that in the 1990s we can use the power of all to meet the potential of each. In the process, we can build a new popular socialism on four foundations. First, a commitment to and strategy for tackling all entrenched interests and unjust accumulations of power and privilege that hold people back; in short a new redistribution of power that gives people more control over their lives. Second, an enabling state offering new pathways out of poverty for people trapped in welfare, showing that the true role of government is to foster personal responsibility and not to substitute for it. The welfare state should not just be a safety net but a springboard. Our guiding theme, to paraphrase an old quotation, is not what the state can do for you but what the state can enable you to do for yourself. Third, a new constitutional settlement between individuals, their communities and the state that offers guaranteed safe-guards to individuals and devolves power wherever possible. I believe that to 'reinvent' government we must first reconstruct the very idea of community. And fourth, a new economic egalitarianism which starts from the recognition that it is indeed people's potential – and thus the value of their labour – that is the driving force of the modern economy, and that the modern economy succeeds or fails through enhancing the skills of everyone. Instead of capital exploiting labour for the benefit of the few, the challenge is to rebuild our economy to ensure labour can use capital to the benefit of all.

We must start, however, by identifying the changes that have taken place over a hundred years to distinguish the old agenda from the new one we must follow, defining what we mean by potential and community, and finally sketching out the social and economic policy agenda we must now pursue.

Socialism one hundred years on

When in 1918 the socialist founders of the Labour Party formulated our socialist constitution, the clauses IV and V they incorporated within it were rallying points for a number of quite distinct ideological propo-sitions and policy positions, including those of Christian socialists, egali-tarians, cooperators, Marxists, Fabians concerned with efficiency, and syndicalists and guild socialists concerned with control of industry. But behind these distinctive positions lay two clear claims about how individual potential or what was then called 'popular emancipation' could be realized. The first was that the economy must be run in the public interest – in the interests of the community as a whole. The second was that there must be fairness in the distribution of wealth, income and opportunities. I believe that it is important to understand that these aspirations grew out of a series of ethical principles applied by socialists to the society in which they lived.

These basic principles hold as true today as they ever did: first, a belief that individual potential is far greater than can be realized in a wholly capitalist society; second, a belief that individuals are not just self-centred but also cooperative; and third, a belief not only that individuals thrive best in a community and that the potential of the individual is enhanced by membership of a community but also that a strong community is essential for the advancement of individual potential. The point in listing them is to show how our basic objectives are wider and more comprehensive than the relief of poverty, more ambitious than what are often 'negative freedoms', the freedoms from unemployment, poverty and ill-health. Of course, as long as there is poverty the relief of poverty will be among the primary aims of the socialist movement. But I want to argue not only that our basic ambitions go to what I will call the politics of liberating potential, but that in recognizing this a fresh agenda opens up for socialists that has relevance and appeal to people whether they are poor or relatively wealthy, well housed or badly housed, in work or out of work.

A hundred years ago, controlling the means to life meant controlling the means of production, distribution and exchange, without recognizing the impact of production and consumption on the environment as a whole. That was clearly wrong. Now controlling the means to life in the interests of enhancing individual freedom clearly means controlling the environment of which the economy is a part, and that requires collective action. Secondly, a hundred years ago it was thought by some that, for the individual to have some control over the productive process in the public interest, the only possible mechanism was expropriation of the means of production, and there was a view that this assertion of the public interest conflicted with the very existence of markets. It is now well understood that both these conclusions do not necessarily follow from the recognition of a public interest, for it is quite apparent that power can concentrate at the expense of individuals within the state as well as within private capital, and that the state can, like private capital, be a vested interest. But it remains clear that while markets can be used in the public interest they are not naturally or necessarily so used; they can produce unfairness, monopoly, and inefficiency. So while the public interest does not require the abolition of markets, it requires that we ensure they be organized to advance the public good. The key question is not whether we abolish markets but how we set standards, or regulate, in a way that ensures that markets work in the public interest.

Thirdly, the socialist answer to the exploitation of labour by capital was, a hundred years ago to advance the public interest by abolishing, or at least controlling, private capital. Now most would accept that the real answer to capital exploiting labour in the interest of a few is to create the circumstances not in which capital is somehow abolished but in which labour can exploit capital in the public interest. Indeed where the success and failure of an economy depend on access to knowledge more than access to capital, individual liberation arises from the enhancement of the value of labour rather than the abolition of private capital.

This last point goes far beyond what is called 'the managerial revolution' of fifty years ago, which recognized that in the organization of the standard company a separation had taken place between the function of owner and the function of manager, and that the manager performed a different role from the owner of capital. Now the skills revolution rather than just the managerial revolution is upon us. While capital remains an essential ingredient for the success of an individual company, it should be treated as a commodity like plant and machinery rather than the directing force of our economy, and we should recognize that it is the skills of all the workforce that are the key to economic progress. The important conclusion we reach is that the Left's basic century-old case – that we must enhance the value of labour as the key to economic prosperity – is now realizable in the modern economy. If this analysis is right, socialist theory fits the economic facts of the 1990s more closely than those of the 1890s.

Fourth and finally, one hundred years ago it was thought that the rights that mattered were primarily the right to vote and the right to basic services, such as health, education and social security like pensions. Now we can see how for individuals truly to realize their potential they must not only have the right to these basic pathways out of poverty but also have an equal right to participate in all the major decisions affecting their lives and a right to the best, not just basic, services.

If we are to succeed in our ambition not just to reverse the unfairness of Conservative rule, but to make the equal right to develop one's potential a centrepiece of socialist politics, we must be clear what we mean by both potential and community.

Potential

I start from the proposition that even in the complex world of the 1990s, human potential is scarcely tapped, and that only a small proportion of our capability as individuals is used. A closed society, one that assigns people predetermined roles and fails to see its role in opening up new opportunities, will also fail to harness potential. When we talk of new dimensions of the idea of potential we mean, for example, new opportunities for freedom for women who are prevented from fulfilling their capabilities at work because of responsibilities at home and the absence of childcare; we mean children denied full opportunities because of inadequate educational opportunities and facilities; we mean young people denied options and choices because they go without the best books, research materials and facilities; we mean not just people out of work but people in work prevented from advancing themselves because of authoritarian structures in the workplace, trapped in cages of low expectation, unfulfilling work, mental drudgery and lack of opportunity. This view of potential does not fit with and rejects the old Toryism that denied the very existence of a problem, where every person had a station in life, and the new liberalism which claims against all evidence that the market is sufficient means to any end. It leads us to reject the narrow 'realism' of the employer who claims no obligation to the worker, and the blindness of accounting conventions which will value every item of stock and every machine but place no value on the people who make them work.

But it is important to recognize that we approach the question of potential in a completely new economic and social context. The conditions of economic development have changed dramatically as a result of the globalization of the economy, and with the creation of global capital markets and the global sourcing of companies. The nature of work and its place in life is changing, and microtechnology has altered our assumptions about lifetime careers; the old idea of a forty-hour week, a forty-eight week year and a fifty-year working life has gone. The threat to our environment is increasingly present and recognized, and thus the need for collective action imperative. People's daily lives are less and less influenced by tradition and habit, whether they are poor or affluent; in other words we have more opportunity to make what we are and what we become. And we have recognized that the state and national bureaucracies can themselves become entrenched interests that deny people opportunity and hold them back.

So in the 1990s we are in new circumstances where traditional ways of living and doing things no longer bind people, where people want the freedom to have more control over their own lives and want to develop their talents to the full. We are in a new world where we mean by potential that every individual is a decision maker in his or her own right, and where markets left to their own devices, which could expand some options, could also, through monopoly, lack of information, short-termism and market failure generally, restrict rather than advance many options for a fulfilling life. And as in the past a strong and supportive community is essential for individuals to advance. But 'community' is changing too.

Community

If the first distinctive feature of modern socialism is the breadth of our assertions about the potential of each individual, the second is our belief in the importance of community in helping individuals realize that potential. Indeed I believe that the dividing line in modern politics is our view on the Left that the well-being of the individual is best understood within the context of the broader community, as we use the community to empower the individual, while the Right believes we do best as competitors in lonely struggle in an impersonal marketplace of buyers and sellers. As well as a manifest denial of reality, the neo-liberal position is an insult to our own sense of interdependence.

But community was never, at root, a reference only to a geographical entity or a description only of class or, most of all, synonymous with the state, but something more fundamental: a recognition of our interdependence, that we emerge from society and are part of it. But we must understand that sustained attack on community by the New Right has been possible for two reasons. First, territorial communities and therefore local identities have broken down under pressure of geographical and upward mobility. Secondly, traditional and static ways of living have had to change as individuals, quite rightly, seek greater personal autonomy and quite legitimately desire to break free from traditional life-styles. In other words community – if defined as merely territorial identity and the preservation of unchanging or static tradition – is out of date and as the defining characteristic of most people's lives has probably gone for ever.

But New Right opponents of community have seized on these two massive changes in the way we live and drawn a more fundamental but erroneous conclusion from it – that the very idea of society or community, in the sense of recognizing and acting upon our interdependence, no longer exists. The truth is that in a world where what happens in a nuclear power station in one continent can influence the capacity for babies even to be born in every other, where the spread of disease in the poorest country can kill thousands in the richest city of the world, where the flick of a computer switch in one capital in one country can affect career opportunities and living standards in town and country in every other, interdependence is even more central to the way we live. Indeed the main characteristic of the emerging global economy is the need for even greater cooperation; our destinies are more than ever linked to each other's, and acting together is not only essential in an interdependent world but the only route to the true realization of individual freedom. Community is not therefore a threat to individual freedom but an essential element of realizing it; true individual freedom is possible only from the recognition that we depend on each other.

In a world where personal autonomy is far more important to individuals than ever before, community – or the idea that people see themselves as mutually dependent – has to be constructed and not just assumed. Indeed when people talk about the reinvention of government let us remember that this must be preceded by the reconstruction of community. It would be simply wrong for us to abandon the ethic of community that derived from the recognition of our interdependence. But the acknowledgment of our interdependence and the duty to act upon it mean two conclusions follow. First, in recognition of our interdependence people must accept their responsibilities as individuals and as citizens, and community action should never be a substitute for the assumption of personal responsibility. And secondly, it is essential that we retrieve the wide and expansive notion of community from the narrow and restricted idea of the centralized state, ensuring first of all that individual rights are protected from any encroachment from the state and secondly examining very clearly how the community can organize its affairs in a decentralized way, more sensitively and flexibly. We must break out of the one-dimensional view of government that too easily assumes that where there is a public interest there must be a centralized public bureaucracy always directly involved in ownership of industry or services. Sometimes the community will work through central government, somethings through local government, sometimes through voluntary organizations, sometimes through collective organizations like trade unions.

To meet the new challenges of a world of new aspirations, diverse needs, changing ambitions, new demands for individual fulfilment, the community in the 1990s must define and organize itself in new ways. With every individual surrounded by a far wider range of options, complexity of choices, diversity of influence, with tradition, custom and life-style no longer having the same hold, what people seek in order to realize their aspirations is not just the provision of uniform services but rights to information, to the skills necessary to make choices, to equal treatment. We need information about options, skills to make choices, and barriers to be removed. While the Right tells us that individuals who are free in the marketplace can achieve their potential without the assistance of the community, it is clear that without the rights I describe many will be left behind. This means, for example, guaranteeing rights to independent information, training in the skills necessary to make choices, rights too to the resources essential for independence, and an assurance that others will not circumscribe their actions. So where the Right's view that individuals are held back by the community and do best when left to their own devices requires them to remove government, how does the socialist belief that an active community is a vehicle for the advancement of opportunity, rather than constraint, work in practice?

Individual potential in a cooperative community

In the economic sphere, if the success or failure of a company is more and more dependent on access to knowledge rather than on access to capital, and therefore the enhancement of the value of labour is not just the key source of prosperity but the basic of any modern economic theory, the principle that will guide our policy is that we will make decisions – and agree investments – in a way that will help people realize their potential. The strategy must be twofold, on the one hand to tackle the barriers to opportunity and potential, including banks that underperform, financial institutions that think short-term, employers who fail to train, and then on the other hand to use the power of intervention to promote economic development.

First, we must emphasize policies for what I will call full and fulfilling employment, not just to enhance individual potential but to end the waste of resources in our economy. The priorities must be to abolish youth unemployment, to end long-term unemployment and to replace the very concept of redundancy with the prospect of retraining for work. Second, if the foundation of economic progress is the modernization of our industry through the expansion of individual economic opportunity, and therefore a policy for the enhancement of the value of labour around improved investment in the equipment, technology and skills available to the worker, we need not just standard employment and training measures but to use the panoply of instruments open to government – the tax system, regional research and development grants, social security rules – to make them a springboard for new employment opportunities and the advancement of skills. Third, we need a new strategy for investment not just in labour but in the equipment, technology and infrastructure that support skills, and we need new relationships between finance and industry, between market and state, between public and private sector, mobilizing the energies of both to invest in our industry and infrastructure. And fourth, we need a radical reordering of our economic institutions. The problem of the late twentieth-century economy is that while our ability to succeed depends on knowledge rather than capital, our institutions are based on capital rather than knowledge. The alternative is not just greater access for employees to training for skills and an end to the old master–servant relationships that restrict opportunities for people to make the most of themselves, but greater access for employees to capital that would enable them to develop their ideas and skills. It is quite wrong that labour has no say in the firm when capital has every say. We should move to a position where employees are seen as members of a firm, with companies built not just around their managers but around the entire workforce and their skills.

In constitutional arrangements, the new settlement between individual, community and government I have described depends on the principle that individuals must have safeguards against entrenched interests, including the state, and that the community must again be in a position to organize its own affairs. That means, in Britain's case, not just a Bill of Rights but proper safeguards and new rights for individuals against the excesses of monopoly and private power. It means genuine freedom of information in relation not just to government but to the dark recesses of the private sector as well. It also means a radical transfer of power from the centre to communities, so the idea of one-dimensional government as the expression of community must end; large, centralized bureaucracies with their one-dimensional structure are simply ill equipped to meet the challenges of a rapidly changing information economy and knowledge-based society. Hierarchical and centralized bureaucracies designed in the 1940s and 1950s simply do not do the job in a rapidly changing, information-rich, knowledge-intensive society.

In education, the socialist objective has, rightly, for a hundred years been to ensure that every person has the opportunity to realize his or her potential to the full. But often this has been conceived in narrow terms: the right to education for all but only until 14, 15 or, as now, 16, and for the last fifty years the right to higher education for a minority. The problem is that while the objective – the best education for all – remains the same, many now see the provision of existing education services as wholly inadequate to the real challenge of the liberation of potential.

The role of government must be far more ambitious than uniform provision of educational opportunities for all to 16 or 18 and for a minority afterwards. It must therefore define the public interest in what we must call lifetime or lifelong learning – the social good and common benefits that cannot be appropriated by the individual or company – and then to implement it, for example through entitlements to learn for 16–19-year-olds, support with pre-school education, personal development advice services, annual career check-ups. But we can go further, to shape not just the education system but the whole tax system to reflect the public benefit in harnessing potential – for example, fiscal incentives for investment in personal development and accounting systems that show real worth of training; setting tough standards and qualifications systems; legislation to provide entitlements to paid leave, rights to training for the young at work and so on. Using the power of modern technology and the experience of distance learning and the Open University, we should establish a desktop university, a telecommunications-based advanced education network, which people can access via their workplace work-station or at home.

Conclusion

Britain's problems, in fact Europe's problems, are too little investment, too little skill and education, too little environmental care, too little long-term thinking, too little fairness and too little social cohesion and community. They have one thing in common: they cannot be solved by free market dogma. They require active but modern government action; they cry out for a democratic socialism that empowers and enriches people with new opportunities. The challenge is to show how our lasting principles of a just society empowering the individual can answer the problems we face. My vision of a fair Britain means not just taking on entrenched interests that hold people back, and pursuing a modern social policy that offers pathways out of poverty, but a new economic policy – a new economic egalitarianism – that not only empowers and enriches people with new opportunities through work but recognizes that to enhance the value of labour and skills is the only sure path to modern economic success.

To modernize our policies – like our organization – is not to change or dilute our values: it is instead to revive them and make them relevant for these new challenges.

Comment: Whose Community? Which Individuals?

Anne Phillips

In his reworking of the socialist relationship between individual and community, Gordon Brown takes a tough line on nostalgic images of community as attached to particular localities and bounded by shared tradition. As the defining characteristic of most people's lives, this kind of community has probably gone for ever. Geographical and social mobility has broken up most of what we describe as traditional communities – a process often brutally accelerated by the closure of major factories or pits – and this is not a trend that can be ignored or readily reversed. We cannot simply recall such communities into existence, and anyway, as Brown rightly observes, we no longer value them as much as before. The community that implied harmonious integration into unchanging or unquestioned tradition was frequently experienced as coercion, and as people have attached increasing importance to individual autonomy and personal choice, they have distanced themselves more decisively from this earlier ideal. What Gordon Brown wants to do is to rescue 'community' in some other senses. My first query is whether 'community' is best suited to the alternative values he wants to affirm.

In his own use of 'community', the term is partly a shorthand for the moral limits of individualism, and partly an assertion of the social – but not necessarily state – regulation that is necessary to empower individuals. The first expresses widespread dissatisfaction with what Brown evocatively describes as a society of strangers: people engaged 'in lonely struggle in an impersonal marketplace' without any sense of their interdependence. However much we value our freedom and individuality, most of us want to pursue these in relations of cooperation rather than conflict. We do not want our individual fulfilment to be at the expense of someone else's subordination – as in the cruelty of an unchecked market, which gives freedom and satisfaction to some while discarding others to poverty and long-term unemployment. In this sense, at least, socialism continues to value what Brown describes as an 'ethic of community', recognizing and validating our mutual dependence.

Community in this sense is not at odds with our growing taste for personal autonomy – a point on which I readily agree – but Brown combines this with a second, more controversial, use of the term. Left to its own devices, the market society has never been able to guarantee the full development of each individual's potential; in the context of today's globalized economy, with the additional and increasing threat to the environment, social regulation is more pressing than ever. This is not something that can be left to the individual; this is something 'the community' must do. But why 'community'? Why not just say – as Brown does in other parts of his chapter – that we need social intervention to set standards and regulate the market, to sweep away barriers to human development, to promote the development of both individuals and economy? Why attribute this role to something called the community – which might prove as mythological as 'the' working class?

The choice of 'community' is deliberate, and reflects Brown's strong sense of the sleight of hand that can transform a case for social regulation into uncritical endorsement of an all-powerful state. Arguing that the state too can become a vested interest, he focuses on the community that potentially underpins it, and leaves it open whether this community will act through the institutions of central or local government, through voluntary organizations or collective organizations like the trade unions. I have no quarrel with his pluralization of the possible avenues through which citizens can participate in decisions. But I do query whether it is useful to base this on a community that does not – and may never – exist. Community control can too easily become an empty form of words, while references to what the community wants or needs have all too frequently relied on what self-styled leaders of 'the' community say. 'Community' is a slippery term, and what most seems to unite its many and varied applications (as in the local community, the black community, the Turkish community, the academic community, the European Community . . .) is a lack of precision over democratic accountability and control. This may not much matter when 'community' primarily works to remind us of the limits of a crass individualism. It becomes a vital weakness in the context of a 'radical transfer of power from the centre to the communities', which would encourage community organizations to take control over some part of service provision, and move resources downwards into their hands. If such a transfer is to increase rather than reduce democracy, it has to be combined with precise and careful procedures for identifying the appropriate bodies and ensuring their representative nature.

The notion of 'community' may not be the best starting point for this. If one of the most pressing problems for democracy today is how to return any power at all to the citizens, another is how to become more genuinely inclusive of all the groups that make up a society. Undifferentiated notions of 'the' community are rarely helpful here, for they tend to obscure significant differences within the supposed community. Think of what in another context Gordon Brown has called the 'unacceptable underrepresentation of women at all levels of our political system'. This was a scandal of democracy that went largely unremarked as long as women's interests were subsumed under men's: political parties simply could not see that they had a responsibility to promote female as well as male candidates, and either gave overt preference to men, or refused to see gender as a relevant consideration. The Labour Party has now made a historic and important commitment to equalizing the representation of the sexes, and has begun, in less formal measure, to address the parallel underrepresentation of citizens from ethnic minorities. But in thinking about the length of time these initiatives took, it is worth pondering the constraints of an undifferentiated community. There may be no intrinsic conflict between affirming an ethic of community and recognizing the value of individual autonomy. There certainly has been conflict between affirming the community and giving due recognition to groups disadvantaged by their gender or ethnicity or race. Perhaps Gordon Brown's notion of the community can be developed in ways that deal with this problem. My own inclinations are to steer clear.

My first comment queries the particular role Gordon Brown gives to community; my second relates to the associated importances he attaches to the individual. In his analysis of economic strategy, Brown lays considerable emphasis on what he calls 'the skills revolution', and much of his resolution of supposed conflicts between individual and community rests on a vision of individuals as freed from the constraints of vested interests, and empowered by a strong community to develop their full potential. An earlier generation of socialists assumed that most people's working lives were fixed, and they looked to changes in the ownership of the enterprise as the main way of increasing labour's power. Today's socialists operate in conditions of more continuous change, where women, in particular, move backwards and forwards between paid and unpaid, full-time and part-time work, and where no worker can be confident of a lifetime's employment in the same job or with the same firm. The priority then shifts towards what Brown calls the enhancement of the value of labour (most specifically, through a lifetime's access to education and training), combined with an end to those restrictions that prevent individuals developing their potential. Once labour is enabled to move freely, both within and between jobs, capital will have been put in its more appropriately subordinate place. It will no longer much matter who owns the enterprise, for with the necessary forms of social regulation and empowerment in place, no one will be condemned to dead-end drudgery or blocked from developing his or her full potential. It is a strategy premised on mobility, one that acknowledges the much greater role mobility now plays in our working lives, and looks to ways of enhancing our free and equal movement.

I very much share Brown's commitment to lifetime education as a means to full and equal development; I also agree that ownership would become largely irrelevant if it no longer constrained human potential. But there is a prior question that has to be addressed, and it arises particularly acutely when we consider the situation of women. Despite major and accelerating change, most women still leave their full-time jobs on having a child, and they commonly return to employment as part-time workers, in less skilled and lower-paid positions. More widely available childcare would undoubtedly modify this pattern, as would more generous parental leave, and a lifetime access to training and education. But the needs of children do not fit the working patterns that built up around the model of the male breadwinner, and short of a major revolution in working hours and patterns for *all* workers (not just women but men), women will continue to 'choose' part-time and low-paid work as the only kind compatible with their other responsibilities. This is not something that can be met by enhancing the value of labour; it depends on more structural change.

The kinds of choice that will be available to a future Labour government will be constrained by an economy recklessly run down and resources gratuitously thrown away, and decisions will inevitably be tailored to what is realistic and possible. But in principle, at least, there seems to be a choice between two alternatives. One accepts, in a sense, the slots that are becoming available in an economy which divides jobs more starkly than before into full-time or part-time, high-paid or low-paid, relatively secure or inherently transient; and calls for a more radical understanding of social and job mobility that will empower individuals to move freely and equally between these slots. The emphasis is on ensuring that no one gets stuck: that no one is permanently condemned to the less favourable working conditions. But this leaves the onus very much on the individual, and it only redistributes within what is currently available. For some workers, notably women, these mechanisms may not be strong enough.

The alternative strategy is to change the slots as well as the people – and as far as the sexual division of labour is concerned, this means changing the absurd distribution of working time that still has men working their longest hours when their children are young, and women doing their notorious 'double shift'. Tackling this would involve a good deal more than lifetime access to education. It would imply legislation, for example, requiring all employers to offer reduced working hours to employees who carry major responsibilities to the young, sick or old; more adequate periods of paid parental leave that could be taken by either mothers or fathers; additional rights to periods of unpaid leave that would allow people to break their employment without losing their rights to their job; and most important of all, a sustained initiative to reduce the working hours of those in full-time employment. None of these is inconceivable, and in a climate of high unemployment, each could contribute to an equalization of opportunities not only between women and men but between those in employment and those out of work. But they all depend on a higher level of social intervention than is implied in strategies for education and training.

Gordon Brown's vision of individual empowerment fits broadly within the first category, and in doing so, it shares some common ground with the arguments developed elsewhere in this volume by Gøsta Esping-Andersen. It injects what may be a necessary note of realism into our understanding of equality. If high-skill/high-wage employment necessarily coexists with low-skill/low-wage employment, then the pursuit of strict equality is utopian, and we would be better advised to concentrate on strategies that allow all individuals, over the course of their lifetime, a good chance at the more favourable slots. I have considerable sympathy with this shift in direction. But in the absence of more structural intervention – I have to say, state intervention – labour's capacity for 'exploiting' capital remains a capacity for redistributing what capital has brought into existence, and may still consign particular categories of individuals to permanent occupancy of the low-skill/low-wage positions. Such an outcome would fall a long way short of what Brown promises to deliver, which is a way of empowering individuals 'to bridge the gap between what they are and what they have it in themselves to become'.

6 Productive Solidarities: Economic Strategy and Left Politics

Joel Rogers and Wolfgang Streeck

We take the crisis of the democratic Left to be obvious enough not to require further description. We also take the traditional goals and self-restraints of that Left – in particular, democracy itself – to be unchanged. Given changed circumstances, we ask only: what new strategy should the Left pursue to advance its traditional goals?

As in any discussion of strategy, this single question is actually two: what should be the intermediate object of transformative energies, and what is the agent of that transformation? In any regime, the best strategies unite the answers in a single practice, progress in which creates the conditions of further advance. Operating under capitalism, successful Left strategies have done this in part by forcing improvements in the material welfare and democratic organization of subordinate classes that also improved the productive capacities of capitalism itself.

Such was the case during the heyday of social democratic progress. The Left appeared, more or less straightforwardly, as a redistributive agent of the working class. Notwithstanding its own rhetoric and self-understanding, however, its success in this project owed a heavy debt to the fact that it was also an important contributor to capitalist innovation and general benefit. Through the alchemy of Keynesian economics, the particular interest of workers in redistribution toward themselves was transformed into a general social interest. Higher wages and wage floors boosted aggregate demand, which increased investment, which increased productivity, which lowered the costs of mass consumption goods for everyone. Organizationally, and bearing on the agency question, workers were united by unions and political parties that sought and were rewarded for the competent administration of this virtuous cycle. Their existence, in turn, materially extended democratic practice in formal institutions of governance.

Today, however, this particular project stands in ruins. Macro-economic demand stimulus is highly qualified as a guarantor of welfare, the 'working class' is a much less integral social fact, worker organizations are in disrepair. The Left no longer has a clear job, the performance of which commands wide social respect, and (or, and so) it lacks a credible agent to get what it wants done. The Left therefore needs to find a new object of its energies – something that satisfies a broad popular interest and is equalizing, the pursuit of which can at the same time enhance a capitalist society's economic performance in ways that underwrite general benefit. Put otherwise, it needs a post-Keynesian equivalent of effective demand. This time, however, the alchemy will have to come on the supply side, in production rather than consumption.[1] The Left also needs to be more attentive to articulating the subject of its project. Consistent with its productive role and without sacrificing its traditional attention to matters of class, it needs to develop organizational forms capable of accommodating and consolidating the heterogeneous interests of the population that project would serve. Just as the working class was partly 'made' through the politics of redistribution, and just as redistribution had its own mechanisms for regulating intra-class transfers, a new solidarity – a new basis for social agency – will need to be created and regulated explicitly through an egalitarian politics of production.

The way to accomplish both things, we argue, is by taking seriously traditional Left commitments both to social control of the economy and to the ideal of democracy of which such control is one instance. The former offers an opportunity for the Left to contribute meaningfully to welfare, the latter an ideological framework for practically uniting otherwise diverse popular interests. We take this recommended strategy to be both discontinuous with recent Left practice and perfectly continuous with the Left's historic self-conception and effective role. It would, on the one hand, require the Left to take leave from traditional perceptions of the economy and the role of Left politics in it, by involving itself in the organization of production and abandoning the pretence, sustained by an exclusively distributionist focus, of 'autonomy' from capital. At the same time, the overall social benefit of doing so is large, as advanced western economies stand to benefit greatly from deep political intervention in their supply side. A new Left productivism would also be perfectly congruent with traditional Left claims to advance the general welfare through advance of egalitarian democratic values – liberty, equality, citizenship, solidarity. Without an active and committed Left, indeed, it is unlikely that western capitalist societies will be able successfully to compete with Asian capitalism without sacrificing such defining values.

Our argument has three parts. The first part ('The good old days and lessons learned') briefly reviews the institutional premises and recent problems of Keynesian social democracy, while drawing some general lessons on the conditions of Left stability and advance. The second part ('Why the Left must again save capitalism from itself') makes the general case for popular, regulative institutions on the supply side, and indicates why the Left is uniquely suited to construct them. The third part ('The new politics of solidarity') focuses on the organizational and ideological reform the project requires of the Left itself.

The good old days and lessons learned

The democratic Left makes progress under capitalism when it improves the material well-being of workers, solves a problem for capitalists that capitalists cannot solve for themselves, and in doing both wins sufficient political cachet to contest capitalist monopoly on articulating the 'general interest'. The Left Keynesian project that did just these rested on three organizational premises.

The first was a nation-state capable of directive control of the environment of economic production within its territory. Most importantly within the Keynesian synthesis, this meant a national economy sufficiently insulated from foreign competitors for the benefits of demand stimulus to be reliably captured within its borders, and a monetary policy apparatus sufficiently insulated from world-wide financial flows to permit unilateral correctives to recession. The second was the organization of capital into large, lead, stable firms dominating industry clusters. Large lead firms provided ready targets for worker organization, and levers in extending the benefits of organization throughout the economy they dominated. Firm stability – itself underwritten by the stabilization of demand that was the goal of the Keynesian system – meant stability for the career paths of workers within them. This also facilitated organization, and underwrote the evolution of the 'industrial' model of union organization centred on administration of the internal labour market. The third was the existence of a more or less determinate working class. Aided by pre-existing 'organic' solidarities and all manner of social restrictions, the distinctiveness and integrity of this class was assured by the levelling organizations of mass production. These both destroyed traditional craft divisions within the working class and, on the assembly line, forcefully clarified the distinctive interests of labour and capital.

Present Left difficulties are owing chiefly to the fact that each of these organizational pillars of the old system is now subject to sharp, and for all practical purposes irreversible, forces of erosion. While product and capital market integration is less than complete,[2] economic internationalization has proceeded far enough for Keynesianism to be limited as a state strategy, and simple wage improvement to be impossible as a union strategy. For the state, the permeability of national boundaries removes assurance that the benefits of demand stimulation will be captured nationally, and compromises efforts at unilateral monetary correction. For unions, even national wage norms no longer succeed in effectively 'taking wages out of competition'.

World-wide, we have seen a reorganization of production that complicates the tasks of worker organization. The dominant 'Fordist' production model associated with the post-war years – high-volume, assembly-line production of standardized goods, and steadily rising productivity with benefits captured in higher wages and lower-priced mass consumer goods – has widely collapsed. Many firms are instead now 'sweating' labour in old-style production, albeit increasingly tailored to niche commodity markets. Others are pursuing one or another variety of 'lean' production. Such strategies characteristically feature more advanced attention to logistics and quality, and more intensive utilization of frontline workers, usually organized in teams. But they are associated with just as fierce downward pressures on wages, and just as much hostility to collective worker representation. World-wide, both 'sweating' and 'lean' firms are increasing their market share at the expense of older, generally larger, unionized rivals. They have become the icons of a new age of 'flexible' production, with most of the costs of flexible adjustment to unstable demand visited on workers.

If the threat such productive reorganization poses to worker welfare is too obvious to be laboured, worth noting are the difficulties attending worker organization on adoption of a more worker-friendly, high-wage response. In theory, and in at least limited practice, it is quite possible for high-wage, unionized firms to survive amid fierce price competition by emphasizing non-price attributes of their products – quality, variety, design, speed in delivery, service, and so on. To capture such quality premia, however, firms need to organize themselves for more or less continuous innovation. Organizationally, this means breaking with traditional divisions of labour among different departments of the firm, deploying workers more flexibly, and investing heavily in workforce training to permit frontline workers to assume more autonomy. As work becomes more differentiated and skilled, however, differences in contribution become more visible. With this comes increased difficulty in holding 'the unit' together and defending the common floor for all, including the less talented or motivated whose 'deficits' are now more observable than ever. Also, as workers become truly involved in substantive decisions in the production process, their distinction from management gets blurred, qualifying their willingness to use power against it. As these complexities are socially negotiated within particular firms, loyalty to a distant and uncomprehending centralized union is attenuated, limiting the ability of that union to enforce and renew the general terms under which things had come to be done 'right' in the first place. And as that ability declines, the temptations to defect from central deals rise, leading to further devolution of governance and attendant further fragmentation.

Even more deeply, the structure of the firm itself is changing. In volatile competitive markets, firms seek to internalize scarcity, externalize risk, and keep their options open. Since they do not know what tomorrow's market will look like, they hedge their commitments in today's. Firms reduce risk while preserving capacity by building contingent capacities – short-term alliances and deals with others that can be folded after a particular job is done. As more and more of their operation takes this form, the boundaries of the firm tend to dissolve. Trying to live up to the fantasies of law-school professors, the firm begins to turn itself into a 'nexus of contracts' – between and among a more or less 'virtual' management and workers, suppliers, production allies, distributors – with very little productive core. Of course, not all firms can do this, as somebody must build and maintain the capacity that is contracted in, and in this sense the strategy is self-limiting if not self-destructive. Nevertheless, it creates very large problems for unions, if only because usually the first thing that becomes contingent in flexible firms is employment, or marginal employment, and because replacement of the employer with a virtual employer, or a 'network', does not precisely facilitate organization of workers. Outside of construction, the organizational life and clout have traditionally been based in firms with more or less stable and continuous production capacity, management and boundaries. Now that base is dissolving.

The effect of all these changes, finally, is to exacerbate *workforce heterogeneity*, and with it, the difficulties of articulating a political project based on the advance of the interests of a determinate, much less unified 'working class'. These difficulties are further compounded by the effects of past success in improving and equalizing living standards, which have had the effect of breaking down the most obvious traditional forms of working-class segregation. And they rise to an almost impassable level of difficulty with the animation of social interests in matters other than class advancement – for example, the environment, gender, racial and 'cultural' justice. Finally, the fact that the state is a less effective guarantor of the general welfare means that the political project of uniting across differences to achieve state power is itself less compelling. With public authority less able to assure well-being, and with firms more prepared to reward those with specialized human capital and less prepared to reward those without, those with and without have less material basis for unity against employers or in public arenas. Without the promise of material gains from unity, however, solidarity becomes more nostalgia.

In brief, the governing institutions and practices that the Left long ago succeeded in imposing on capital – thereby both civilizing capitalism and saving it from its underconsumptionist competitive self – are in advanced decay. The effects of their decline are registered in rising unemployment, growing income inequality, rapid expansion of a junk work sector employing low-skilled labour at marginal wages, intensification of work, rising and growing pressures on social welfare benefits, a profound coarsening of social life in our cities, and more. Even as untold technological marvels and fantastic wealth have increased the welfare and amusement of the few, the decline of egalitarian Keynesianism has made life nastier and more brutish for the vast bulk of the population. All this, we believe, is familiar enough. The question is what to do about it.

Why the Left must again save capitalism from itself

How, under the changed circumstances, can the democratic Left be revived? Can it still hope to satisfy the general organizational maxima of Left advance – provide something of value to individual workers, solve general economic problems that capitalists alone cannot solve, and assume, largely by doing so, a clearly contributory role in the broader society? Is there something in the new capitalism that may 'require' a new, or renewed, Left to save it from what used to be called its own contradictions, just as the old capitalism 'required' the old Left? What is that, and how might a renewed Left position itself to seize that role?

Before answering these questions directly, we emphasize that the renewed Left we have in mind is about *power*, not just moral impulses, and that differences in power owe ultimately to differences in actual contribution to the production of material life. All politics is materially conditioned. However morally superior its project, the Left needs strongholds in the economy to guarantee that the democratic interests it speaks for get the resources they need.

More precisely, the democratic Left will be powerful under capitalism only if it has the capacity and competence to make capitalism an offer it cannot refuse – the offer of an indispensable and unique contribution to the viability of capitalism as a mode of production. If no such offer can be made, either because capitalism has become self-sufficient and can prosper on markets, hierarchies and property rights alone, or because the Left prefers to concern itself only with immaterial goodness or material redistribution,[3] the ambit of realized Left demands will always be set by the 'needs' of 'the economy' – as unilaterally defined by those who run it. This is not power, but subordination.

Returning to our questions, then, and beginning to offer answers, the current opportunity we see for the Left is this. The just-described disorganization of capitalism in the name of 'flexibility' generates need for organizing the institutional base on which flexibility can rest. The more decentralization of decisions and specialization of functions, the greater the need for coordination and cooperation; the less formal the structure, the greater the need for trust; the more market and con-tract, the more need for social integration and social cohesion. The new production systems that western capitalism needs to remain economically viable can fully mature only with a social infrastructure of collective goods – from 'trust' to 'goodwill' within the context of shared norms of contribution and reward, from general worker skills to facilities for joint research and development, from an organizational ecology of other flexible firms with comparable productive capacities to regional develop-ment plans and centres for technology transfer. Without this social and institutional infrastructure, it is impossible simultaneously to maintain productive flexibility *and* realize gains to cooperation within and across productive units. Either 'flexibility' simply describes the unilateral imposition of risk, or 'cooperation' becomes limited to firm-specific, and thus inevitably unstable, initiatives.

As in any collective goods problem, rational economic actors, acting individually, have little or no incentive to contribute to the cost of maintaining this social infrastructure. Neo-liberal regimes of governance – based on respect for the fundamental value of 'liberty', enamoured of its exercise in competitive markets, and limited in their appreciation of authority to the hierarchical commands of property owners to their subordinates – are thus singularly ill equipped even to notice, much less to solve, this problem. Neo-authoritarian regimes may do better on contribution, but definitionally through direct threat to defining norms of liberal, republican civic culture. Whatever the decline of popular demo-cratic organization, we do not think it overly optimistic to assume that such a rollback would meet with widespread individual resistance. The administrative feasibility of such schemes, moreover, is undermined by the very 'disorganization' of capital that presently confounds the Left.

A familiar hybrid of these positions, offered by the managerial Right, combines commitment to free markets and to traditional values of obedience and internalized acceptance of authority in vertical social relations. The success of such 'corporate culture' as a vehicle for the social reintegration of a fragmented production process and society, however, will depend on whether the Right will be able to deliver the goods of social peace in spite of growing insecurity and inequality. This we consider unlikely, at least to the point of fully crowding out the obvious Left alternative – the popular construction of cooperation through citizenship and authentic participation, in politics and at the workplace. At a minimum, in any case, the managerial Right's project can be complicated by the Left's ability to mobilize the republican values it threatens – again, best done in the process of articulating an explicit alternative that is more attentive to them.

In a nutshell, our argument is that the present organization of capitalism relies heavily on realizing gains from cooperation, that such cooperation is facilitated by social cohesion and social integration as well as less intangible public goods, and that no prominent non-Left forces are well positioned to provide the infrastructure of institutional capacities and behavioural constraints on which such cohesion, integration and other goods rely. Providing such, in a way consistent with its democratic commitments, is what we see as the new job for the Left. Now, some details.

Effective supply

In the Keynesian age the Left helped itself and the broader society by helping capitalists solve the puzzling cooperation problem of effective demand – a problem because in a competitive economy each individual employer has incentives to cut costs. Today, with competitiveness a more immediate concern than underconsumption, the pressing cooperation problem is on the supply side – in the provision of the collective goods on which optimal productive flexibility depends.

By *effective supply* we mean political interventions directed to providing those goods, and perforce overcoming the market and hierarchy failures now barring their adequate provision. More particularly, the term denotes provision of the range of inputs (institutional supports as well as attendant behaviours) needed to drive capital beyond mere price-competitive responses to present competition, and towards 'quality' strategies that can sustain high and passably equal wages, and some significant democratization of power within the firm itself.

Again, individual firms cannot be expected to produce these goods on their own. They prefer free riding on collective goods to contributing to their provision. Their managers prefer to make profits in ways that put fewer constraints on their autonomy. In many cases, whatever their individual effort or motive, they lack relevant capacities for production.[4] Nevertheless, the imposition of a regime supplying such goods would benefit capital, as well as workers.

Consider training. Capitalists as well as workers are hurt by the non-availability of effective systems of advanced training. For workers, casualization of employment and firm restructuring means that career ladders to higher skills are both more important (to preserve their position on the external labour market onto which they are even more routinely thrown) and less available (given the absence of a stable core inside firms themselves). And within production itself, it becomes difficult for workers to advance their interests in the advanced forms of combined 'team-work' production – involving episodic agglomerations of differently skilled workers and managers for the execution of discrete production tasks. For employers, however, the absence of such a system is also problematic. For it means that they cannot draw on a reservoir of diverse and deep worker skills, even though it is the availability of such a reservoir – if not, alas, its full utilization at any given moment, let alone of course its actual production – that advanced production requires.

Similarly, capital as well as workers is hurt by gross inter-firm variation in work rules, mechanisms of adjudicating intra-firm disputes, compensation and benefits. Workers are hurt by this because it guarantees inequality, and with that a lack of cohesion. Individual workers are hurt by it too, however, both in the obvious sense that many workers have lousy jobs, and in the ways that such incomparability of position limits worker mobility to exploit new employment opportunities. Workers in a job with decent pension rules, for example, may stay there, even if their productivity and satisfaction would be enhanced by a move, because the jobs in which such increased productivity and satisfaction are achievable lack the social protections of the old. But capitalists are clearly disadvantaged by this as well. As more production becomes joint production, just who owns the employment contract is less determinative of whom one works with and how. Firm A sends a delegation of workers to firm B to work on a joint project involving intense collaboration. That collaboration is threatened if firms A and B treat their employees radically differently. Both sides of the class divide, then, have an interest in assuring some comparability in the terms and conditions of employment. And what is true of training or generalized wage or other norms, we here assert, is true of the diffusion of new technology, advanced forms of work organization, desirable accounting practices, joint marketing arrangements, and all manner of other elements of a well-managed, passably egalitarian and generally productive economy.

Constraints and opportunities

Would capitalist firms consent to being governed in their own interest? We suspect they eventually would, and to this extent a Left economic strategy of effective supply does stand a chance of finding allies on the other side of the class divide. But while all firms may eventually be willing to live under a demanding social order of production, and many may even come to support it, and at least a few may find it in their interest to extend its terms – if only to punish less viable competitors – we cannot emphasize too strongly that all this will as a general matter occur only after that regime has become a social fact. Long-term profitability becomes an interest for firms only if short-termism has been made unprofitable, and intangible production factors are attended to only if strategies that can do without them have been ruled out. Acceptance by capitalist firms of a demanding pattern of production follows its institutionalization rather than precedes it. The regime must be imposed, and alternatives foreclosed. And initially at least, this imposition and foreclosure will be sharply resisted.

Recognizing this, and its own current weakness, the Left must be clear from the beginning that implementing a strategy of effective supply requires a double-barrelled approach of *opportunities* and *constraints*. An economic policy that only provides inducements to investors – for example, in the form of infrastructural provisions, from transportation systems to social peace – falls short of what is needed for advanced capitalism to progress. Constraints are needed to prevent firms from defecting from virtuous production patterns, and to force them to learn to observe social rules more complex and exacting than those of markets, contracts and hierarchy. Social institutions must be put in place that pose problems for firms that behave unacceptably, while also offering solutions to those willing to accept high social standards as a basis of their operation.

Equity and efficiency

Aiming at the structure of production, a Left supply-side strategy rejects conventional notions of a trade-off between economic efficiency and social justice. Social democratic economic 'realism' today often accepts the idea that an economy maximizes its efficiency if it is left to itself, enabling political intervention later to detract from such efficiency within reasonable limits in pursuit of social justice. The politics to which this gives rise is one that concedes production and efficiency to management, and economic policy to the Right, as their privileged areas of competence, whereas labour and the Left resign themselves to specializing in distribution, equity and social policy. However, if social integration is recognized as a productive resource, this distinction breaks down, as does the very idea of an efficient economy independent from society and politics.

A productivistic Left economic policy conceives equality and democratic participation not as consumptive benefits taken out of an efficient economy by distributive politics, but as a source of productive progress. Social policy, instead of countervailing economic policy, thus becomes part of it.[5] Equality, rather than being wrought from the economy at the expense of efficiency, is built into the organization of the production process itself. High wages, low wage differentiation and democratic participation serve as supply-side constraints as well as opportunities: ruling out low-wage adjustment strategies while facilitating skill formation and cooperation, and thus high investment in new products, flexible technology, flexible work arrangements, training, etc., that may sustain high wages. Wage bargaining remains important, but the productive contribution of high and stable wages is no longer primarily to provide for high and stable demand, as wages – and social policy in general – become a tool for unions and Left politics to influence the direction of industrial restructuring and work reorganization.[6]

A Left policy of effective supply defends the welfare state as an indispensable instrument for imposing high and egalitarian labour standards on a capitalist economy, as well as for equalizing and enhancing the productive capacities of individuals and organizations, in both ways improving the economy's performance potential. As it does so, however, it insists on productivity within that state. An inefficient public sector may in the past have generated low-paid but secure employment for the clientele of socialist parties and unions, but today's needs for effective public support of competitive quality production have made such shelters too costly to defend. It is not shelter from markets that Left social policy can provide, but equal participation in the productive capacities and collective choices necessary to conquer markets without being conquered by them.

The strategy we recommend, in short, seeks to respond to the limits of both kindness and greed. Mere kindness is dependent on greed providing its material conditions. Mere greed provides material conditions that increase the need for kindness while generating fewer resources for it. While kindness is not enough for a good society, greed is not enough for a productive economy. Left economic policy today can capitalize on the economy's growing need to be supported by virtuous social institutions if it is to progress as an advanced economy. The Left can mobilize power for the purpose of kindness by inserting itself in the construction of such institutions, making equality and participation both its contribution to capitalism's competitive performance and the price of that contribution.

The new politics of solidarity

More products, more choices, greater variation in jobs, less connection between work and community, greater returns to unevenly distributed human capital, and casualized employment can unmake not just a working class, but a public. And without a public, it is difficult to produce the very public goods on which quality-competitive production depends.

At the outset let us say that this problem is, perhaps, not quite as bleak as many students of 'disorganized capitalism' would have us believe. The reason is that the very changes just described – while clearly disruptive of traditional solidaristic practices – prepare the grounds for new ones. Thus far we have chiefly witnessed the ways in which increased competition and firm restructuring have eroded individual and firm tolerance for those who cannot 'pay their own way', while opening up new opportunities for those with unique niches or endowments. Where all is competition, all life is a search for narrowly defensible rents. At some point in the competitive maelstrom, however, it becomes obvious even to the lucky that their luck is unlikely to be eternal. And as this experience becomes general, so too does the social interest in finding some insurance against risk. We cannot assume, however, that the agent of this new system, and its requisite institutional supports, will arise naturally. Both will have to be aimed at to be achieved, and doing so will require the Left to break with some past orthodoxies.

Association and its artifice

Just as the productivist contribution of the Left during the post-war period went on 'behind the back' of established Left rhetoric, so too did the Left's discovery of a central organizational feature of modern capitalism. To work in even passably egalitarian ways, mass democracies require the support of a wide variety of 'secondary' associations – unions, employer associations, community organizations, other civic associations – of a certain kind. These are needed for the representation of social interests, the conveyance of information to the state, the monitoring and enforcement in private arenas of state commands, and the development of trust and cooperation among social actors in all kinds of social project. Given the inequalities of capitalism, however, the right kinds of associative support do not arise naturally. More commonly, indeed, the associations that do form incline toward pathologies of particularism – excessively narrow assertions of interest – or pathologies of inequality – more heavily resourced actors find it easier to organize and use organization to enrich themselves further. And this may leave democracy enfeebled rather than strengthened.

This problem might be 'solved' by limiting associational rights, but this of course is a cure much worse than the disease. Alternatively, and this was the Left's discovery, the 'right kinds' of association might be explicitly encouraged as a counterweight to the 'wrong kinds' that naturally emerge. Political organization, in other words, might be subsidized, as part of the administrative costs of democracy.

As with its own productivism, this Left discovery was seldom explicitly thematized. In practice, however, the Left made sure that its mass popular organizations (as well, in some measure, as those of business) received ample support from the state – subsidies and other supports to political parties and other overtly political organizations, unions and other institutions of economic governance, community organizations and other institutions of representation. With the decline of old forms of solidarity, and the need to encourage new ones, this lesson must now be made public. Just as the economic world is constrained by the social, so the social should be constrained by the requirements of democracy itself. An explicit 'politics of association' is needed on the Left – the aim of which would be to use traditional state powers (taxes, subsidies, other supports) deliberately to provide democracy with its needed associative base.

A prominent example of such use is state mandates on representation itself. In our studies of works councils – to take just one example – we have been impressed with how very important explicit state support is for the viability of such representative forms.[7] Even as, in their mature form, councils may be welcomed by management and labour, their welcome depends (especially at their beginning) on dynamics only set in motion by an absence of choice about their existence. Equally, one cannot fail to be impressed at how important deliberate state subsidies and supports are for the management and union participation in European apprenticeship systems and skills standards setting. While private associative actors can relieve the state of much unnecessary work, they themselves need to be fed.

Here then the orthodoxy the Left needs to break with is its own silence about its own practice. Just as deliberate attention to the narrowly economic institutional bases of productive economy is a recommended focus of its public energies, so too should be construction of the broader associative bases for a deliberative, competent public.[8]

Democratic agency

The Left needs a view of agency simultaneously more encompassing and more demanding than that of Marx. The subject of the Left is no longer best characterized as 'the working class'. Few members of that class think of themselves exclusively as workers; ambiguities in class position confound easy organizational boundaries drawn on the basis of it; and even some clearly non-working-class actors have a stake in what we are about. The agent of the Left, instead, is something more like 'the democratic public' – all those (the working class certainly squarely among them) with an interest in the autonomy and mutual respect that is the foundation of democratic politics, and in the protection of social life and 'nature' from the wreckage inflicted on them by unregulated market forces. At the same time, the 'universal subject' can no longer (if it ever could) be reasonably expected to take a determinate social form, from which solidarity will more or less naturally arise. Now more than ever, solidarity will need to be constructed discursively, and explicitly, with a practice informed by the democratic commitments that ground it. The notion of a constructed rather than found agent makes explicitly imperative, moreover, what we in any case believe to be the case, namely that the universal interest in democracy must be declared before the subject will be found to carry it forward. It is the articulation of that interest that the Left should first and foremost in these days be about. The subject, we believe, can follow. Considering the number of people at risk, under modern capitalism, of finding their lives and their social relations disrupted by 'market forces', we are sanguine about its size.

Without forsaking the Left's traditional attachment to modernity, moreover, we recommend that the Left come to franker terms with its deep affinities with at least some aspects of conservative thought. The Left, including the Marxist Left, has always in some measure been conservative – devoted to protecting the human substance of individuals and societies from being destroyed by marketization. If ever there was a fundamental claim that united the Left's various factions, it was that the lives of human beings must not be made subservient to the laws of motion of the market. In Marx, this became the central motif of a theory of capitalist crisis, premised on the belief that human society would ultimately prove itself ungovernable, and thus unproductive, under a market regime. Marxist crisis theory, in turn, was linked to a theory of class, which served to identify the social and political counterforces that would be activated by capitalist development and would ultimately subject it to social control. It is quite possible that it was the sociological realism of Marxist class theory, especially as it came to be constructed by Marx's followers, that blinded the Left to the powerful commonalities it always had with conservative critics of capitalism, such as Durkheim and, in particular, Polanyi.

Re-reading Polanyi today, one finds another theory of capitalist crisis, like Marx's asserting the ultimate incompatibility of human nature with commercialization, but without the ballast of a realist theory of class. For Polanyi just as for Marx, society under capitalism faces the task of organizing a 'counter-movement' against the anarchy of the market: a task of institutional reconstruction for the sake of protecting both the human and natural substance and the productive capacity of industrial society, and indeed both in one. With capitalism's post-1945 institutional containment broken, this problem poses itself again today, with exactly the same urgency as in the past, and in fact on an even larger scale. For the Left, building its political strategy around the need for institutional protection of society and nature in a global economy should not be ideologically difficult, in the light of its fundamental historical insight that *capitalism's social as well as economic viability depends on the limits society manages to impose on it*. And having been forced by history to abandon its class-theoretical realism, there should be no reason why the Left should not today seek and find allies far beyond its traditional constituencies.

Beyond defeat

Finally and most immediately, however, a renewed Left must take leave from traditional perceptions of the economy and the role of Left politics in it. Sheltered by the Keynesian synthesis, the Left felt free to operate at arm's length from production. Either wealth creation and economic efficiency were taken for granted, or providing for them was left to capital, management and the market. By concentrating on distributive politics and avoiding involvement in the production sphere, the Left protected its autonomy from capital and established for itself an independent base for corrective intervention in capitalist economies – conveniently overlooking its own essential contribution to the wealth that gave credibility to its redistributionist claims.

The problem of Left economic policy at present is that the power it used to derive from its tacit contribution to the performance of the Keynesian–Fordist production system has disappeared together with that system. Lacking an alternative, and with mounting confusion, the Left waffles between marginalizing defences of traditional redistribution and a resigned acceptance of the view that restoration of competitiveness and productive performance requires deregulation, less public intervention, restoration of managerial prerogative, less egalitarianism, and higher rewards for 'initiative' and 'risk'. To the extent that unions and social democratic parties find such policies difficult to execute themselves, they more or less openly concede the management of the economy and the creation of material wealth to the Right, hoping to pick up later some of the benefits of neo-liberal supply-side revitalization to hand out to their clientele. In the meantime, other, less odious subjects are preferred, the farther removed from the economy the better.

We have argued here that contenting itself with, as it were, neo-liberalism with a human face is unnecessary and dangerous for the Left. Ultimately restoration of competitiveness in western capitalism is not possible without attention to the productive contribution of citizenship and social justice. Leaving efficiency to capital and limiting Left intervention to distributive justice not only surrenders the Left's claim for power, but results in less than optimal efficiency and thus hurts society as a whole. If the Left misses its opportunity, the social and economic decline of western capitalism – from growing inequality to stagnating productivity and declining competitiveness – will not be halted. It is only an egalitarian popular Left that understands the productive benefits of regulation that can establish a new bargain between equity and efficiency – one that has been made both possible by the opportunity to move towards quality-competitive production, and indispensable for competitiveness by the changes in the world economy.

Notes

1 This is emphatically not to say that the supply-side project we recommend should be inattentive to the structure of demand, much less that it can succeed without active state intervention in the economy (for example, in foreclosing low-wage options on restructuring, providing material supports for more appropriate sorts of restructuring, ensuring appropriate material and immaterial infrastructure for the more socially controlled economy we seek). It is to insist that demand stimulus alone, especially undirected stimulus, will no longer suffice to assure the general welfare.

2 This issue deserves more attention than can be given it here. Briefly, however, those who argue that capital and product markets are now completely integrated mistake stylized facts for reality. National savings and investment rates still correlate closely, and national manufacturing tends overwhelmingly to trade with itself. More pertinent, even within sectors directly exposed to international competition, the home economy retains considerable discretion in shaping their strategy of response. For purposes of this essay, we assume residual social capacity to set the terms of economic activity.

3 That is, redistribution without productive side effects, intended or unintended. As we have argued, it was the beauty of the Keynesian period that the Left could actively contribute to production and productivity without knowing, or at least without having to admit openly, that this was what it was doing; it could be *de facto* productivist, and collect the political dividend of productivism, while at the same time maintaining the illusion of itself as exclusively distributionist and without 'responsibility' for the management of capitalism. This luxury, we are saying, is no longer available.

4 Even the largest and most decentralized firm, for example, cannot keep track of all that is happening in labour markets. When it comes to competence, moreover, what is true of firms is true as well of the state. Despite its much greater supervisory, monitoring and enforcement capacities, the 'all thumbs no fingers' state is not optimally suited to providing the continuous microadjustments needed for effective supply.

5 Rather than, as in neo-liberalism, economic policy becoming social policy.

6 Supply-side Left economic policy therefore rejects a strategy of increasing employment by lowering wages at the bottom end of the wage scale, resulting in higher inequality. In addition to the obvious inequality effect, a lower wage level and higher wage differentiation reduce the pressure on employers to train, to invest in customized quality products, and to organize work so as to accommodate high skills and broad, decentralized responsibility, all of which reduce productivity.

7 See Rogers and Streeck (forthcoming).

8 For further consideration of a deliberate Left 'politics of association' see Cohen and Rogers (1992).

References

Cohen, J. and Rogers, J. 1992: Secondary associations and democratic governance. *Politics and Society*, 20, 393–465.

Rogers, J. and Streeck, W. forthcoming: *Works Councils*. Chicago: University of Chicago Press.

Comment: Don't Forget the Demand Side

Robert Kuttner

Joel Rogers and Wolfgang Streeck begin their chapter with the paradox that in its heyday the social democratic/Keynesian Left advanced the condition of wage-workers by helping capitalism operate more efficiently. They suggest that the economic, political and social conditions today make the social democratic project far more difficult than a generation ago. The internationalization of capitalism has weakened the state and put pressure on wages. Post-Fordist production obscures class relations, weakens workplace solidarity and undercuts unions, even as it relies on new forms of 'sweating'. How, then, might a Left concerned with democracy, equality and worker empowerment once again save capitalism from itself – and in the process recover its ability to carry out a Left politics? The answer, say the authors, is to offer it a more competitive and dynamic workforce, and in the process to revitalize that workforce as a political agent of progressive politics. This analysis is very powerful and convincing in its broad strokes. However, it needs to be qualified in several respects.

My first friendly quibble is on the issue of why the cure for the decline of social democracy is primarily a human capital cure. The chapter seems subtly to shift emphasis as it proceeds, insisting on a purely supply-side remedy as it begins, but adding, almost in passing, the need for more traditional elements later on. This is a matter of emphasis, and my concern is that the early claim that productivism is *the* cure exaggerates what the supply side can accomplish alone, and dismisses other necessary elements. Why does it follow that the cure for the changed structure of industry, the revised basis of class politics, and the relative weakness of the nation-state as Keynesian stabilizer must be on the supply side? Why is this approach superior or more feasible – economically, politically or institutionally – than reinventing Keynes or bringing the state back in? Why not attack both the supply side and the demand side, too? I shall return to this shortly.

Secondly, it is important not to overstate the degree to which the post-war Left emphasized distribution at the expense of production. In fact, the social democrats of our fathers' and mothers' generation hardly took the economic efficiency of a market economy for granted. The New Deal in the US, the post-war Labour governments in the UK, and continental labour and social democratic programmes all included policies of high growth/full employment as well as significant economic regulation, and also a substantial degree of public ownership and public planning. The Left in the forties and fifties was rather more productivist than the Left in the seventies.

My third point concerns the question of just how much capitalism needs the new bargain Rogers and Streeck proffer. They say that there are in advanced capitalism crucially important gains to be reaped from cooperation. That is certainly true. They also accept that the newly flexible productive economy contains new forms of vulnerability, which require new forms of social integration and cooperation. But capitalism has a long history – some would say a logic – of tolerating arrangements that are far from optimal for the economy or the society but which are convenient for owners of capital. And as long as flagrant crisis is averted, the system marches on.

The new economy includes a profusion of contingent relationships. This new contingency is destructive of personal security, of social solidarity, and ultimately of society itself. But there is a good deal of evidence that it suits the new capitalist economy just fine. As the core long-term staff of large firms shrinks and more people become contract workers, freelance workers, and 'temps', the individual absorbs risks and shocks that used to be absorbed by the firm. Yet despite this new insecurity, people do learn necessary skills, acceptable trust relationships are forged, and at the end of the day the firm saves a lot of money.

At the high end of the economy, a large number of engineers, architects, designers and consultants actually thrive on the new flexibility. At the bottom end, there are losses in living standards and in employment security – but not enough to impair the functioning of the production system. Indeed, innovation is proceeding at ever accelerating rates and for the most part industry has little difficulty finding or training people with adequate skills. And of course these new arrangements have the useful side effect of weakening labour.

Where the system does suffer is at the level not of the productive economy, but of the *society*. As living standards drop, especially for the bottom one-third, a variety of social pathologies recurs – unemployment, homelessness, crime, violence and the decay of public services, of public spaces, of public safety and public amenities, and of the perceived quality of life. But the connection between the change in the economy and the damage to society may be too indirect for owners of capital to seek a different bargain.

Rogers and Streeck contend that the new conditions of production require a new social contract of high skill and trust. But it may not necessarily require the one they commend. If it is social cohesion but not production that requires such a new contract, it is not at all clear that owners of capital will feel constrained to make a new bargain. This is surely the history of capitalism. Roosevelt's New Deal and Attlee's post-war Labour government resulted not from a change of heart on the part of capitalists, but rather from a shift in the relative power of wage-earners acting both as trade unionists and as voters. (German, French and Japanese capital is a somewhat different story.) Today the damage to unions and Left parties and governments may be so severe that progressive forces lack the political power to inflict what capitalism does not know it needs.

I fear that despite their attempt to apply a new analysis to the new high-flex economy, the authors tacitly retain a lingering Fordist conception in which the workers ultimately have residual power because they are able to stop the machine if they so choose. In this case, the equivalent of stopping the machine is withholding trust or failing to apply necessary skills. But there is just not enough evidence for this proposition. To a significant degree, corporate managers are succeeding in imposing a Japanese-style workplace – discipline, loyalty, total quality, zero defects, team work, etc. – even as capital fails to reciprocate a long-term commitment to labour. And even as workers are discarded at increasing rates, the post-Fordist illusion that there is no longer a working class makes it far more difficult to engender social solidarity and Left politics in response.

Rogers and Streeck note elsewhere in the chapter that most capitalists will not take the social high road voluntarily, even though this high road would ultimately yield a more efficient as well as a more just economy. But if the choice belongs to the capitalists because they have the power, what is the bargain labour is to offer that capital cannot refuse? The evidence to date is that managers will happily take the subsidized training, the tax credits, the public contracts, the anti-trust exemptions and whatever else the state has to offer, as well as the new flexibility and the other concessions from unions – but not offer much in return. A more highly skilled workforce is not necessarily synonymous with a social contract.

This raises my fourth concern – power. A test of the Rogers/Streeck programme is whether it would be empowering as well as conducive to economic efficiency. Here, the approach is fine as far as it goes. A Left committed to 'effective supply' – efficient, empowered, well-trained loyal and flexible workers – would win praise from industry and from its own rank and file. To the extent that industry reciprocated by offering greater job security, more rewarding work, and genuine influence on the shop floor and in the boardroom, the strategy would be truly empowering. But it is not clear that the Left, or the labour movement, or their allies in public office have the power to impose their version of the high-skill model; but it may serve as what André Gorz called a 'non-reformist reform', ineluctably leading to a greater degree of equity and a shift in the political power balance.

Further, the 'quality-competitive' path may not by itself add up to a political strategy. For one thing, the imperative of more highly skilled, autonomous workers describes only a section of the total workforce. What about McDonalds, or the back offices of banks, or nursing homes? If anything, the well-documented bifurcation of the labour force is intensifying. Many new jobs require workers with only miminal skills. Moreover, even higher-order skills do not necessarily imply empowerment or durable worker–employer relationships. According to Manpower, Inc., which is now the largest employer in the US, semi-skilled computer operators who know graphics programs are now the fastest growing category of temporary workers, and such workers can be trained in a week.

A new, quality-competitive social contract will be a real gain for the workers in firms whose managers agree that they need it. But can it be expanded to the rest of the labour force without a vastly stronger state and labour movement? Here, I return to the demand side and its connection to the power of labour. As Rogers and Streeck concede, it is impossible to guarantee employment security in one job description or in one company or even in one industry. To assure that productivity gains in one factory add up to gains in living standards for workers rather than technological unemployment requires a macro-economic context of high growth and full employment.

Rogers and Streeck do acknowledge that just as training is a public good, so are consistent work rules, fringe benefits and mechanisms for adjudicating disputes. This is also hard to deny, but most employers (at least in the Anglo-Saxon countries) would rather suffer the inefficiencies than tolerate the increased power of the state and the labour movement that an alternative policy regime would entail. The Clinton administration is baffled and dismayed that even though its proposed health legislation would save most large corporations significant costs in the form of reduced or capped health insurance premiums, few large companies support the plan because they resist an expansion of the reach of the state.

Thus, although Rogers's and Streeck's 'quality-competitive' model is attractive in its own terms, as well as being economically efficient and good for labour, the political fact is that it would probably have to be imposed on capital rather than be welcomed by industry as a gift. That said, one must ask what other sorts of power shift would be necessary for this imposition to occur and for the model to become the kind of self-reinforcing economic and political system that the Keynesian welfare state was in its glory days.

Rogers and Streeck hope that a new politics of association can help to rebuild solidarity, relying on state subsidies to political entities and novel instruments of political democracy. A notable example is the works council, which presumably would be an instrument for the linkage of the productivist model with greater political empowerment of workers and hence with a revived democratic Left. This all seems quite sensible and insightful. But does the process begin with a series of new laws facilitating associationism and productivism at the workplace? Or with a new emphasis to labour organizing, stressing productivism? Or with an appeal to economically vulnerable wage-earning voters and a new programme for Left parties? Presumably, each would reinforce the other.

In sum, the productivist model is very appealing as far as it goes, as is its connection to a revived political base. But, and here is my final point, it cannot exist in isolation from other Left strategies and it may not be as novel as the authors claim. For, on close reading, Rogers and Streeck are also calling for a good deal of regulation as well as substantial public investment in physical and social infrastructure. Implicitly they also presume a macro-economic context with plentiful jobs that allows wokers some bargaining power, and they call for constraints on global *laissez-faire* via social tariffs. Like the economist in the well-worn joke who falls into a hole and blithely assumes a ladder, they assume a state that has somehow regained much of its lost power to regulate capital domestically and globally – the same state whose new weakness they lament in the first section of the chapter. Thus, in the end, almost in spite of itself, their model concedes the need for several familiar elements of a social democratic mixed economy beyond workplace productivism, and rightly so.

To add a productivist emphasis as a strategy of overcoming the recent weaknesses of the Left makes sense. To offer this approach as something entirely new or as a replacement for other necessary elements – full employment, public investment, regulation, broadened electoral participation, revived state capacity – would overreach and mislead. We surely need all of the above, not just one element.

7 Social Solidarity in a Mixed Economy

Michel Rocard

I have organized this chapter into four parts, concerning the nature of the current 'crisis of social democracy', the values that continue to motivate the Left, the relationship of the state to the market, and the generation of social solidarity.

The social democratic crisis

Our social democratic project has obviously been in deep crisis. There can be no dodging this diagnosis. Politically and ideologically, it has been in crisis because we live in western democracies in a phase of development when the market has come to embody efficiency, and when market laws seem to have triumphed over collective action. The descent of the Soviet experiment into the gulag cannot easily be set aside. The historical contest is clear, and voters have been conditioned to a philosophy which says that whenever the state touches anything, it is inefficient, and fails to deliver, whether in health, the environment or even education.

But whatever this ideological and electoral controversy, in fact the social democratic project is in crisis for more serious reasons. The first is that we have to acknowledge that to have a successful economy there is no alternative to the market. There was in our historical project a share, a part for the 'administered economy', in other words collective property of exchange and production goods, but it did not work in the Soviet bloc where it was most comprehensively applied. We have to recognize that the market economy is the only possible performing economy. The issue is its nature and its limits, the distinction between the things which should be submitted to the market and those which should not.

The second element of the crisis of our social democratic project is the triple challenge to the welfare state. Financially, the growth of spending outstrips the growth of resources – there are large deficits everywhere. The health and pension system is under the control of anonymous bureaucracy. And there is a crisis of local adaptation to needs, which adds to the financial crisis. Third, we have difficulties in the form of the political party: what is its viable form, and what is the link between membership and leadership? All our systems were organized on a national, inter-class vision of solidarity – but is it still pertinent?

At this stage, a point of reflection must be to ask why these problems should have arisen. For myself, I do not think we have finished with the heavy work of philosophical criticism on our recent history. I want to suggest paths for research and thinking with three remarks. First, the social democratic founding thinking privileged the collective fields, economic and social, the individual not being sufficiently involved and considered as such. I think that we have not devoted enough thinking to human nature – above all its consistency and its principal needs. Can we organize society, make politics, as if the basic needs of a human person were exclusively in terms of income and of money? Of course not. The basic needs include recognition, identity and cultural connection with the world. But the main reason for action of any human being is always interest – not only monetary interest, but including it. And if we accept that, the result is that it was a completely false way of thinking to believe that we could control a global economy in which the behaviour of people could be disinterested and not connected with those interests.

This means, and this is the second point in answer to the question 'why?', that in a century-long struggle for social democracy, including the communist perversion of social democracy, we have underestimated the power of competition. Competition is the definition of existence in the modern era. Human life is made of competition. How can we imagine an economy which would not have competition as its first element? By this mistake we produce scarcity, economic paralysis and the rejection of our excessive orientation to administrative organization. Every time we think something must be state-controlled, or state-regulated, we must also think in new ways about how to do it, not through police or statutory organization, but through incentives and disincentives, adapted to the market, according to collective needs. Although the market is irreplaceable, I do not make the confusion of identity between capitalism and market. After all, we can imagine a very competitive market in which every firm would be worker-owned, or every firm could be local-authority-owned. Competition is one thing; the strength of private property pushing to concentration and creating norms or standards on the market is something different, logically linked naturally, but which we have to recognize as different.

The third point of this discussion is that I do not think we have devoted enough thinking to *power*. We are the heirs of a way of thinking in which power was derived from the accumulation of capital. But there are distributions of power that have nothing to do with the main economic structure. We need, in the social democratic movement, a more accurate reflection on these fields, which would probably go back to the fact that any type of power is dangerous when it is unaccountable. Our vision of democracy should include counter-powers – checks and balances – at every level, including the regional, national and international levels, and should include also the media system. In a computerized society, information technology creates the conditions for communication to revive democracy, rather than pervert it. We are just at the very beginning of the exploration of new forms of democracy which are opened or permitted by the new technologies developed in the last fifteen years. So to what ends should we drive our engagement with democracy?

Values

I think successive technical rationalizations of our project have failed. We are not here to impose social justice through a planned economy, through the extension of collective property or collective goods. But the essential point, enunciated by Karl Kautsky seventy years ago, is important: we are here to enforce social justice and social solidarity in a market economy. There is no question we need both. We need a market economy, but creating a society of social solidarity means more than a free market. By definition, the effects of markets increase inequalities. The market creates growing disequilibria. It encourages not only concentration of consumption but concentration in the means of production. A society of solidarity in a market economy requires a public authority with the responsibility to preserve social cohesion.

Can we be more precise on the set of principal values? I think so, because we need to regain the symbolic authority that comes from principal values which we can present to public opinion and on the basis of which we can win their confidence. You have to confirm what are your principles, and I think we can delineate seven that are our values.

The first is freedom. That is uncontroversial and not very new, except that if you have a freedom that is not only freedom of expression and the like, but freedom of the consumer, it implies the market economy is included in the definition of freedom right at the beginning – it is not a concession. It is a substantive element of the concept. The second value is democracy, which insists on pluralism and competition. I think we have to link the economic and the political project.

The third value is solidarity. But solidarity of which kind? Eduard Bernstein was already, at the end of the last century, predicting white-collar growth and the dilution of class borders. Now it is clear that class solidarities are weakening, and we have problems of solidarity generated by region, nation, ethnicity, gender and increasingly generation. On the one hand, we have youngsters, aged 18 to 25, with the threat of unemployment, with hardly any resources, their links cut, and young families with small children, without the capacity to live, earn and eat, and on the other hand we have the older generations, isolated maybe but receiving pensions which have distorted the income pyramid. The solidarity on which support for the economically inactive depends is not evident at all, but it is what we promise and struggle for. We want to build a society in which no one is left behind.

The fourth value should be primacy of law in all spheres. I am not sure market operators, business people, are really used to thinking that there is in the economic field primacy of law, which covers social treatment of employees and respect for the environment. We live under a hypocrisy according to which the economy does not deserve any types of limit or regulation. Curiously enough, we live in a world in which the fact that there can be no freedom without rules to organize it is supposed not to be true for the economy. In the economic field, freedom means absence of rules, and I feel it is time to go back to civilization based on the primacy of law and responsibility. Then we have to argue for a society in which the forms of collective organization, even very local, are such that every citizen has the greatest share in the shaping of his or her own destiny. I think it is time to come back to civilization, which is the basis of our claim to control and improve the market.

The fifth value is decentralization. One could call it autonomy. It aims at the trend according to which every human being should in the future get a greater and greater share of responsibility for his or her own destiny. The sixth value is to recover human control of nature, but this brings in the crisis of development. In Africa, for instance, we have proposed techniques to societies which were not able to adopt them, which would destroy the social and natural environment, even before permitting them to benefit from the results. We have to reintroduce techniques under a social, human, cultural control. Naturally, the seventh principle must be peace, maintaining peaceful organization on the planet.

Now some of these fields need to be explored and their ramifications debated. I want to focus on the market, on the state, on solidarity and on the multinational dimension of Europe and the world.

Market and state

Let me begin with the market. As soon as we accept that there is no substitute for the market, we are immediately confronted with the problem of its excesses. And I think the time has come to define them in order to get legitimacy for their regulation. If you want to make a plea for a government decision using taxation, you have to say why. The question depends on a type of ethics. We should isolate problems which are linked to non-renewable goods and services, natural environments and land. Towns are in a terrible mess because we cannot control the use of the land. So that is the first category – non-renewable goods and services. A second problem is the production of goods and services the nature of which would call for a treatment which is not market-led because of our own human criteria. For example, the teaching system is the responsibility of public education, not of the market. Naturally, I would say the same thing for the health system, for the police and justice and research. The market can push developmental research, but fundamental research is not amenable to market organization. The third category of limits to the market is brought on by the permanent push of the market in the direction of concentration – concentration of capital, of companies, of regional capacities, which all call for some regulation. We can introduce a fourth category, because internally to itself the market has a tendency to short-termism, which means that the market is not efficient in the production of infrastructure. There can be a deep antagonism between the general long-term interest and the interest-rate situation, even for those infrastructures which are not market determined and under state regulation.

The market is continually pushing against the search for security, and for this reason to the constitution of rents, any rent, land rent, monopoly rent. Social democracy can be defined as the struggle against the rent. More than that, even the best theoretician of market forces would accept that we need state intervention to get rid of rents or at least to avoid their excessive growth, and that social protection has to be incorporated in the market for the long-term satisfaction of the health of societies.

Social solidarity

I am convinced that in this period of political apathy – witness the diminution of voting numbers – we cannot renew the dignity of democracy without having a greater practice of local management, local democracy. But I do not think at all that nation-states, and politicians struggling on political lines in their nation-states, can proclaim any more any solutions to unemployment, to social protection, to environmental protection, to peace and war on the planet only within the nation-state.

The main claim which probably we have to make popular – probably we have to make a symbol of it – is that we want an *organized planet*, concerning the former Yugoslavia, concerning the environment, concerning interest rates, concerning the damaging volatility of rates of exchange between the dollar and the yen and European currencies. 'We need an organized planet': this can be made to sound silly, but is now real. For example, how do we save Antarctica from pollution? The beginning was a Franco-Australian communiqué, but the end is in the Madrid Treaty, which is a world-wide decision on the fact that we should preserve our white continent because it is fragile. We want world regulation of the human environment, and we cannot escape the fact that the monetary invasion of the planet has to be solved through the G7 and the international monetary system. The rules have to be extended to the whole planet. Probably it makes sense to extend some prudential ratios from the banks to any financial intervention, and draw Mr Soros and his like into a system of prudential regulation which would not permit them to destroy any strategy between civilized nations. The Continental level is a living level.

Jean Monnet decided at the inception of the European Community that nothing could be hoped for from the politicians, and that transferring or sharing some recognition or sovereignty was too difficult for them. The idea was to integrate the EC by creating technical interconnections and technical interdependence to create a technical solidarity. But it failed on symbolic issues because they are not technical. The first was defence in 1952, and the second is the monetary field in our era.

The only way forward is to say that we have a civilization contest. The identity card of Europe is simple – human rights and social protection. And this is not only worth protecting, it is worth exporting. But to do that, we have to be very powerful economically, competitively capable of defending it instead of being protectionist. And that is why we should write down the reasons why we want a common Europe, and then discover that it can only be a federation, and that we want to delegate to a central federation what has to be done in common. It is no use being hypocritical again: we have to learn that politics and values count. The social democratic movement from its birth in the nineteenth century was defined as internationally minded, and the case today is strengthened because our nation-states are too small. We have to get to a superior degree of unity, which cannot be done at the national level. Fidelity to functionalism is not the answer.

Comment: The Social Market in a Global Context

Will Hutton

The Left may have lost its way, but its mission has rarely looked more valid or its values more pertinent. The market experiment is everywhere progressing less confidently – indeed is beginning to be seriously questioned. The associated unemployment, instability, societal fracture and collapse of what is held in common are not matters of indifference – even to the Right.

In this respect Michel Rocard has made an important statement of social democratic belief; but he has yielded too much ground. The notion that markets are the only successful form of economic organization, as he claims, requires more caution. The failure of collectivization on the Soviet model does not mean *per contra* that marketization on the US model has succeeded. Rather it has failed less. More than that, there are many forms of market and capitalism with varying degrees of efficiency and social cohesion; the Left must discriminate between them.

For while the Right may insist that economic efficiency can only be achieved by society submitting to the logic of market Darwinianism, the mounting international evidence is that social well-being and solidarity are inseparably linked with wealth creation. At bottom the Right, and its business mentors, have conflated individual gains with social gain; but the Left cannot and must not make a similar concession. Social solidarity and wealth creation are indissolubly interconnected, and those societies whose institutions point their capitalism in those directions are those that succeed. This is and must be the Left's core argument.

The advance of the New Right and the implantation of market thinking across the West have not settled the argument over what forces make for human happiness; quite the contrary. The trumpeted gains in efficiency from dismantling the regulations that bind capitalism have been slight, but the costs have been huge. And as for the distrust that Rocard believes ordinary men and women have of the welfare state, education, health and public service, I suspect again he has made too big a concession. They certainly want standards of service to match what they find in the private domain, and an extension of choice, but they are keenly aware of the limits of their means and the vital importance of the welfare system to their lives. It is an objective truth that the majority cannot afford, for example, to make provision for old age as cheaply as they can through the state. They know it.

Nor has the new direction of policy been voluntary, as Michel Rocard seems to suggest, with governments and societies yielding to the more compelling logic of market organization over all others. The story, from Sweden to New Zealand, has surely been that governments have been unable to resist forces compelling them to move in this direction – and those forces are anti-democratic, invoking the ideas of the New Right to justify their position. In particular, the globalization of finance has imposed a *de facto* veto on expansionary economic policy, prohibiting budget deficits and the growth of national debt. Here there is frequently a confusion. Belgium and Italy, for example, have real problems of debt and deficit which constrain their economic options, but the same cannot be said of the whole of the OECD, yet the whole of the OECD is governed by the same policy injunction. There must be 'fiscal consolidation', 'flexible' labour costs, downward pressure on inflation, 'privatization' of state enterprise, reduced 'social costs', and taxation that favours entrepreneurial incentive. The OECD is thus recommending all governments to weaken the institutions of social cohesion, in particular trade unions, progressive tax structures and strong welfare systems, in order to dynamize the so-called wealth-creating sector of the economy. What is inhibiting wealth creation, runs the argument, is obstacles to entrepreneurship, risk taking and enterprise. With lower budget deficits come lower interest rates – but only so far as justified by the prospects of lower inflation. In the long run, it is claimed, there is no trade-off between low inflation and growth; low inflation is the precondition of growth.

Michel Rocard accepts this paradigm, but wants to pursue social democratic politics within it. He is the nice guy who will find the least damaging societal trade-offs whilst respecting the new imperatives. He will preserve the values of the Left – freedom and democracy – whilst making necessary concessions to the economic world of the Right. He will patiently argue about market failures, thus hopefully winning himself permission to make interventions that the OECD New Right would otherwise forbid. He will be a more successful midwife to the new forces than the hard men to his right.

This is not a plausible position for the Left. Either it represents an alternative paradigm and philosophy or it is dead. Its crisis is not that it belongs to the same tradition that brought us the gulag, as Rocard suggests, but that it has decided in the face of awesome financial power to temporize and accept the paradigm of the Right. The tradition of the Right can fairly be criticized this century for having brought us the Holocaust and totalitarianism too, but that has not prevented it from continuing to develop as a democratic force. Either paradigm carried to extremes can be and has been contorted into totalitarian excrescences; even Christianity in its times has begotten the crimes of the Jesuit inquisition. The Left can and should keep its nerve and protect the roots of the tradition from which it springs.

By surrendering too much philosophical ground, social democrats can open themselves up to the charge of being the Right *en travestie*. It is always open to the Right to humanize themselves a little and soften their edge, presenting the voter with the choice of voting for the real thing or its imitation.

The Left has to represent an alternative paradigm. It must argue that markets are unstable, inefficient and inequitable. It must represent the millions of ordinary people whose lives are touched adversely by these forces. Of course it will want to preserve the best of markets; but to get that best they must be socially regulated, and the risks faced by ordinary people underwritten. It must therefore talk the language of democracy and social justice, of enfranchisement and fairness. Above all it must stand for social cohesion and inclusiveness; for recognizing that without public goods and common values life for all is nasty, brutish and frequently short.

This is not to deny that the Left's old constituency of the unionized working class in large factories pumping out standardized products has shrunk, or to say that it is any longer plausible to sustain socialism's claim to represent a scientific analysis of society and the force of history. After the events of the twentieth century we cannot be sure that history is on the side of socialism, or that there are scientific solutions to the problems of economy and wealth creation.

In this respect Rocard is right and his chapter offers a way ahead. Socialism is the placing of human values before impersonal ones; it accents inclusion rather than exclusion; it emphasizes the role of the social and society in the construction of individual well-being and personal opportunity. Its roots lie deep in the battle-cry of the Revolution: liberty, fraternity and equality. Those values endure and their purpose has never been more appropriate. Indeed I would argue that the Marxist episode was an unhappy diversion in a much more longstanding progressive tradition.

The operation of markets and deregulated capitalism has reproduced in our times the forces of a hundred years ago. Absolute living standards may be higher, but the same stark inequalities are emerging, and in relative terms exceed the degree of inequality then. Nor are the inequalities only in income; they range from access to fertility treatment to the social skills necessary for new forms of interactive work. Those at the bottom of the income pyramid find themselves increasingly offered work whose terms are insecure, and the trends making for short-term contracts and insecurity are spreading throughout the workforce. The market principle is being extended into areas of social life, like surrogate motherhood, that are repugnant, while television which has a capacity to cement society and carry culture and laughter to millions, is being suborned by the same forces.

Above all, the dynamics of deregulated markets are exhibiting the same instability and proclivity to waste as markets in the nineteenth century. And this is part of the very fabric of the market experience. The fact that economic agents cannot know the future means that markets have a tendency to overshoot into booms and busts, and equal tendencies once they have reached some point of balance to stay there. Thus after the 1970s' oil shock all industrialized economies' unemployment shot up to some 10 per cent, but unemployment has stayed locked at that level.

Across the OECD there is now a reserve army of the unemployed, bidding down wages and living conditions and creating uncertainty for all in the employed workforce. This is not the result of exports from the newly industrialized countries, whose labour is cheaper, or of the new world opened up to trade liberalization. The total volume of merchandise trade is some two-thirds of American GDP; it is just not large enough to generate such powerful forces. Rather they are the natural tendency of the wave of deregulation, marketization and restrictive economic policies whose *a priori* efficiency the advocates of the New Right urge we accept.

But markets do not dance to music conducted by an invisible hand; they are the instruments of powerful private actors whose interests cannot be relied on to be coincident with a wider public interest – and whose fruits cannot be guaranteed to be distributed fairly. The nature of this divergence differs, and observation of the structure of capitalist economies reveals that the way the welfare, financial and educational systems are structured can bias behaviour strongly to be more or less civic. The injunction not to permit strong unions, for example, in the name of labour market flexibility is not the result of a value-free judgement. It is made to weaken labour and strengthen employers, because that is considered to produce economic growth. Yet if it does not, all that has been served is the transfer of power.

It is because markets are not political or moral neutrals that they must be regulated and managed. They must be socially controlled and directed. Indeed it is only if they are so managed that they can give of their best by inhibiting their natural tendency to monopoly, instability and inequity. The question for the Left is therefore two-fold. It is a technical question of how such management can best be delivered at both the micro and macro level; and it is a question of how it can breathe life and legitimacy into the public agencies that necessarily must be the tools of such management.

This can only be done through democracy; not the static democracy of mass parties representing electorates in national parliaments, but a much more engaged democracy reviving the life of the citizen at work, home and play, offering a multiplicity of sites for association and community. There needs to be a whole new interlinking web of public agencies, ranging from training boards to development banks, from transport institutes to science laboratories, to which are delegated the job of setting boundaries to market behaviour. The only possible legitimacy for this new wave of public agencies is that they be plainly democratic; indeed without reinventing democracy we cannot reinvent the Left. Here I am at one with Rocard in arguing that left-wing political parties have to solve their own internal problems of democracy before they can make a plausible case to a wider electorate.

It is democracy that will guide the new public agencies that must revive the social control of the market – regenerating trade unions, reconnecting finance to the world of value added, enfranchising workers in decision making, making evident the real cost of policies that despoil the planet, and finding new ways of legitimizing supranational governance within the European Union and beyond. Rocard's European commitment is refreshing. Yet he needs to go beyond his statement of values and belief in the democratic spirit, to make a more confident appeal about how these forces could be used to return to full employment and reassert the social dimension. This is what the Left must promise. The language is not difficult. It invokes opportunity and better-lived lifes, personal fitness and well-being, and an escape route from the marketplace when it has become tyrannous. It is the same call the Left has always made; designed for our times but never more relevant. Citizens must take arms to create and defend human institutions they hold and control in common – nothing more, nothing less.

Part IV

Politics Beyond Labour

8 Equality and Work in the Post-industrial Life-cycle

Gøsta Esping-Andersen

Modern social policy has its mainsprings in the great wave of industrialization in the latter part of the nineteenth century. But the modern welfare state is the child of post-World War II reconstruction, an institutional companion to the second industrial revolution of mass production and consumption. Put differently, the post-war welfare state became integral to the 'Fordist' economic order; the risks it addresses, and the ideals of equality and social citizenship it promotes, reflect the historically specific image of the prototypical post-war (male) industrial production worker.

The 'Fordist' welfare state, then, founded its identity on the basis of a set of assumptions about the family, life-cycle and work of the standard worker. The family was assumed to combine a full-time, stably employed male breadwinner with a wife primarily devoted to family social reproduction. This model family depends, of course, on a breadwinner who is assured a secure income throughout working life as well as in retirement; the breadwinner's earnings and social transfer income must suffice as a 'family wage'. Secondly, it was assumed that citizens' life-cycles were orderly, standardized and predictable. The life-cycle could be summarized as 'once a worker, always a worker': early entry into employment, sustained work activity throughout the productive years with little if any occupational or job mobility, and retirement to follow was the norm. The third assumption was that the political economy would assure permanent employment, and from this it followed that the welfare state would concentrate on the beginning and end of the life-cycle, childhood (schooling) and old age (pensions). The Fordist welfare state was thus meant to be passive during the active part of a person's life-cycle. It

I would like to thank Frances Fox Piven and David Miliband for their excellent comments and suggestions on this chapter.

espoused, in a sense, a 'Fordist egalitarianism' – a promise to minimize differentials in status and living conditions.

The advance of post-industrial society, I shall argue, poses new demands for which the Fordist welfare state is ill prepared. For the advanced economies, globalization and industrial decline, combined with the revolution in manufacturing products, technology and work organization, help accelerate the marginalization of the erstwhile standard manual worker. The emerging dominance of administrative and servicing occupations, combined with the changing economic status of women, implies new social differentiation and a radical change in the skill and occupational mix. Also the family is being revolutionized, and the conventional male and female life-cycle applies to an ever-decreasing part of our population: the typical woman is no longer a housewife, and men's careers are decreasingly stable, flat and predictable. What used to be called non-standard employment is today becoming quite mainstream, while the standard job trajectory is becoming atypical. The transformation of working life and the family gives rise to radically different welfare needs, particularly during the active, adult period of the life-cycle.

Such post-industrial trends are partly technology-driven, but they are also produced by the welfare state. Much of the ageing crisis of advanced societies is attributable to declining fertility, longer life-expectancy and government efforts to facilitate industrial restructuring via induced early retirement. The rise of the dual-earner household has been nurtured by welfare state provision of social care and of maternity and parental leave. Also, there is the claim that Europe's labour-market ills, such as jobless growth, the severe youth unemployment rates and the spread of informal employment, are related to the heavy fixed labour costs that employer social contributions incur.

In the debate on 'Eurosclerosis' conservatives tend to put the blame on the welfare state, arguing that it creates labour-market rigidities and, hence, impedes flexible adaptation and employment growth. These critics favour the American model for its lower fiscal costs and greater reliance on the market, which, it is held, permit better adaptation to a world that craves individualization and flexibility. It may be less egalitarian but this, many fear, is the price we must pay if we wish to regain full employment and a competitive economy. It is this case that I tackle in this chapter. My treatment begins with a synopsis of the principal differences between the post-war European and American welfare states, since these differences have a profound impact on how they affect, and are affected by, post-industrial change.

Post-war welfare states: divergent models

The US welfare state is usually regarded as residual or 'incomplete'. What is clear is that American social policy has evolved quite unlike the two great European traditions. The first European tradition, dominant on the Continent, links social rights to compulsory membership in occupationally differentiated social insurance schemes. It can be seen as a modern form of corporative solidarity in which duties and entitlements (and hence the domain of equality) are status-exclusive. Post-war reforms have helped universalize social protection to a degree, partly by consolidating the myriad occupational funds under one larger umbrella, and partly by extending basic income guarantees to those groups that have only a weak attachment to the labour market. However, the single most important post-war change was to introduce the *adequacy principle* in income transfers. Since the early 1960s, most Continental European welfare states have linked social transfers to previous earnings rather than, as earlier, to contributions. The goal was to maintain a family's relative consumption standards and social status.

The second European tradition, primarily associated with Scandinavia and to some extent the UK, was based on universal social rights with equal, but basic, flat-rate benefits for all, regardless of prior employment, earnings or status (the 'people's pension' model). The strength of this approach lay in its all-inclusive model of solidarity; its weakness in the inadequacy of the benefits. Scandinavia and Britain parted ways in their response to the adequacy issue. The Scandinavian solution was to sustain universalism with the introduction of an essentially all-inclusive second tier of earnings-related benefits. In contrast, Britain moved in an 'American' direction, favouring private sector supplementation (chiefly via employer plans) of the basic flat-rate public schemes.

Common to both European models is their stress on social *rights* (citizens' in Scandinavia, employees' in Europe) as opposed to demonstrable need. The bias in favour of rights (Britain is a partial exception) has effectively marginalized the role of private welfare. Welfare in Europe thereby became an affair of the state. Also, the European welfare states' embrace of near or complete universalism matched with benefit adequacy helped eliminate the mass worker's classical cycles of poverty. In this respect, both European versions of the Fordist welfare state helped secure for the working classes not only a guaranteed family wage, but also a homogeneously secure, linear and predictable life-cycle.

The two European models diverge, however, on two critical counts. The first has to do with social service provision. The strong Catholic (and Christian Democratic) influence in much of Europe has favoured a familialist social policy which has prevented the collectivization of traditional family social reproduction responsibilities, such as care for children, the elderly and the sick. This contrasts with the Scandinavian welfare states' drive for social service expansion. As a consequence, the former continues to encourage the traditional gender division of labour, while the latter actively nurtures the dual-career family.

The second difference lies in the redistributive profile of the welfare states. The occupationally distinct insurance approach is meant to reproduce accustomed status differences when people are retired, sick or disabled. Where risk sharing is narrowly occupationally defined, redistribution will be intergenerational rather than between the social classes. In contrast, the universalistic Scandinavian approach emphasizes a broader equalization of resources between the social classes.

The American welfare state evolved according to much more residualist principles, favouring, on one hand, targeted means-tested assistance to the poor and, on the other hand, private market supplementation for the 'middle class'. American residualism has also meant a significantly less comprehensive welfare state in terms of risks and needs covered. The United States is unique in having no national health-care system, no legislated sickness or maternity pay, and no child-allowance scheme. Federalism, combined with weak unionization, the absence of a labour party, and the racial divide, is crucial in accounting for America's 'incomplete welfare state'. These factors account for the often huge local variations in benefit and eligibility standards, in particular with regard to social assistance (Aid to Families with Dependent Children – AFDC) benefits, and also for the bias in favour of means-tested targeting and privately bargained welfare.

The American model assumes that the 'adequacy' goal will be satisfied via private employer plans or individual insurance, both of which are heavily tax-financed. The core American working class came to enjoy fairly solid coverage under private schemes, thus granting it 'middle-class' living standards and, like its European brethren, assurance against the risk of poverty. The dualism of the American model lies in the weak (or non-existent) private insurance coverage among a huge stratum of the population, including both regular workers in the 'secondary' sector, the less regularly employed, and especially vulnerable groups such as single parents. This population suffers high risks of poverty and dependence on means-tested assistance: for example, child poverty has risen from 14 per cent in 1970 to more than 20 per cent, while the poverty rate of single-parent families is nearly 40 per cent (Sawhill, 1988: 1084).

The model of American residualism has its exceptions. The elderly have been granted a basic citizens' right to Medicare, and the means-tested Medicaid plan covers a substantial share of the poor. Also, benefit targeting has become gradually less stigmatizing, at least with regard to the 'deserving poor'. Thus, the introduction of the Supplemental Security Income in the 1970s implied a less onerous, income-tested, basic 'social' pension to the elderly poor, and eligibility rules for AFDC were to a degree liberalized in the 1970s. Nonetheless, full income maintenance at European-type levels still assumes private, occupational supplements.

Measured as a percentage of GDP, American welfare state expenditure is only about half that of the European average, but this does not imply that Americans consume less welfare than do Europeans. The principal difference lies in how it is packaged and distributed. If we combine private and public social expenditures, the United States spends about 25 per cent of GDP, which is more or less in line with average EU costs. But, in America, half is private welfare. The American welfare state also stands out in terms of its social assistance bias: a full one-third of public social outlays are means-tested, whereas in Europe these typically account for no more than 5 per cent. America's unique combination of social security, assistance, and private welfare results in a much more inegalitarian distribution of social welfare. Poverty among the elderly has been all but eliminated in Sweden, but was recorded at 11 per cent in West Germany and 24 per cent in the United States[1] (Rein et al., 1988: 96).

It is often believed that the European welfare states began to drift in the American direction during the austere and conservative 1980s. At the aggregate level, such a trend is not visible. Real per capita average benefit expenditure continued to grow everywhere throughout the 1980s, even in Thatcher's Britain, albeit at a much slower pace than in earlier decades. Expressed as a percentage of GDP, social expenditures have not declined, except very marginally in a couple of nations such as (West) Germany and Sweden. There is discussion of means-testing and privatization of pensions and health, but the differences cemented in the post-war decades remain essentially intact. The European welfare states have, so far, avoided any dramatic changes, let alone privatization, of welfare responsibilities. Instead, they have been kept afloat by a combination of deficit spending and cost-containment measures at the margin.[2]

Welfare state responses to economic change

The post-war welfare state promised full employment; it also depended on it. In line with its assumptions about the standard worker, the definition of the full employment commitment was narrowly masculine. All nations relied on the growth of industrial production for its attainment. But from the 1970s onwards, industrial employment has shrunk everywhere. This coincided with the emerging impossibility of traditional Keynesianism, since the stimulation of domestic purchasing power would mainly generate jobs in Osaka and Seoul rather than in Düsseldorf or Manchester.

The changing international economic order has already altered the welfare state's traditional role in the economy, compelling it into active management of labour demand and supply. On the one side, the welfare state became a key actor in managing industrial workforce reductions. On the other side, it plays an indispensable role in nurturing alternative service job growth. We can identify three distinct welfare state strategies for managing 'deindustrialization', each one flowing logically from the peculiarities of existing welfare state characteristics.

Among the EU nations, the paradigm case being (West) Germany, the dominant approach has been to reduce labour supply, especially through early retirement provisions. Their extremely high labour costs (due to social contributions and the 'family wage' principle), combined with welfare state fiscal incapacity and/or ideological resistance (Catholic familialism), meant that these countries could not count on any major employment growth in either the private services or public welfare services.

Scandinavia's welfare states, in contrast, adhered to an expansionist strategy, combining supply-side policies (mainly programmes for worker relocation and retraining) and demand-side policies within sheltered sectors (massive growth of welfare state social services). While the EU model produced sharply falling male participation rates, the Scandinavian strategy was much more successful in sustaining full employment while vastly increasing female employment. One approach perpetuates the conventional family structure, the other produces a convergence of male and female employment rates, and the dual-earner (and dual-career) family has become the norm.

The third, North American response is intimately related to its residual welfare state. Early retirement has been a favoured instrument of industrial reorganization, but this has mainly involved the system of private occupational pensions which has always been concentrated within traditional industries, like car production and steel. America's spectacular job growth during the 1980s was fuelled by a combination of defence spending, the ballooning budget deficit, and a dramatic deterioration of the minimum wage. By 1990, the legislated minimum wage had dropped to only one-third of average manual worker hourly pay. In addition, social assistance programmes were not allowed to grow in tandem with the rise in poverty, implying a substantial increase in the proportion of poor American families. As many studies have argued, the American job miracle of the 1980s occurred via a labour-cheapening strategy, not only within the 'secondary' labour force, but affecting also the traditional core working class – hence the concept of the 'declining middle' (Levy, 1988; Burtless, 1990).

The three strategically very different welfare state responses to unemployment and industrial decline produce profound consequences not only for the welfare state itself, but also for the ways in which nations' post-industrial futures are shaped. Two challenges of the new social and economic order are paramount. The first relates to the consequences of an economy dominated by services and necessitating greater labour-market flexibility; the second to demographic and family change.

The welfare state and the service economy

The transition from an economy dominated by corporate industrial mass production to what can broadly be labelled a post-industrial economy has produced massive upheaval in the structure of the labour force. All evidence suggests that the new, leaner and much smaller core industrial workforce will be biased in favour of better-skilled and functionally more flexible workers. The need for flexibility may also produce a secondary labour force of precarious stand-by workers with lower wages and little, if any, job security or social insurance. Since industrial employment is in any case contracting, most new jobs must come from the services. Today, industry typically accounts for no more than one-quarter of total employment, while the share of services exceeds 50 per cent and, if we include distribution also, almost two-thirds. Since employment in distributive services and in administrative jobs is unlikely to grow considerably – in fact many traditional jobs in administration are rapidly contracting – the post-industrial employment profile will depend on three sectors: business services, social services and personal consumer services. Their logics are highly divergent.

Business services tend to be biased in favour of 'good' jobs like managerial, professional and technical occupations; their rapid growth over recent decades is essentially caused by industrial restructuring and the sub-contracting of traditional tasks, such as accounting, marketing, product design and engineering. Although its relative size remains modest (about 7–10 per cent of total employment), it is a key source of recruitment into the new professional elites, and it is a sector in which the share of autonomous, or self-employed, workers is high (Elfring, 1993).

Massive employment growth (and the hope for full employment) must depend on trends in the two other service sectors, social and personal services. Herein lies the real problem, since both are characterized by their low productivity growth. In the case of personal services, which are predominantly offered in the market and overridingly based on low skills, employment growth depends on affordability, which means wage costs. In contrast, social services growth depends primarily on the welfare state and is therefore less contingent on wages than on tax tolerance. A hallmark of social services is their dual skill profile: a strong bias in favour of professionals, but also in favour of unskilled workers (cleaners, homehelpers, caretakers, etc.). The growth potential in both these service sectors is closely connected to welfare state policy. Here we can identify three clearly distinct responses: a Scandinavian, welfare-state-led, social services model, an 'EU-nation', jobless-growth model, and an American emphasis on market services.

Jobs and wages

The Nordic countries are powerfully biased against the growth of personal consumer services, partly because of the high fixed labour costs due to employer social contributions, partly because of their strong egalitarian wage policies. The low skill content and productivity of most personal services imply that high wages will price them out of the market.[3] As a result, this sector has contracted sharply over recent decades and, today, accounts for only 4–5 per cent of all jobs. The unique feature of Scandinavia is the massive growth in public social services, which, given wage costs and wage equality, also remained the only viable source of employment creation. Indeed, since the early 1970s, social services have accounted for more than 80 per cent of total net job growth in Sweden, and now constitute 30 per cent of total employment (half the jobs are part-time). A number of attributes combine to produce female domination of employment in this sector: first, social services catalyse female labour supply, and the two have expanded in tandem; secondly, social services often address traditional female skills and, at the bottom end, these are easy first-entry jobs; thirdly, social services are particularly attractive to women workers because government employment is sheltered, offering job security, decent pay, and flexible working-time schedules.

The EU countries face a different situation. The costly social insurance system, pegged as it is to the family wage, tends to outprice workers in the private personal services. Yet, a trend in favour of self-employment (with family labour), combined with informal (that is, black market) employment, has helped offset the cost problem in some European countries, most notably in Italy (where self-employment accounts for 60 per cent of the hotel and catering economy), but increasingly also in Britain where self-employment was once regarded as virtually extinct (Rodgers and Rodgers, 1989). Still, from the point of view of addressing Europe's unemployment question, the self-employment option is but a drop in a huge bucket. The problem within many EU nations is that a social-services-led strategy is both fiscally and politically blocked. It is fiscally blocked because the huge social transfer burden on the welfare state allows little additional room to finance public service growth – a problem that has worsened considerably due to the additional costs of massive early retirement and unemployment compensation. In addition, Catholic social doctrine remains a powerful political force in perpetuating traditional familialist social policy.[4] These factors combine to produce jobless growth, high unemployment, and the emergence of an insider-outsider cleavage in the labour market: a stagnant, or even shrinking, largely adult male, insider labour force enjoying high wages with job security and social entitlements on one side, and on the other a ballooning but heterogeneous outsider population of youth (EU youth unemployment rates can be up to five times higher than in either Scandinavia or the US), early retirers (the participation rate of males in the 55–64 age group is almost half that of Sweden), and women, all of whom must depend on either the family or the welfare state.

It is easy to see why the European insider–outsider cleavage helps reinforce the traditional Fordist welfare state structure. First, an ever larger share of the population comes to depend on social transfers and the 'family wage' principle, which implies that the insiders become additionally dependent on the dual high-wage/high-social-wage guarantee. Secondly, the insiders come to rely even more on the traditional, orderly career life-cycle profile, especially so because it has been dramatically shortened from the conventional 16–65 age-span to the now typical 20–55 age-span. Since full pension benefits normally stipulate at least thirty-five years' unbroken employment, very few can risk any job uncertainty, let alone experimentation across their work careers. Thirdly, the pro-familialist policy paradigm in many countries helps attenuate the problem. Thus, both unemployed youth and the long-term unemployed are usually forced to depend on family help. In most countries, eligibility for benefits presumes substantial prior employment. Even in Germany, unemployment assistance is not paid to individuals (including adults) if their parents' income is too high.

Many observers claim that the third, American model has the solution to the Gordian knot of post-industrial unemployment. While the EU nations suffered from job stagnation and actual decline, the United States added millions of new jobs; while European unemployment rates sky-rocketed, they fell in the United States. The American job miracle was not, as in Scandinavia, achieved through the public sector (indeed, public employment declined throughout the 1980s); it occurred *exclusively* in the private economy and was spread quite evenly across the diverse service sectors. The 1980s defence build-up helped delay redundancies, and the deindustrialization wave within the old 'rustbelt' industries was offset by the relocation of manufacturing in the 'sunbelt' states. Via plant mobility and a host of other corporate strategies, the traditional backbone of primary sector manufacturing could escape the problems of uncom-petitively high wage costs and job security provisions by shifting pro-duction to non-unionized regions with lower wage rates. The classic division between a primary and secondary labour market that so power-fully characterized the post-war American economy is eroding as the status of primary sector workers increasingly comes to approximate that of their secondary sector brethren.

These trends have potentially huge consequences for the American system of employer-provided occupational health, sickness and pension plans. To reduce production costs and gain flexibility, corporations reduce or even entirely eliminate their fringe benefit packages, especially for newly hired workers. When we add to this the fact that a huge proportion of total service job growth occurs in low-paid, non-unionized and non-protected employment ('McJobs'), the result is a marked decline in the share of stably employed American workers covered under private wel-fare schemes.

The American 'job miracle' is often described as polarized, with the growth of elite professional occupations at one end, and an ocean of lousy 'McJobs' at the other. This is incorrect in so far as we are concerned with skills and occupations. While it is true that the absolute number of unskilled service jobs has risen, in relative terms the share of qualified jobs has grown considerably faster. The real polarization that does exist applies therefore not to skills but to the attributes of jobs, in particular to earnings, fringe benefits and employment security. The traditionally stable relationship between jobs and pay has been ruptured. The concept of the 'declining middle' conveys the fact that the once well-paid and secure 'Fordist' jobs (especially manual and clerical jobs in the corporate sector) are being eliminated or transferred to non-unionized, low-wage areas, or of course abroad. Inequalities of earnings, and the proportion of people in precarious jobs, have risen sharply. The unskilled and new labour-force entrants are the two groups that have been most severely affected. All available evidence indicates that the new cohorts of American workers will not be able to count on the kinds of 'Fordist' guarantee of secure and well-paid employment that their fathers enjoyed (Levy, 1988; OECD, 1993; Burtless, 1990).

Employment dilemmas

We arrive, then, at a curious paradox: the very same attributes of the American model that European pro-market liberals wish to emulate in the name of flexibility are facing an ever-deeper crisis precisely because they are seen as impediments to flexibility and international competitiveness. American industry is engaged in a vast and systematic effort to reduce or entirely eliminate its occupational welfare commitments. Hence some corporate support for a national health-care plan.

The peculiar American enigma is that poverty, inequality and sheer destitution have grown in tandem with a historically unparalleled expansion of jobs. Those most vulnerable to poverty are, of course, the unskilled in general, and especially those who are geographically removed from the centres of job expansion, or who are unable to work maximum hours, for example single parents. The kind of flexibility that is built into the American labour market via greater wage differentiation, less job security, and a greater reliance on private sector welfare generates huge social costs in terms of poverty, social exclusion and crime (see, for example, Auletta, 1982; Wilson, 1987; Jencks and Peterson, 1991).

There is some evidence that a similar spectre is raising its head in the European economies. Thus, after decades of equalization, wage differentials are widening in most European countries (especially in Britain). This is partly attributable to government policies to diminish wage costs in the youth labour market, but is mainly due to the changing industrial and occupational structure, to the weakening of trade unionism and, as in the United States, to a widening gap between the unskilled and the skilled. In addition, there is also evidence of a rise in precarious employment, such as temporary contracts, part-time employment below the minimum for contribution purposes, and other forms of contingent labour (stand-by workers hired out by agencies, homeworkers, etc.). But, with few exceptions (such as outwork in Italy, which, according to Dallago's (1990) estimates, involves between 1 and 2 million people), non-standard and irregular employment still remains marginal in Europe

(Buchteman, 1991: 251–78).[5] It is not temporary work as much as part-time and self-employment which has grown, and it is difficult to regard these as either novel or atypical (Pollert, 1991; Rodgers and Rodgers, 1989).

The employment scenarios that I have depicted force a set of apparently irreconcilable dilemmas upon the contemporary welfare state. There appears in particular to be a zero-sum trade-off between job expansion and equality. In a service-dominated economy, any major employment growth will depend on greater wage inequalities, at least to the point where earnings reflect productivity differences and consumer-demand elasticities.[6] In the Fordist economy, many were employed in lousy, unskilled factory jobs, but they could count on decent pay. In a full-employment post-industrial society, probably fewer will find themselves in lousy jobs, but probably more will be ill paid. If, instead, we opt for a homogeneously upgraded, high-pay labour market, the consequence is likely to be a large outsider population. This dilemma summarizes the traditional EU–US confrontation. But what about the Scandinavian alternative?

For a long period, the Nordic welfare states seemed capable of harmonizing egalitarian goals with full employment by opting for a social-service-led post-industrial order. However, this model is in the long term incapable of cutting the Gordian knot. To begin with, its huge social service system includes a large share of unskilled jobs. Also, its extreme female bias has resulted in the western world's most sex-segregated labour market. Regardless, the welfare state will not in the long run be able to finance wage increases that far exceed productivity. In the short run, it could finance the burden of service employment expansion via the extra tax revenue that accrues from maximizing labour-force participation. Also, very high individual tax rates can be tolerated in so far as households can rely on two persons' earnings. But there is a paradox in the Scandinavian model: it has emancipated women from dependency on the male's earnings but has, instead, made both men and women dependent on the joint income of two spouses.

The Achilles' heel of the Nordic model in the long run is that a social-services-led expansion must reach a natural as well as fiscal limit, and that the more it expands, the greater is the intensity of wage conflicts between the public and private sectors. As the fiscal burden of public employment mounts, governments are compelled either to curtail expansion or to ask for sustained wage moderation. With a substantially better productivity performance, the private sector workers will be unwilling to participate in broad wage-equality bargaining. The result, as we have seen in dramatic form in the Nordic countries during the 1980s, is severe wage differential conflicts between public and private sector unions. The Nordic model postponed, but did not resolve, the basic trade-off between equality and jobs in a service economy.[7] I return to the way out of this problem in the conclusion.

The welfare state, family change and demography

Societal ageing is frequently held to have cataclysmic consequences for the welfare state. In a narrow sense, there are two equally unconvincing solutions: one lies in a spurt of productivity growth, but this is unlikely in a service-dominated economy; the second is to engineer a combination of increases in financial contributions with a decrease in benefits. The latter is not very likely since higher contributions will only worsen the existing wage-cost problems, and the political lobbying power of the aged today is probably sufficient to rule out any substantial deterioration of benefit standards. An alternative technical adjustment is to raise or even abolish the mandatory retirement age, which, despite a leap in longevity and health conditions, has actually fallen over the past decades. I will suggest below that post-industrial life-cycles, if nurtured by the welfare state, might help diminish the problem substantially.

In general, the ageing burden will automatically be eased via an increase in labour supply, which can be effected through immigration and/or greater female participation. Besides the controversy surrounding an open border policy, the key problem for such a strategy is that it will require a very different, and much more flexible, labour market to that which exists in Europe today. Being largely unskilled, immigrant workers can only be absorbed where there exists a huge market of unqualified, easy-entry jobs. In the past, seasonal agricultural jobs performed this function. But given the potential magnitudes, a contemporary immigration strategy will have to rely primarily on massive job creation in the lower end of the service economy. In brief, Europe would need 'McJobs'. The alternative, or complementary, strategy is to promote female labour-force participation, which, as we know, presumes widespread availability of social services, care for children and the aged, and substantial improvements in many nations' programmes for maternity, sickness and parental leave. Hence, if our chief concern is to safeguard the welfare state against the looming ageing crisis, we again find ourselves forced, first, to resolve the original dilemma of full employment in a service economy.

Post-industrial society is usually identified in terms of the rise of services and the new professionalized knowledge class. However, post-industrial society also involves a revolution in the family and in the life-cycles of its members. To begin with, the growth of social and personal service jobs is closely linked to family behaviour. Personal services will only grow when households prefer to purchase their leisure, laundry or meals in the market rather than reverting to self-servicing via home videos, washing machines and microwave ovens. A similar logic applies to social services: the family can satisfy its caring needs outside (daycare or old-age homes) or by traditional family care work. In both cases, the choice depends on the price. The more families are capable of satisfying their service needs outside the home, the greater will be the impact not only on job creation but also on our life-cycle. The availability of affordable social services outside the household is the *sine qua non* for both men's and women's capacity to depart from the traditional Fordist lifecycle; women in the sense that they will be enabled to pursue sustained employment and thus careers; men because their individual responsibility for securing the family wage will be lessened, and they will thus be better equipped to risk interruptions and changes in their career cycle. It is important to add that these are exactly the same conditions that will permit service employment growth and the kind of labour-force flexibility that a post-industrial economy is said to demand. In brief, postindustrial society presumes a post-industrial family, and a post-industrial family presumes widely available social services.

It is therefore not surprising that it is in Scandinavia that people's life-cycles have been most revolutionized. On the one side, almost universal (and sustained) female labour-force participation has meant that women's life-cycle has increasingly come to resemble the typical male's; the classic rupture in employment and return to the family that occurred (and still prevails in most of Europe) at marriage and childbirth have been reduced to a brief interruption. And male life-cycles have to a degree become feminized. For example, in the first years of Sweden's new parental leave legislation, only a tiny proportion of men chose to use it; today, more than 30 per cent of married men take parental leave and thus interrupt their employment (usually for shorter periods than women). Bolstered by Sweden's active training and retraining programmes, there has also been a significant increase in the proportion of employees who change careers throughout adulthood. In brief, the conventional, orderly and linear life-cycle is rapidly becoming atypical, and the more this is so, the more citizens will demand that welfare state efforts shift their emphasis to the active, adult part of the life-cycle.

The welfare state is of course not the only possible provider of social care services and, as we know from the United States, a remarkable growth in female labour supply can occur through alternative means, be they delayed fertility, informal arrangements, employer provision or private purchase of care. As in Scandinavia, American women's life-cycles are converging with the typical male career trajectory (Oppenheimer, 1988). In part the explanation is to be found in employers' attention to women's needs within their occupational benefits system, and in part it has to do with the low-wage (heavily immigrant) labour market, which makes it affordable for an average middle-income earner to purchase private childcare or eldercare.

It is in the 'EU bloc' of countries (excepting Denmark) that the barriers to life-cycle revolution are the greatest, due to the combination of high labour costs and traditional familialistic social policy. Thus, both men and women remain largely dependent on the male breadwinner's family wage. Of course, female employment growth has occurred in these countries, with Britain leading the way. Here, sustained female employment careers come to depend primarily on personal solutions: delayed marriage and childbirth, the availability of a family member (the grandmother, typically) and, for the elite classes who can afford it, the employment of nannies and maids. There is little doubt that the first solution is becoming increasingly dominant, and this has doubly negative social policy consequences. As fertility rates decline, the ageing crisis worsens. Additionally, the class selectivity in marriage patterns means that the income gap between dual- and one-earner families will polarize, especially so since a dual-career family will bring home two 'family wages' and two sets of welfare state entitlements, each of which is assumed to suffice for the entire family.

The real problem for EU Europe is that a perpetuation of the traditional Fordist life-cycle will seriously inhibit a policy for labour-market flexibilization. The average male earner is trapped in his guarantees of a stable job and high earnings, and he will naturally perceive demands for flexibility, re-education or job change as risky. The labour-market institutions, especially the trade unions, thus find themselves today compelled to safeguard erstwhile Fordist victories and resist modernization.

Conclusions

The panorama of change that I have presented here hardly suggests a happy ending. A return to full employment, let alone any growth in participation rates, necessitates a huge expansion of service jobs, many of which are bound to be badly paid. And this is likely to be accompanied by an inegalitarian thrust in the earnings distribution, together with rising poverty. In brief, we seem to face the prospects of either greater job inequality or a society of mass unemployment.

If our policy goal were limited to employment expansion, the low-wage American job miracle model would be convincing. But we also know the considerable, and unacceptable, social costs that the American strategy incurs. Political preferences aside, the real risk of an American-style trajectory is an unacceptable degree of social polarization at great public cost.

If, however, we retain the classic welfare state goals of full employment with equality, my analyses suggest that a necessary first step must be to 'post-industrialise' the family and the life-cycle. In effect, a family capable of being flexible and adaptive must be able to count on an adequate supply of welfare-state-provided social services. In addition – and herein lies, I believe, the crux of the problem – the flexible life-cycles of a post-industrial family require revolutionary change in our system of income maintenance.

It should be obvious that privatization of the welfare state is no solution – the new, flexible, lean and mean firm cannot (or will not) shoulder the costs of heavy occupational benefit schemes in the first place. In addition, dependency on employer welfare runs counter to the needs for a flexible and mobile workforce. But our earlier discussion actually does suggest one obvious alternative solution.

Let us illustrate this with fiction. Imagine the prototypical post-industrial family: the welfare state provides it with services and care, encouraging both spouses to work and pursue careers, interrupted for some periods in order to give birth or care for infants, and in other periods to change or augment skills or to embark upon an alternative career path. In this kind of family, the idea of temporary retirement from work in mid-career might be as appealing as (if not more so than) the traditional promise of permanent retirement in old age.

Let us now imagine that our post-industrial family lives in a full-employment service economy. One or maybe both spouses will have a high probability of finding themselves at some point in an unskilled 'McJob'. Now if, instead of encouraging and consolidating Fordist employment permanency, the welfare state's principal activities were dedicated to maximizing the life-cycle opportunities of individuals, most obviously through education and training, then our imaginary post-industrial family would know that their 'McJobs' experience would be brief, and that life could improve.

Viewed in purely static terms, it appears socially unacceptable that a large share of the population is condemned to work in lousy service jobs: our imaginary post-industrial husband works at the carwash, and the wife cleans hospitals. But viewed in a dynamic perspective, the welfare problem of badly paid, dead-end service jobs will hardly matter if the welfare state extends a basic guarantee of life-cycle opportunities. Our post-industrial family's spell of inferior employment matters little if it remains but an interim in a welfare-state-guaranteed process of career mobility.

The point is clear. The Fordist welfare state slices up the life-cycle and ignores the active adult part on the assumption that a Fordist economy guarantees decent pay and secure employment. The post-industrial economy is less likely to provide such guarantees; indeed, the average worker's life-cycle risks will increase substantially. Hence, the average post-industrial family may be much less concerned with old-age retirement than with optimal chances for mobility and career success during adulthood.

We know that education and training give a very good assurance that people will be able to move up the job hierarchy (see Esping-Andersen, 1993). Data from Scandinavia and North America show that the vast majority stay in such jobs for only a brief spell. There is, of course, the risk that a hard core remains imprisoned in life-time 'service proletarian' status. This risk is primarily associated with two factors: lack of training, and lack of access to family care services. The, albeit small, 'service proletariat' is mainly composed of the unskilled and, in the United States, also single parents. In contrast, the upwardly mobile 'McJobs' workers are either youth hovering between education and careers, or people capable of acquiring training and education in the midst of their employment career.

In sum, if the welfare state can extend a citizen's guarantee of skill acquisition and social servicing at any point during the life-cycle, labour-market inequalities, worker flexibility and a mass of poor jobs are not necessarily incompatible with an egalitarian ideal. Put differently, if we were to abandon our traditional 'Fordist' notions of equality in favour of a more dynamic life-course guarantee, post-industrial society need not be a predestined zero-sum trade-off between full employment and equality.

Notes

1 Poverty rates are defined as below 50 per cent of median income, adjusted for family size.

2 On the cost-containment side, there have been marginal reductions in benefit replacement rates, some efforts to tighten eligibility (say, waiting days for sickness pay), and funding caps for services. It may, however, be that the seeds of much more radical change are currently being sown. A standard cost-containment approach is to fail to uprate pension benefits in line with incomes or inflation. Such marginal adjustment practices will have virtually

no immediate effects but will, in the long run, seriously undermine pension standards and push people towards private pension plans.

3 To illustrate, the average cost of having a shirt laundered and ironed in Scandinavia is about US$8–10; in Germany and Italy, around US$5: and in the United States, about $1–2.

4 In this light it is telling that, in comparison to Scandinavia's gender equalization via services and employment, the German CDU's response has been to recognize the wage-equivalent value of family work in terms of, for example, pension entitlements.

5 Perhaps the most reliable data come from Germany, where it has been estimated that irregular, temporary-contract employment grew from 4.0 to 5.6 per cent of total employment between 1984 and 1988.

6 It is important to bear in mind that low productivity need not imply low pay. This would be the case, for example, where service workers produce positional goods (you have your hair cut at Chez Pierre rather than at the local barber shop), or where consumers desire a service for its quality rather than its affordability.

7 The point finds confirmation in the Swedish government's plan (October 1993) to cut 80,000 public employees from the state payroll.

References

Auletta, K. 1982: *The Underclass*. New York: Random House.

Buchtemann, C. 1991: Does (de)-regulation matter? Employment protection and temporary work in the FRG. In G. Standing and V. Tokman (eds), *Towards Social Adjustment*, Geneva: ILO.

Burtless, G. (ed.) 1990: *A Future of Lousy Jobs?*. Washington, DC: Brookings Institute.

Dallago, B. 1990: *The Irregular Economy*. Dartmouth: Aldershot.

Elfring, T. 1993: Structure and growth of business services in Europe. In H. W. de Jong (ed.), *The Structure of European Industry* (third edition), Amsterdam: Kluwer Publishers.

Esping-Andersen, G. (ed.) 1993: *Changing Classes*. London: Sage.

Jencks, C. and Peterson, P. (eds) 1991: *The Urban Underclass*. Washington, DC: Brookings Institute.

Levy, F. 1988: *Dollars and Dreams*. New York: Norton.

OECD 1993: *Employment Outlook*. Paris: OECD.

Oppenheimer, V. 1988: A theory of marriage timing. *American Journal of Sociology*, 94, 563–87.

Pollert, A. 1991: *Farewell to Flexibility?*. Oxford: Blackwell.

Rein, M., Smeeding, T. and Torrey, B. 1988: Patterns of income and poverty. In J. Palmer, T. Sneeding and B. Boyle Torrey (eds), *The Vulnerable*, Washington, DC: Urban Institute Press.

Rodgers, G. and Rodgers, J. 1989: *Precarious Jobs in Labour Market Regulation*. Geneva: ILO.

Sawhill, I. 1988: Poverty in the US: why is it so persistent? *Journal of Economic Literature*, 26, 1073–113.

Wilson, W. J. 1987: *The Truly Disadvantaged*. Chicago: University of Chicago Press.

Comment: Economic Imperatives and Social Reform

Frances Fox Piven

Gøsta Esping-Andersen is correct to say that welfare state programmes have become a major influence on labour market and family patterns and, he might have added, on politics as well. Still, the moral he draws is troubling. He calls for a 'revolutionary change' in systems of income maintenance so they will mesh with the pattern of low-wage, service sector employment of the post-industrial economy. But welfare state arrangements reflect fundamental conflicts of interest in market societies as much as or more than they attenuate them. A 'reinvention' of the welfare state should take account of these conflicts as one basis for Left politics.

The European welfare states, Esping-Andersen tells us, have run up against implacable fiscal, political and demographic limits. Designed to meet the imperatives of a Fordist mass production and mass consumption economy, and of a patriarchal family system reliant on a single male earner, they are badly misfashioned for a post-Fordist economic and social order. Industrial employment is contracting as a consequence of technological innovation and competition from low-wage countries abroad. The resulting high unemployment not only adds to the fiscal drag of welfare state expenditures, but also promises to create a society divided between employed insiders and unemployed outsiders.

For a time, the Scandinavian model seemed to provide a benign solution, through expanding public service employment. That model has now also reached its fiscal and political limits. The only path open is the expansion of low-wage, private sector service employment. But this path has heretofore been blocked by the high non-wage costs with which an outdated Fordist welfare state has saddled European economies. And the problem compounds itself, since the unavailability of cheap services prevents women from entering the labour force, where they could offset the growing burden on the welfare state of an ageing population. Hence, the policy moral: an adaptation in systems of income maintenance so that they are consistent with the realities of patterns of employment, family and life-cycle in a post-Fordist world.

Esping-Andersen does not say very much about the design of this post-Fordist welfare state, but what he does say is not at first glance unreasonable. Instead of concentrating on programmes which support the non-productive young and the old, presuming an industrial-era life-cycle of regular and well-paid employment, income maintenance programmes should make it possible for people to move in and out of employment, maximizing opportunities for flexibility and mobility over the life-cycle. Is this sort of direction feasible? And is it likely to strengthen a Left opposition?

The debate in the EU about the direction of European welfare and economic strategy, and about the European Commission White Paper on Employment presented to the December 1993 European Summit by Jacques Delors, rotates around the dilemma that Esping-Andersen addresses. Conservative political leaders want to stimulate job creation by lowering minimum wages and scaling back social security costs, no doubt influenced by what they perceive to be American experience, and particularly the American record of expanding low-wage, service sector employment. But that achievement, if such it is, is made possibly by the distinctive harshness of the American welfare state. Hence the logic that leads Conservatives from deregulation of the labour market to an attack on the welfare state.

Esping-Andersen's discussion of the American model of a means-tested and employment-based welfare state identifies some of its glaring faults, pointing especially to the widespread poverty, insecurity and stigma it helps produce. Presumably, this is not what he means by a revolutionized, post-Fordist welfare state that can be a component of a Left programme, even while meshing with a labour market that relies on expanding low-wage service employment. Rather, and here I have to surmise, Esping-Andersen imagines a system in which income supports are adequate, and readily available to people throughout the life-cycle, as they move from job to job, or take sabbaticals for retraining, or do a stint of family care.

But there is a lesson of sorts to be drawn from the American experience. Success at creating low-wage service employment is not the result of innovative programmes, but rather the result of generally low benefits and narrow coverage. If anything, the American reliance on private sector welfare programmes impedes labour-market adaptation because workers are likely to cling to particular employers for fear of losing their health or old-age benefits, an arrangement that might better be likened to serfdom, not post-Fordism. Nor does the American success at job creation reflect supportive public income maintenance programmes, in the sense that the programmes allow people to live at a reasonable level as they adapt to a more flexible labour market and family form. To the contrary, labour-market expansion at the bottom is made possible by programmes which systematically restrict access to benefits, stigmatize those who get them, and in any case provide only very meagre benefits. Moreover, as the low-wage job miracle unfolded in the 1980s, the programmes were contracted even more. Unemployment insurance was cut back, with the consequence that less than a third of the unemployed received benefits, and means-tested benefits were slashed, in tandem with the declining minimum wage. Meanwhile, a kind of societal psychodrama unfolded, in which black single mothers were made to play the central role, as politicians with little to say about steadily declining wages, or the growth of part-time and temporary employment, declaimed instead about the purportedly growing problem of welfare 'dependency'.

The welfare state which permitted these developments was not particularly post-Fordist. If anything, it was more pre-industrial than post-industrial. More to the point, it was simply restrictive. A residual welfare state permitted a 'labour-cheapening' strategy which encouraged a huge expansion in low-wage service jobs, at the cost of growing inequality, poverty and sheer destitution. Together these developments also helped to destroy American unions, whose membership rolls in the private sector plummeted from 30 million in 1970 to 12 million in 1990, a development which in turn also contributed to the low-wage job miracle. It is hard to see how programmes designed along the lines that Esping-Andersen suggests could have done as well in channelling people into low-wage (and irregular) jobs. After all, his scheme must include ready access to reasonable benefits if it is to support people as they move from job to job, or retool for another career, or change their family care arrangements. But ready access to reasonable benefits would also have constituted an alternative livelihood for Esping-Andersen's prototypical post-industrial family, allowing them to resist the downgraded wages and deteriorating working conditions which job expansion entailed.

To put this point another way, the European problem is not only, and maybe not mainly, the problem of a welfare state which is ill-designed to mesh with the shifting work patterns made necessary by a post-Fordist economy, family structure and life-cycle. It is much more simply the result of programmes that are more widely available, more generous and less stigmatizing. Under these conditions, social benefits cushion market (and family) sanctions, and permit resistance to the changing imperatives of the labour market, and in some ways to the imperatives of dominant forms of family organization. This is the problem created by a Fordist welfare state in a post-Fordist world, and it may well be that it is a problem the Left should try to exacerbate, not solve.

Let me make this point about the political possibilities that inhere in the tension between welfare states, economies and families in a more general way. Esping-Andersen argues that welfare state programmes have in the past sustained a Fordist economic and family order. They were, to invoke a now unfashionable term, 'functional' for a mass production and mass consumption economy, and for the patriarchal family. Yet, writing elsewhere (Esping-Andersen, 1985:31), he sounded a very different note. He wrote:

> Only when workers command resources and access to welfare independent of market exchange can they possibly be swayed not to take jobs during strike actions, underbid fellow workers, and so forth. Where the market is hegemonic, the labor movement's future depends on its ability to provide an 'exit' for workers that concomitantly ensures collective solidarity.

As Esping-Andersen knows, the welfare state was never simply a complement to industrial capitalism. Welfare state programmes have also generated tensions for market and family relations because they were shaped by a complex and conflictual politics. True, some aspects of the programmes shore up market and family imperatives, by making old-age or disability protections, for example, conditional on long-term labour-force participation, or by making the eligibility of women conditional on attachment to a male wage-earner. The work-enforcing aspects of the programmes largely reflected employer interests in crafting programmes that would not interfere with labour-market incentives. (The 'family-wage' premises of the programmes seem to have been largely tacit and assumed, rather than the subject of contention.)

My point, however, is that it is hard to see how any public programme which guaranteed income as a matter of right, no matter how fenced in by conditions, could improve upon the stark imperatives of the market in human labour, or the stark dependence on male family heads enforced on women and the aged by biology and their marginalization in the labour market. The programmes were inaugurated and shaped over time not mainly to shore up the labour or family requirements of an industrial economic order, but to satisfy to some degree the broad popular quest for security from the vagaries of unstable markets. Karl Polanyi (1944) was right when he said that human beings could not long endure the 'stark utopia' of the 'self-adjusting' market. In other words, what Esping-

Andersen describes as the stability lent by the welfare state to a Fordist order was forged by efforts to manage the persistent conflicts of industrial capitalism. And the variations in welfare states reflected the way distinctive national institutional and cultural heritages shaped the conflicts that unfolded – between labour and capital, the metropole and the hinterlands, traditional and modernizing sectors, production and reproduction – as industrial capitalism developed.

The American case again illustrates the point. Because popular forces were feebler, the welfare state was underdeveloped, the protections it offered weaker, and the conflicts it nourished less marked. At bottom, this was probably the result of the underdevelopment of American democracy, and particularly of the failure of a strong national party system to emerge, for reasons including a fragmented governmental structure which privileged the southern section and the racist arrangements on which it relied. But whatever the reasons, the result was a welfare state shaped more to accommodate employer interests, and less to reflect popular aspirations for economic security. Institutional arrangements not only reflect the power relations of the past, but help to shape the power relations of the present. The American welfare state reflects the historic feebleness of popular political forces, and it also contributes to the weakness of contemporary popular politics, thus smoothing the low-wage path to post-industrialism.

I share Esping-Andersen's view that there is little hope of recovering the working-class constituencies which in the past gave the Left political muscle and an *élan* born of a sense of historic mission. Nevertheless, I firmly believe that, as the new world order takes shape, so will new insurgent constituencies emerge, with new strategies, and new grand theories about history and popular power.

But what to do now? The question is painfully difficult. Still, I do not think we should assume the responsibility of contriving solutions which take for granted the new power alignments constructed by an internationalizing capital. We should not imagine ourselves a shadow government, working out more benign if unlikely programmes for administering austerity. Rather, we should defend the programmes built by Left power in the past because these provide some economic protection, and some political space during a period of often wrenching transition. And we should begin to search for the new constituencies, the new power strategies capable of leverage over a mobile capital, and the new imaginary of history through which the hope that politics matters can be regained.

References

Esping-Andersen, G. 1985: *Politics Against Markets: the social democratic road to power.* Princeton, NJ: Princeton University Press.
Polanyi, K. 1944: *The Great Transformation.* Boston: Beacon Press.

9 Sustaining Social Democracy: The Politics of the Environment

Stephen Tindale

Ecological politics ought to be natural territory for social democrats. It binds together traditional concerns of the Left – social justice, the need for collective action and (in theory at least) internationalism – with the emphasis on individual rights and local autonomy that has come to the fore in the late twentieth century. It offers the Left a new paradigm in which to apply old concepts; a vision which could invigorate social democratic ideology for the twenty-first century. Yet, across Europe, the Left has failed to integrate environmentalism into its thinking in a coherent and compelling way. This chapter explores the paradox. It considers the concept of sustainable development, the extent to which social democracy needs to be transformed to encompass ecological politics, and the policy choices that need to be faced.

Social democratic neglect of ecological politics stems partly from poverty of vision on the Left. Most social democratic politicians (indeed, most politicians of all persuasions) regard environmentalism as virtuous but not much fun. The environmental 'issue' is ignored in favour of concerns thought to be more pressing, such as unemployment, tax and health. But the fault lies also with environmentalists. Green parties are notoriously fractious and disorganized, making even the Left seem disciplined and united. There has also been a damaging tendency to present environmentalism as being in conflict with the normal aspirations of the majority. Gro Harlem Brundtland, one of the few successful politicians to have made the green agenda the central part of her politics, explains the perceived marginality of environmental issues as follows: 'The environment does not exist as a sphere separate from human actions, ambitions and needs. Attempts to defend it in isolation from human concerns have given the very word "environment" a connotation of naivety in some political circles' (Brundtland, 1987). The word 'environment' is, in fact, a large part of the problem. It smacks of middle-class concerns, in stark contrast to the real issues facing 'ordinary people'. As one trade union leader put it: 'Why should my members worry about holes in the ozone layer when they have holes in their roof?' Yet few people would dismiss preventative public health strategies as a luxury or superfluous. One reason for seeking to protect the ozone layer is to reduce the number of people who develop skin cancer. The main reason for tackling urban air pollution is to stop children suffering from asthma. And the main reason for providing clean drinking water world-wide is to prevent thirty million people dying every year from diarrhoea (Chivian et al., 1993).

Similarly, few people would suggest that famines, floods or hurricanes are peripheral issues. These 'natural' disasters can be brought on by human activity which fails to respect environmental limits, like overintensive agriculture, deforestation and, above all, industrial and transport patterns which lead to global climate change. Of the world's population, 70 per cent live on coastal plains, many of which will be vulnerable to flooding as the greenhouse effect causes sea levels to rise. The recent Californian drought and series of severe hurricanes have led to a dramatic increase in environmental concern in the USA.

Environmentalism is an essential part of genuine egalitarianism because inequality is far more pervasive than simple differences in wealth. Though no one can escape the consequences of global environmental problems, local environmental degradation often impacts most heavily on poor communities. Those who suffer most from air pollution are inner-city dwellers, mostly too poor to own cars, and not the suburban residents whose driving habits largely cause the problem. Those who suffer most from water pollution are those who cannot afford to drink bottled water.

The widespread perception among commentators and newspaper editors in the UK that 'the environment is no longer an issue' is not borne out by events elsewhere in Europe. In Italy, the Greens have been one of the groupings to capitalize on the anti-party mood, and triumphed in the Rome mayoral elections. In Germany, the Greens appear to have overcome their internal crises and have the capacity to become a serious force again. Before the 1993 French general election, Michel Rocard called for an alliance with environmentalists to revive the Left: the so-called Big Bang. In the elections, the two green parties together won 10 per cent of the vote – disappointing only in that they had registered nearer 20 per cent in the pre-election polls. As the Socialists come to terms with their crushing defeat, the Big Bang may yet develop into something more than a slogan.

Of course, environmental concerns can be temporarily eclipsed by seismic political developments or by economic hardship. The German SPD's programme of ecosocial democracy – the most ambitious attempt yet to integrate the environment into left-wing politics – was unable to protect the party from the consequences of its failure to judge the mood of the electorate on German unification. 'The Red-Green marriage of social market and ecological ideas, [the SPD's] major contribution to the European centre-Left, was swept aside by the more basic economic and political problems thrown up by German unification', writes David Goodhart (1992:4). In the UK, the percentage of poll respondents citing the environment as the most important issue fell from 35 per cent at the end of the 1980s (when it was placed in first place, well ahead of issues such as health) to 14 per cent at the depth of the recession. The environmental agenda will not go away – indeed the issues are getting more serious. Ecological politics are the inheritor to the radical, grass-roots political culture that was previously dominated by the extra-parliamentary Left. Direct action is now more common in pursuit of environmental goals than any other. Environmental groups were at the forefront of the revolutions which swept eastern Europe in 1989. In western Europe, environmentalists have the ability to mobilize at local level, most notably in the burgeoning anti-roads movement, in a way which few political parties of Left or Right can match.

Sustainable development

Sustainable development is, according to the most widely accepted definition, development which meets the needs of current generations without compromising the ability of future generations to meet their needs. It is thus a paradigm with two central, closely related concepts: the demands of intergenerational equity and the requirement to meet current needs. The idea that we have a responsibility for future generations is certainly not new. It is the basic premise of parenthood. But is it new to politics, as some ecologists claim? The answer is that it is not so much new as rediscovered. Pre-industrial methods of agriculture took fully into account the need to preserve the fertility of the soil, water resources and so on for the societies of the future. But the industrial revolution, together with scientific advances and the belief that human beings could conquer nature, led to this approach being abandoned. Because we can now produce the basic means of survival with considerable room to spare, the need to respect ecological limits has been rendered less immediately pressing. It is one of the paradoxes of industrial society that as longevity has increased, so our psychology has become increasingly short-term.

Sustainable development demands that we reverse this cavalier attitude. It could be summed up as equity plus futurity; or social justice plus environmental protection. The former is the central tenet of social democracy; the latter is, with some notable exceptions (Owen, 1991; Thompson, 1977; Williams, 1983), at best a newcomer in the pantheon of the Left. There is substantial common ground between ecological politics and the traditional concerns of the Left. At the level of principle, sustainable development offers powerful support for social democracy by linking the concept of equality between generations (which is at the centre of sustainability) to the concept of equality within generations. At an applied level, the concepts and tools which social democrats have developed to promote social justice – the positive role of government action; the importance of planning; internationalism – are also the concepts and tools of environmentalism. The 'free' market cannot deliver sustainable development because it takes no account of 'externalities' such as pollution, and regards the global commons as a free resource. More fundamentally, the market depends on the private preferences of individuals acting in what they perceive to be their own interest. Even where each of these private decisions is wholly rational, they do not necessarily add up to the best outcome for the community or for the individuals. To be on the Left is to recognize that there exists a community or public interest. It is to accept the concept of a common good which can be embodied through government action. It is through the individual acting within the community framework that sustainability can be attained. As the German SPD's Basic Programme, adopted in 1989, puts it: 'ecology and social justice require a binding framework against capitalist interest.'

Ecological politics therefore assigns a central role to planning to create this framework. So too does social democracy; or at least, it did in the past. Economic planning has fallen out of favour since the perceived failures of the 1960s and 1970s in western Europe and the implosion of the centrally planned economies of the eastern bloc. In contrast, physical planning remains very much in favour. The UK's town and country planning system is one of the greatest legacies of the Attlee Labour government. Sustainable development requires a strengthened and democratized local and regional planning system. It also requires a broader national economic and industrial plan, but one which stops well short of the stifling central control typified by earlier efforts. It can best be seen as a framework within which private enterprise can flourish, which lays down the overall objectives for society, against which success can be measured, and sets the ecological limits beyond which development cannot safely be allowed to go.

Sustainable development also requires a greatly strengthened political framework at the international level (Brown, 1992), and this, too, coincides with longstanding social democratic concerns. The notion that increased wealth has made redundant the Left's analysis of power and opportunity is scarcely credible when applied to developed western societies; when applied on the global scale, it is ludicrous. A world in which billions live below the poverty line, suffer from malnutrition and intermittent famine and have few opportunities for even the most basic self-expression or development is a world with ample scope for traditional notions of social justice and redistribution of wealth. The Left's failure to inspire in the late twentieth century is in part a result of its retreat into narrow nationalist perspectives.

National chauvinism and egalitarianism are incompatible; so too are nationalism and environmentalism. It is a truism to state that pollution does not respect national boundaries, and that countries need to act together to protect their common environment. Ecological politics refutes the idea that a nation-state is entitled to do whatever it wishes with the resources inside its borders; resources are part of the common inheritance of humanity, cogs in an interdependent global ecosystem. There is a clear supranational imperative.

It cannot, however, be assumed that environmentalism is the sole preserve of the Left. Neo-liberalism, with its desire to deregulate and its denial of community, clearly cannot address the environmental agenda. But other strands of right-wing tradition can comfortably embrace environmentalism. Edmund Burke's concept of trusteeship is an obvious starting point for those of a green-blue persuasion (Waldegrave, 1978). Conservatism can easily be defined to encompass conservation (Paterson, 1989). It is conceptually possible (though practically difficult) to achieve sustainability – the conservation of the environment for successor generations to inherit – within current social and political structures. As long as there are powerful police and paramilitary forces, environmental protection and social injustice can, in industrialized, urban societies, coexist. (This is not the case for Third World countries, where poverty and environmental degradation are inseparable.)

Environmentalism becomes undeniably of the Left when it moves from conservation to sustainable development. It is not possible to achieve sustainable development without major social, political and economic reform. The needs of the current generation are not met, and those of future generations will not be met (irrespective of any ecological consideration), by the dominant model of social organization. Radical political transformation, which spreads wealth, power and opportunities more equitably, links sustainable development to the Left; even centrist creeds such as Christian Democracy will baulk at the radicalism it implies.

Sustainable social democracy

It is not enough to view sustainable development as traditional social democracy with an extra bit bolted on – conservation as an ideological conservatory put up at the back of our existing structure. To take sustainable development seriously, social democratic thinking requires transformation. The goal of politics and the objectives of political intervention cannot be maximum growth, but maximum sustainable economic activity. Economic growth has, however, been elevated from a means by which a dividend can be secured to an end in itself. Without growth, the argument has run, no redistribution is possible. There is thus a need to maximize economic output – generally defined as production of manufactured goods – ahead of all other objectives. Meanwhile, the labourist tradition, narrowly interpreted as a defensive and often sectional attempt to protect existing employment patterns, has often succeeded at cost to the environment, and often in the face of the real benefits in employment and standard of living that change could bring. It is this conservative 'producerist' mentality which has led many environmentalists to reject social democracy as incapable of respecting ecological limits or of developing a sufficiently radical approach to politics to reap the benefits of ecological transformation (Porritt and Winner, 1988).

Sustainable development is not anti-growth or anti-materialist. It recognizes that the industrial revolution has brought immense benefits, and that most people want increased personal prosperity; hence the need to increase economic activity. But it also recognizes that industrialization and increased material consumption have had a high environmental and social cost, primarily because such factors have not been considered by decision makers (Durning, 1992). In future, decisions should be taken within a framework designed to ensure that future generations inherit a legacy which enables them to meet their needs, while current generations are not damaged by the ill-health or aesthetic impoverishment which accompany environmental degradation.

The aim of sustainable social democracy would therefore be to achieve the maximum possible level of economic activity and wealth generation within the ecological framework. This is not the same as saying that growth must be limited. The important point for a sustainable economic policy is to measure the quality as well as the quantity of growth. Not all forms of economic activity have an equal impact on the environment; this is the basis of the notion of environmental productivity.

The second half of the twentieth century has seen dramatic advances in the productivity of labour; the twenty-first century must see similar advances in the efficiency with which we use natural resources and the amount of economic activity we can attain per unit of pollution. The Dutch government has set a national target of a tenfold increase in environmental productivity within fifty years. This is of the same order of magnitude as increases in labour productivity over the last fifty years. The environment therefore becomes what Vice-President Gore calls the 'central organising principle of society' (1992). This does not mean that the environment must become the single or overriding goal – the Left would certainly see the alleviation of poverty as at least as important. Gore uses the concept of ecological security to illustrate his view that unless the environmental threat is repelled, democratic politics will be unable to pursue any of its other goals. This requires the integration of ecological thinking into all areas of policy. The rest of this chapter will simply outline some of the implications in three key areas: planning, economic policy and transport.

Creating the ecological framework

An 'ecological framework' is designed to identify the environmental limits – in terms of resource depletion and pollution levels – which cannot be breached without damaging the prospects of future generations. This depends on science rather than subjectivity. Sustainable economic activity will stop short of polluting or degrading the environment beyond its ability to assimilate and recover. An ideology which takes sustainability seriously will accept these ecological factors as absolute constraints. Politics should have no part in deciding what constitutes the maximum load of pollution which an environment can bear; this is a matter for debate among environmental scientists. There should be no debate about whether to exceed the capacity of the receiving environment to assimilate pollution. If the environment is damaged beyond its capacity to recover, intergenerational equity will have been forgotten (Blowers, 1993).

In this respect, ecological politics has more in common with the 'blue-print politics' of old-style Fabianism than with the generative or process politics discussed elsewhere in this volume. Indeed, there can be a tendency to go too far in stressing the importance of process: the Left must have a view on the outcome of the decision-making process as well as its form. And since future generations do not yet have a vote, democracy may well fail to respect the environment. A course of action is not necessarily sensible simply because most people support it.

However, ecological politics is not irredeemably paternalistic. The environment cannot ultimately be protected by a benevolent elite telling the rest of the population how to behave. Sustainable development can only be approached in the context of far-reaching political, legal and constitutional reforms which empower citizens to take control of their own environment. In particular, freedom of information on environmental matters is a prerequisite. When individuals know the state of the environment in which they live, they are much more likely to act to protect it. Conversely, where there is no freedom of information, as in the old eastern bloc, environmental degradation proceeds almost unchecked.

Democracy is also necessary because, within the ecological framework, sustainable development ceases to become an absolutist creed and becomes an exercise in weighing up trade-offs and making subjective decisions. And unless every individual and every section of society is able to participate equally in deciding what is or is not an acceptable trade-off, patterns of economic activity and environmental change will simply reflect the preferences of the powerful. Some ecological features are so valuable that they should be regarded as inviolable, safe from development whatever the potential benefits to the current generation. But if this principle is clear and relatively uncontentious, the process of deciding which features should count as inviolable can only be carried out democratically. Arbitrary designations are unlikely to be respected.

Creating a green economy

The need for an environmental revolution, similar in its scope and significance to the earlier agricultural and industrial revolutions, offers an opportunity to restructure European industry and working practices to maximize employment, conserve resources and minimize pollution. The notion that, at a macro-economic level, environmental concerns are a threat to industry and employment is increasingly recognized to be wrong. The SPD Basic Programme, drawing on years of experience in the old West Germany, states unequivocally that 'ecological renewal creates jobs.' All the macro-economic studies done in the UK suggest that a green industrial strategy would lead to higher GDP and higher levels of employment (Barker, 1991). Studies in the Netherlands, Norway, the USA and the EU bear out these findings (Pearce, 1992). Most of these studies look only at the costs of environmental policies; they do not attempt to quantify the benefits. These can include not only intangibles such as a better quality of life, but also concrete economic gains which can be given a monetary value, such as the lower cost to the health service and the higher productivity which will result from a healthier population (Barker, 1991, Pearce, 1992).

In the short term, an environmental 'New Deal' could help overcome the crisis of mass unemployment by creating work on a wide range of environmental protection and modernization projects. In the longer term, a sustainable economic policy would shift taxation off 'goods' such as employment or savings and onto 'bads' such as pollution, waste or resource depletion. This shift would eliminate the perverse market signals which make it cheaper to replace labour-intensive production with energy-intensive, highly polluting, capital-intensive production. A reduction in employment taxes would contribute directly to the creation of a vibrant and expanding economy. Both the European Commission and the OECD have recently issued papers calling for a shift in the burden of taxation, away from employment and onto environmental 'bads' (European Commission, 1993; OECD, 1994).

An area of taxation which has proved controversial both in the UK and in the EU is energy. The European Commission has proposed the gradual imposition of a carbon/energy tax, which would increase costs of domestic, industrial and transport fuels. The British government has attempted, with little success, to present the recent imposition of VAT on domestic fuel as a green tax. There are two problems with using price to try to encourage energy efficiency in the domestic sector. The first is its regressive impact: poor households spend a greater proportion of their income on fuel than rich ones, and there are already many millions of people living in fuel poverty across Europe. The second, linked problem is that price is a blunt instrument in this instance. For those not on low incomes, fuel costs represent a small outgoing, and there will be little change in their behaviour unless the increase in price is very great.

However, responsiveness to price is far greater in the commercial and industrial sectors, where the amount of energy used is often large, and in some instances there are dedicated energy managers. The way to avoid hurting the poor while helping cut pollution is therefore to increase non-domestic energy prices. And to do this without hurting industry, there should be a simultaneous reduction in employment taxes. This is what Commission President Jacques Delors proposed in his recent White Paper on employment (European Commission, 1993).

Ecological tax reform could contribute significantly to the parallel goals of maximizing employment, regenerating European economies and improving environmental productivity (Repetto, 1992). There are, however, difficulties. As the above discussion of energy taxation showed, environmental taxes – like all indirect taxes – tend to be regressive unless carefully designed (Johnson et al., 1990). Any significant shift in the burden of taxation would need to be integrated with a reform of social security to ensure that the burden of environmental improvement did not fall on those least able to bear it. Major fiscal reform would also run the risk of the 'tobacco tax' problem, where a tax is introduced to discourage a particular activity, but the Exchequer then becomes in effect 'addicted' to the revenues raised, to the extent that the government can no longer afford to discourage the activity. The need for progressivity and buoyancy in the tax system restricts the scope for ecological reform. It seems unlikely, for example, that it will ever be open to a left-of-centre government to replace or significantly reduce income tax – politically attractive though this might be.

A sustainable economic policy must stimulate environmentally beneficial or benign forms of growth while discouraging pollution and resource depletion. Concentration on the 'growth versus no growth' debate has obscured the real issue, which is that there are limits to industrial production. Economic activity in future will need to be less centred on manufacturing, which will be constrained by the ecological limits placed on pollution and resource depletion, and more service-oriented (Daly, 1992). The manufacturing base is an icon of the Left which is due for a rigorous reappraisal. It is not clear, beyond the level of rhetoric, why making and selling a motor car or a washing machine is in any sense more 'real' than making and selling a television programme.

Transport

The environmental impact of current transport patterns is highly visible – the destruction of beautiful scenery; the filthy air in cities. Equally visible is the cost, in terms of human misery, of road accidents – 60,000 people a year are killed or seriously injured on the roads in Britain alone. Much less widely recognized is the way in which current transport patterns, in particular society's worship of the car, have contributed to the breakdown of a sense of community. Roads built in urban areas divide communities and lead to the loss of people's homes. Planning policies based on the car lead to the dispersal of economic and social activity. Car travel is an anti-social form of transport in more senses than one. Drivers do not come into contact with anyone outside their own vehicles; they are often alone with their stereo. There is no common experience; other road users are simply an aggravation. Cars have contributed to the atomization of society.

Perhaps the most dramatic impact of the car culture is the loss of freedom for children. The recent decline in road traffic accidents has been achieved in large part by a retreat from the streets. In many parts of Europe, children no longer play in the streets, or walk or cycle to school unaccompanied. They are taught to be fearful and wary. There are also considerable health impacts resulting from the car culture. Motor vehicles emit a range of toxic pollutants, including nitrogen dioxide, carbon monoxide and hydrocarbons such as benzene, a known carcinogen. These pollutants are damaging to respiratory systems, and are particularly harmful to children and old people.

The car is often hailed as having extended the choice and freedom of ordinary people. But has choice really been extended? For non-drivers, of course, the answer is no; their lives have been made ever more difficult as everything is arranged for the convenience of the car. Even for car drivers, it is not clear that the car culture has improved the quality of life. Certainly car owners have more mobility, but this has increasingly led to life-styles which involve long journeys, for business rather than pleasure. For many people, particularly in rural and suburban areas, motorized mobility has become a necessity rather than a choice. Motoring to new parts of the world or into the countryside to get away from the pressures of urban life or to broaden one's experience is becoming a self-defeating activity – there is less tranquillity in the countryside, and towns and cities are becoming increasingly similar; noisy, dirty, smelly streams of traffic with occasional islands of architecture or culture.

The car provides a classic illustration of the prisoner's dilemma. If fewer people drive, pollution and congestion levels would fall, walking and cycling would be safer, the streets would be more pleasant. But if an individual chooses not to drive when everyone else continues in the car, he or she will be at a disadvantage. So everyone drives, and everyone is worse off. Only public policy can break this spiral, by providing alternatives to the car, and creating the conditions in which individuals choosing not to use the car do not suffer a decline in their quality of life. Through the use of the planning system, through the creation of extensive car-free areas and cycle networks, through the provision of better public transport facilities, through the provision of compulsory delivery services by major shops, a sustainable transport policy could offer people not just choice but security.

The fiscal contribution made by drivers to the public purse does not nearly cover the full cost of motoring. Even introduced alone, with no accompanying measures to boost alternative transport modes, increasing the cost of motoring (through fuel duties or road pricing) is progressive rather than regressive because most poor people do not own cars. Hypothecating some or all of the revenue raised to public transport would make the approach highly redistributive.

Reflecting the true cost of transport in the price of fuel would also promote more diffuse patterns of economic activity. The combination of low transport costs and an ever-increasing roads infrastructure has not, contrary to expectations, spread economic activity and brought prosperity to peripheral regions. Instead, it has facilitated centralization, since it has become easier and more cost-effective to manufacture in one place and then distribute nationwide or, increasingly, Europe-wide.

Sustainable development and democracy

Tackling the car culture is not an easy political option. Indeed, it is issues such as this which have led to environmentalism being seen in terms of sacrifices demanded, rather than opportunities offered. Environmentalism is generally thought to be an appeal to people's better natures, stressing the need for more responsibility and taking the moral high ground. If this were all the green agenda had to offer, it might help the Left in the task of appealing to the young and idealistic, and perhaps help win back some cynical and disenchanted former radicals. But it would not, in all probability, appeal to the majority. Fortunately, ecological politics is more complex than this picture suggests.

Across Europe, social democrats are trying to develop a new approach which combines the politics of the public interest with the politics of self-interest. It is emphasized that increased economic efficiency, better education and training, higher skills levels and more investment in the infrastructure will benefit everyone in the community. This approach is undoubtedly more likely to succeed than one based solely on altruism, which will appeal only to a committed minority. It will also fare better than a strategy based on an appeal to narrow self-interest, since the Right is always liable to do better on straightforward pocket-book issues (recent events in Britain notwithstanding).

There are, however, a number of problems, of both style and substance. With the important exception of education, the Left's new agenda is not dealing in concepts likely to inspire. Investment and infrastructure are without doubt important, but are not rallying cries to set the pulse racing. They are, or are perceived to be, essentially technocratic responses, accepting the framework and general approach of liberal capitalism. They do not appear to offer bold solutions to what are undoubtedly deep-seated problems of unemployment and decline. More substantively, economic modernization of a particular nation-state is, by its very nature, a nationalist agenda, not an internationalist one. Even a pan-European social democratic industrial strategy would be a regional rather than global response. There may be, as Marx and others have asserted, a global interest of labour, but it is proving extremely hard to discern. Competing successfully with the Asian tigers means, ultimately, depriving Asian workers of jobs. The community to which Left theorists appeal is national or European, not global. Europe's industrial base of course needs modernization, but a political agenda aiming to strengthen the ability to *compete* is not going to strengthen an ideology based on the notion of cooperation.

A further problem relates to the social democrat's age-old dilemma: whether redistribution is possible in the absence of rapid economic growth. It is of course this which lies behind the desire to strengthen Europe's competitiveness. The perceived need for growth is made stronger by western electorates' increased hostility to high taxation, which appears to rule out redistribution by any other means. Meanwhile, the credibility of a strategy based on rapid rates of growth is dented by the inability of any government in charge of a major economy to overcome the various international impediments and make an appreciable difference to its economic performance. The feeling that governments are relatively powerless to influence the economy is a major cause of the increasing disillusionment with the political process which is discernible throughout the developed world. A final problem is closely related, and hampers all attempts by left-wing parties to shed the 'tax and spend' label. Since the Left believes in the public good, it must in some circumstances also believe in the merits of public rather than private spending. If the Left is genuine in its protestations that it will not increase taxation, then what is the Left for?

The Left thus faces four key difficulties. It appears to have no idealistic or radical solutions to the crisis of mass unemployment and social disintegration; its revamped ideology has replaced a key tenet of left-wing thought – world-wide cooperation – with a desire to sharpen regional competition; its entire strategy is predicated on the achievement of higher levels of economic growth, which sceptical electorates tend to find less than wholly convincing; and it cannot convince people that it will not increase taxation, because the demands of egalitarianism require higher public spending. Without egalitarianism, the Left is nothing.

Ecological politics can help overcome all these barriers to success. It is bold and idealistic. It is wholly cooperative and unremittingly global. It is credible; or at least, it has not yet been discredited. Perhaps most significant of all, it offers a project which could deliver redistribution without higher taxation, by improving the quality of life of all, but benefiting poor communities disproportionately.

This takes us back to the question posed at the outset. Why have so few mainstream politicians taken the environmentalists' message to heart? It is not because ecological politics need be unpopular. Nor is it because ecological politics is incompatible with traditional social democratic concerns. The real reason why the Left has yet to embrace ecological politics is that social democracy, originally a creed to conquer capitalism, now uncritically accepts its assumptions. Social democrats are trapped in the language and concepts of the materialist, individualistic Right or the producer-oriented tribal politics of old labourism. For all the talk of community, there is little vision other than of continuing wealth creation. The vision of a society in which government plans for the long-term public interest while promoting well-being as well as wealth is one which a timid Left, sadly lacking in self-confidence following the demise of socialism in eastern Europe, dare not articulate. We approach the twenty-first century offering not a cooperative community, but more successful competition.

A synthesis of social democracy and environmentalism could break this log jam. Ecological politics can contribute the idealism and ambition the Left currently lacks, while social democracy still offers a compelling analysis of the structures of power within which politics takes place. Environmental concern is not the property of the Left; but the Left can make ecological transformation its issue.

References

Barker, T. (ed.) 1991: *Green Futures for Economic Growth*. Cambridge: Cambridge Econometrics.

Blowers, A. 1993: *Planning for a Sustainable Environment*. London: Earthscan/TCPA.

Brown, L. R. 1992: *State of the World 1992*. London: Earthscan.

Brundtland, G. H. 1987: *Our Common Future: the World Commission on Environment and Development*. Oxford: Oxford University Press.

Chivian, E., McCally, M., Hu, H. and Haines, A. 1993: *Critical Condition: human health and the environment*, Cambridge, MA: MIT press

Daly, H. 1992: *Steady State Economics*. London: Earthscan.

Durning, A. T. 1992: *How Much is Enough?*. London: Earthscan/World Resources Institute.

European Commission, 1993: *Growth, Competitiveness and Employment*. Com (93)700. Brussels: European Commission.

Goodhart, D. 1992: Back from the ruins of 1992. *Fabian Review*, 104(5), 4.

Gore, A. 1992: *Earth in the Balance*. New York: Houghton Mifflin.

Johnson, P., McKay, S. and Smith, S. 1990: *The Distributional Consequences of Environmental Taxes*. London: Institute for Fiscal Studies.

OECD, 1994: *Employment/Unemployment Study*. SG\EUS (94) 1. Paris: OECD.

Owen, R. 1991: *A New Vision of Society and Other Writings*. Harmondsworth: Penguin.

Paterson, T. 1989: *The Green Conservative*. London: Bow Publications.

Pearce, D. 1992: *Growth, Employment and Environmental Policy*. London: Employment Institute.

Porritt, J. and Winner, D. 1988: *The Coming of the Greens*. London: Fontana.

Repetto, R. 1992: *Green Fees; how a tax shift can work for the environment and the economy*. Washington, DC: World Resources Institute.

Thompson, E. P. 1977: *William Morris: romantic to revolutionary*. London: Merlin.

Waldegrave, W. 1978: *The Binding of Leviathan – Conservatism and the future*. London: Hamish Hamilton.

Williams, R. 1983: *Towards 2000*. London: Chatto and Windus.

Comment: Sustainability and Environmental Policy: Five Fundamental Questions

Susan Owens

Stephen Tindale presents the new environmental agenda as both a challenge and an opportunity for the Left. Green issues undoubtedly impinge on the lives – and the quality of life – of every citizen; they have grown rapidly in political significance; and it is clear that socialism and environmentalism have many roots and values in common (Cotgrove and Duff, 1981; Lowe and Goyder, 1983; Paehlke, 1989; Williams, 1984). Why then, as Tindale also suggests, has the Left been divided and equivocal in its response? If the necessary policies are self-evidently beneficial, why is consensus in practice so difficult to achieve? At one level, this paradox might be explained by the need for persuasion, recognition of communalities of interest and assimilation of new ideas. More fundamentally, however, its roots lie in conflicts and contradictions which are rarely confronted in the rhetoric on sustainable development. Important issues arising from Tindale's chapter concern values, obligations, limits and the role of science in environmental policy. Here I identify five fundamental questions related to these issues. If environmental policy is to be based on a coherent environmental philosophy, it is crucial that these questions are addressed, for to paraphrase Aldo Leopold (1937, quoted in Meine, 1992: 40), sustainable development 'without a keen realisation of its vital conflicts ... falls to the level of a mere Utopian dream'.[1]

Values, needs and sustainability

The Brundtland definition of sustainable development is simultaneously compelling and frustrating because it deals with the very basic question of human need. But the relation of needs to environmental quality is complicated by the frequent elision of quite different social meanings of 'environment' under the general heading of sustainability. In part this explains why environmental concerns can seem both radical and bourgeois, and why sustainable development does not, after all, fully reconcile old, polarized positions on growth and the environment.

Brundtland's most influential argument was that '[e]nvironment and development are not separate challenges; they are inexorably linked. Development cannot subsist upon a deteriorating environmental resource base' (WCED, 1987: 37). This thesis is most convincing in relation to what we might call the *material* dimensions of sustainability, arising from concerns about resource degradation, health and ultimately survival; the ozone layer and a functioning biosphere can hardly be dismissed as luxuries. Indeed, though the scale has increased to encompass global concerns, sustainability in this sense has clear antecedents in the much older concept of 'prudent resource use' (see, for example, Meine, 1992). In relation to material concerns about health and survival, needs can be defined without great difficulty and environmental protection, as Tindale argues, can quite readily be aligned with socially progressive intentions: it is indeed the poor who suffer disproportionately from resource degradation and pollution.

But sustainability is about more than survival. The concerns which inspire environmental activism – and the passions which Tindale argues that the Left should harness – are often post-material (Inglehart, 1977): they encompass amenity in its broadest sense, cultural and aesthetic satisfaction and often a non-instrumental appreciation of intrinsic value in nature (this is the 'spiritual reverence' to which Tindale refers). The outrage felt over Twyford Down is not about health or survival.

These post-material dimensions of sustainability are fundamental to much environmental conflict. It is simplistic to regard them as optional luxuries: rather, as Goodin (1992: 56) argues, they 'reflect concern about the value and meaning of life'. And it is unsatisfactory to assume that these issues 'pale into insignificance' beside the major material concerns of health and survival: if so, future generations could look forward to a safe and sanitized but aesthetically and culturally sterile environment. Definition of what is sustainable in the post-material realm will therefore be impossible without a theory of value. Issues of landscape and habitat preservation,[2] for example, raise profound questions about values, how they are expressed and measured, whether they are widely shared and how to act when they are not. Though some authors suggest that a large 'attentive public' is broadly sympathetic to environmental ideals (Lowe and Goyder, 1983), it has long been observed that attitudes towards nature vary significantly among different social groups (see, for example, Cotgrove and Duff, 1981; Kreiger, 1973; Rolston III, 1988; Sagoff, 1974, 1981). Sagoff (1981: 210) claims provocatively that '[i]f the pleasures of the poor were measured equally with those of the rich, then quicker than you can say "cost-benefit analysis" there would be parking lots, condominiums and plastic trees.' If this view is uncomfortable, can it be refuted without incurring a charge of elitism? It is more important to confront these issues than to base a false and temporary consensus on the notion that environmental policies are of equal and positive value to all. The first fundamental question, therefore, is whether 'principled positions' (Squires, 1993) can be worked out in relation to the post-material and non-instrumental dimensions of sustainability.

Obligations and the boundaries of moral significance

Other fundamental questions underlie notions of obligation in environmental discourse. The most familiar in the context of sustainable development is that of an obligation to future generations; this is an extension of the human-instrumental emphasis reflected in the definition itself. However, theories of the intrinsic value, moral significance and in some cases the 'rights' of nature also imply obligations to the non-human world (Goodin, 1992; Hargrove, 1992; Johnson, 1991; Leopold, 1949; Nash, 1989; Regan, 1981; Rolston III, 1988; Stone, 1972; Taylor, 1986; Varner, 1987). These are important issues, vigorously debated in environmental ethics: we have certainly moved beyond simple dichotomies of 'plants or people' to much more taxing questions about the form and significance of values inhering in nature. For many, this extends to a thoughtful critique of the subject–object dualism characteristic of post-Enlightenment western attitudes towards the environment and the associated treatment of nature as a repository of resources for human use, prudent or otherwise.

Once again, these are issues where uncritical rhetoric is too often a substitute for rigorous analysis. Again, the result is that conflicts are ignored only to surface in any attempt to define sustainable policies. A number of philosophers have raised difficult questions about the limits to obligation (Fishkin, 1982; Parfit, 1984; Norton, 1982). Parfit (1984), for example, poses the 'non-identity problem' – policies adopted now affect not only the environment inherited by our descendants but also their *identity*: in a sense, therefore, whatever choices we make will 'benefit' these people, because alternative choices would have meant that they did not exist. Norton (1982: 337) cites this problem as an example of the inadequacies of individualistic ethical reasoning in supporting our 'intuitively felt obligations concerning environmental protection', and suggests that it will be preferable to recognize new forms of generalized obligations. But as Fishkin (1982: 170) shows, when general principles are no longer restricted to those close to us, 'any plausible principles of general obligation will *routinely* range over so many cases as to overwhelm us.' These are profoundly difficult issues, but they cannot be evaded in any truly radical rethinking of political philosophy: and they are particularly relevant for the Left, which has in the past been instrumental in extending the boundaries of moral considerability. A second fundamental question, therefore, is how, and on what ethical basis, these boundaries should now be drawn in environmental policy.

Environmental protection: the role of state, market and citizen

Questions of obligation lead us into another set of issues, concerning the respective roles of the citizen, the market and the state in environmental protection. The limitations of the unregulated market in this respect are well rehearsed.[3] Environmental degradation can often be characterized as the outcome of a many-person prisoner's dilemma, in which 'if we all pursue self interest, this will be worse for all of us' (Parfit, 1984: 111). Since in such circumstances appeals to altruism will conflict with self-interest, political solutions which change the context for individual decisions are likely to be required. As Tindale points out, collectively we choose outcomes that diverge from the aggregation of our individual preferences, in part because we have different values as consumers and citizens. (Sagoff (1988) provides an extensive discussion of this distinction; see also Brown (1984).) But in environmental policy there is currently a resurgence of an individualistic market ethos, reflected in the increasingly influential view that the environment must be 'priced', and weighed in cost-benefit analysis, in order to make convincing and efficient environmental policy decisions (this is pervasive even in such notions as the 'true cost' of transport). Where markets do not exist, revealed preference theory is invoked, and 'willingness to pay' becomes a measure of environmental value (for different perspectives, see Cropper and Oates, 1992; Pearce et al., 1989, Price, 1993). It is sometimes implied that application is limited mainly by methodological difficulties, but some critics focus on conceptual problems, including flaws in the utilitarian underpinnings of cost-benefit analysis (see, for example, Bowers, 1992; Brown, 1984; Kelman, 1990; Neuburger and Fraser, 1993).[4] The important issues to be resolved relate to Tindale's tension between paternalism and the tyranny of the majority; they are not entirely new to the Left. They also point to the third fundamental question. When the aggregation of individual preferences is an inappropriate basis for policy, on what grounds should environmental policy decisions be made?

Growth, limits and sustainability

The politics of altruism has limitations in a different sense, relating to the specific impacts of environmental policies when net social benefits are clear. It is frequently argued that environmental policy will boost the economy and generate jobs: Tindale presents considerable evidence to challenge the old 'jobs versus the environment' dispute. But to understand real policy outcomes, it is necessary to distinguish between macroeconomic effects and specific impacts. In a representative democracy, what generates public and political pressure is concern about *these* jobs in *this* locality. There are very few policy changes that 'benefit everyone in the community', and for the Left, the question of who benefits and who loses has always been of central concern. The answer can certainly not be to defend the status quo, but must involve seriously addressing the interaction between social, spatial and environmental inequalities and their reproduction in communities dependent on environmentally harmful activities (Blowers and Leroy, forthcoming). In the rhetoric of 'greening the economy', these conflicts are evaded: hence the awkward contradictions on coal and the silence on Sellafield.

In the macro-economic sphere, it is worth probing some other tenets of the emergent conventional wisdom. One is the failure of GDP to take account of the negative effects of pollution and depletion of natural resources: indeed, pollution may *add* to GDP, because clean-up generates economic activity (a phenomenon that Daly (1973) once called 'hypergrowthmania'). These criticism are widely accepted. There is therefore something inconsistent about the claim that environmental policies are good for economic growth because there is a large and growing market for pollution-control equipment. The argument is more convincing when it refers to investment in clean, low-impact technology, but then we need some assurance that the 'dirty' industries are not simply relocating in countries with less stringent environmental regulations: exporting unsustainability does not amount to sustainable development.

Finally, in this context, there is the question of growth and sustainability. The rhetoric here is fraught with contradictions, because advocates of sustainable development often struggle simultaneously to assert and deny the existence of limits to growth. This tension emerges in Tindale's chapter when he refers both to 'ecological limits' and to 'absolute constraints', yet insists that sustainable development 'is not anti-growth or anti-materialist'. His argument depends on a broad interpretation of 'development'[5] and on the potential to reduce the 'environmental co-efficient of growth', defined by Jacobs (1991: 54) as the degree of impact or amount of 'environmental consumption' caused by an increase of one unit of national income. As long as this coefficient is positive, however, and as long as there is growth, demands on the environment will continue to increase, and have the potential to exceed environmental capacities. Furthermore, the *scale* of economic activity and its 'environmental intensity' matter, as well as its rate of growth, though attempts to address this issue tend to be dismissed as neo-Malthusian. Connections between efficiency of resource use, the environmental coefficient of growth and the achievement of sustainability merit more rigorous scrutiny.

To argue that there is scope for growth within limits is not to deny that limits exist. In both its material dimensions (where we identify, for example, maximum sustainable yields for renewable resources and critical loads for pollution) and in relation to post-material values (where we may deem certain culturally and ecologically important assets 'inviolable'), the assessment of what is sustainable often reduces to the identification of limits to growth. (Interestingly, this is clearly the case in land-use planning, which Tindale offers as a model: Collis et al., 1992; Jacobs, 1993; Owens, 1994.) It is misleading to deny the conflicts between growth and environmental protection, for they will certainly resurface during the policy and planning process.

These issues together can be distilled into the fourth fundamental question. In what circumstances does environmental sustainability imply constraints on economic activity: when it does, what are the distributional consequences?

Science and objectivity

A final set of issues concerns the relation between science and policy in this very complex field. Tindale implies that science will define the limits to resource depletion and pollution, but that in the post-material realm sustainability constraints (essentially, what to conserve) must be determined through the democratic process. But these distinctions themselves cannot be sustained. Environmental science, as many authors have argued, is itself socially constructed (see the essays in Oelschlaeger, 1992; also Harvey, 1993; Weinburg, 1972; Wynne, 1992). Even in relation to the material dimensions of sustainability, though the *concept* of limits is easy to grasp, limits themselves are strongly contested and environmental standards emerge out of conflict rather than consensus. Even here, many issues fall into the realm of what Weinburg (1972) calls the 'trans-scientific'. When it comes to landscape, habitat, amenity and cultural assets, we have hardly begun to address the question of how to define environmental limits or the respective roles of public, political and expert judgement in this process. Environmental science is indispensable in defining sustainable development, but it is inseparable from politics, economics and ethics. It cannot in isolation provide the answer to the final, and perhaps the most fundamental question, which has already been posed by Beck (1992: 28): '[H]ow do we wish to live? What is the human quality of human kind, the natural quality of nature which is to be preserved?'

Notes

1 Leopold said this of conservation.
2 Habitat preservation, contributing to protection of biodiversity, has both material and post-material dimensions. It is linked to instrumental concerns about human health and survival, but this is not always its primary rationale.
3 The orthodoxy of 'free trade' is less consistently questioned, but critics are increasingly alarmed at the potential environmental and social effects of the Uruguay round of GATT – see, for example, Lang and Hines (1993).
4 Interestingly, one of the most vitriolic recent attacks has come from the Right, on the grounds that such methods give *too much* significance to environmental considerations (Bate, 1993).
5 This interpretation itself tends to be post-material, if not anti-material.

References

Bate, R. 1993: What am I bid?. *Economic Affairs*, Vol 14, No 1 (Sept./Oct.), 33.
Beck, U. 1992: *Risk Society: towards a new modernity*. London: Sage.
Blowers, A. and Leroy, P. forthcoming: Power, politics and environmental inequality: a theoretical and empirical analysis of the process of peripheralisation. *Environmental Politics*.

Bowers, J. (1992) 'A conspectus on valuing the environment', *Journal of Environmental Planning and Management* Vol 36, No 1, 91–100.

Brown, T. C. 1984: The concept of value in resource allocation. *Land Economics*, 60 (3), 231–46.

Collis, I., Heap, J. and Jacobs, M. 1992: Strategic planning and sustainable development. Paper prepared for English Nature, Peterborough.

Cotgrove, S. and Duff, A. 1981: Environmentalism, middle class radicalism and politics. *Sociological Review*, 28, 333–51.

Cropper, M. L. and Oates, W. E. 1992: Environmental economics: a survey. *Journal of Economic Literature*, 30, 675–740.

Daly, H. E. 1993 'The steady state economy: towards a political economy of biophysical equilibrium and moral growth' in H. E. Daly (ed). *Towards a Steady State Economy.* San Francisco: Freeman 149–174.

Fishkin, J. 1982: *The Limits of Obligation.* New Haven: Yale University Press.

Goodin, R. E. 1992: *Green Political Theory.* Oxford: Polity Press.

Hargrove, E. 1992: Weak anthropocentric intrinsic value. In M. Oelschlaeger (ed.), *After Earth Day: continuing the conservation effort*, Denton: University of North Texas Press.

Harvey, D. 1993: *The nature of environment: the dialectics of social and environmental change.* In R. Miliband and L. Panitch (eds), *The Socialist Register 1993: Real Problems, False Solutions.* London: Martin Press, 1–51.

Inglehart, R. 1977: *The Silent Revolution.* Princeton, NJ: Princeton University Press.

Jacobs, M. 1991. *The Green Economy: environment, sustainable development and the politics of the future.* London: Pluto Press.

Jacobs, M. 1993: *Sense and Sustainability.* London: CPRE.

Johnson, L.1991: *A Morally Deep World: essays on moral significance and environmental ethics.* Cambridge: Cambridge University Press.

Kelman, S. 1990: Cost-benefit analysis: an ethical critique. In T. S. Glickman and M. Gough, (ed.), *Readings in Risk*, Washington , DC: Resources for the Future.

Kreiger, M. 1973: What's wrong with plastic trees? *Science*, 179, 446–55.

Lang, T. and Hines, C. 1993: *The New Protectionism.* London: Earthscan.

Leopold, A. 1949: *A Sand County Almanac and Sketches Here and There.* New York: Oxford University Press.

Lowe, P. and Goyder, J. 1983: *Environmental Groups in Politics.* London: Allen and Unwin.

Meine, C. 1992: 'Conservation biology and sustainable societies: a historical perspective'. In M. Oelschlaeger (ed.), *After Earth Day: continuing the conservation effort*, Denton: University of North Texas Press.

Nash, 1989: *The Rights of Nature: a history of environmental ethics.* Madison: University of Wisconsin Press.

Neuburger, H. and Fraser, N. 1993: *Economic Policy Analysis: a rights based approach.* Aldershot: Avebury.

Norton, B. G. 1982: Environmental ethics and the rights of future generations. *Environmental Ethics*, 4, 319–37.

Oelschlaeger, M. 1992 Introduction. In M. Oelschlaeger (ed.) *After Earth Day: continuing the conservation effort*, Denton: University of North Texas Press.

Owens, S. 1994: Land, limits and sustainability: a conceptual framework and some dilemmas for the planning system. *Transactions of the Institute of British Geographers NS* (forthcoming).

Paehlke, R. C. 1989: *Environmentalism and the Future of Progressive Politics.* New Haven and London: Yale University Press.

Parfit, D. 1984: *Reasons and Persons.* Oxford: Oxford University Press.

Pearce, D. W., Markandya, A. and Barbier, E. 1989: *Blueprint for a Green Economy.* London: Earthscan.

Price, C. 1993: Landscape economics: a personal journey of discovery. *Journal of Environmental Planning and Management,* 36 (1), 51–64.

Regan, T. 1981: The nature and possibility of an environmental ethic. *Environmental Ethics,* 3, 19–34.

Rolston III, H. 1988: *Environmental Ethics: duties to and values in nature.* Philadelphia: Temple University Press.

Sagoff, M. 197x: On preserving the natural environment. *Yale Law Journal,* 84 (197), 205–67.

Sagoff, M. 1981: Do we need a land use ethic? *Environmental Ethics,* 3, 293–308.

Sagoff, M. 1988: *The Economy of the Earth.* Cambridge: Cambridge University Press.

Squires, J. (ed.) 1993: *Principled Positions: postmodernism and the rediscovery of value.* London: Lawrence and Wishart.

Stone, C. 1972: *Should Trees Have Standing? Toward legal rights for natural objects.* Los Altos: William Kaufman.

Taylor, P. W. 1986: *Respect for Nature: a theory of environmental ethics.* Princeton, NJ: Princeton University Press.

Varner, G. E. 1987: Do species have standing? *Environmental Ethics,* 9, 57–72.

WCED (World Commission on Environment and Development) 1987: *Our Common Future.* Oxford: Oxford University Press.

Weinburg, A. M. 1972: Science and trans-science. *Minerva,* 10, 209–22.

Williams, R. 1984: How socialists and environmentalists can get together. *Guardian,* 11 June, 10.

Wynne, B. 1992: Uncertainty and environmental learning: reconstructing science and policy in the preventive paradigm. *Global Environmental Change,* Vol 2, No 2 (June), 111–27.

Part V

Instruments of Change

10 Reinventing Federalism: Europe and the Left

David Marquand

Europeans have lived for so long in the warm cocoon of the Community system that we have almost forgotten what our history was like before the astonishing burst of institutional inventiveness that culminated in the Treaty of Rome a generation ago. If present trends are allowed to continue we may be brutally reminded, with consequences we cannot now imagine. The demons of European history – chauvinism, xenophobia, irredentism, racism and scapegoat-hunting – are on the march all over the former Soviet bloc. In Community Europe they are still relatively quiescent. But no one who has watched the rise of the French National Front or the German Republicans – no one, for that matter, who watched the 1993 Conservative Party conference in the UK – can pretend that they strike no chords on this side of what used to be the iron curtain. There is an ample supply of combustible material lying about in western Europe as well as in the east. If anyone puts a match to it the entire Community system may be destroyed.

To be sure, its institutional structure is not at risk. Institutions, particularly international institutions, often limp on, pale shadows of their former selves, long after events have squeezed the life out of them. The real danger is that they will bombinate in a vacuum; that the mountains of paper, the hours of talk, the agitated comings and goings of self-important personages will be so much spitting in the wind; that, while preserving the forms of a supranational Community, the reality of European life will be one of beggar-my-neighbour attempts to sneak competitive advantages in an ever more cut-throat world economy, accompanied by increasingly raucous chauvinistic drum-beating and deepening national rivalries in politics as well as in economics.

For the current trend in the brave new European Union inaugurated by the Maastricht Treaty is emphatically towards a two- (or even a multi-)

speed Europe. Like the currency upheavals which destroyed the snake in the 1970s, the currency upheavals which have inflicted so much damage on the European Monetary System in the recent past have shown that the mere exercise of political will cannot force through the economic convergence which is the necessary condition of a monetary union between the 'strong' currency core of the European Community and the 'weak' currency periphery. If present trends continue there is not much doubt that the Deutschmark-dominated core – with or without France – will continue along the path to further economic and monetary integration. In the periphery, meanwhile, a vigorous 'race for the bottom', led by the United Kingdom, is likely to accelerate.

Britain's social chapter opt-out is a classic example of free-rider politics. In effect, Britain has been allowed to escape its share of the social costs of the single market. It is riding free on the backs of the other member states, in an attempt to make itself that much more attractive to inward investment, and that much more competitive in the cheap and shoddy end of the global marketplace. And it is justifying itself by banging on a peculiarly crass and nasty xenophobic drum. The Community can survive one free rider. It could not survive several. Yet, if John Major's free riding succeeds, it is hard to believe that all the other member states will refrain indefinitely from following suit. If he is followed, the process of competitive social dumping which the social chapter was designed to stop is likely to start after all. If it does, member states with high standards of social protection will be under enormous – and understandable – pressure to defend themselves against unfair competition from those who have followed the British road. And the lesson of history is that that sort of self-defence quickly spreads, and quickly becomes self-stultifying.

It is equally clear that, on present trends, the institutional framework of the Union will, for the foreseeable future, remain essentially inter-governmental rather than supranational; that an unholy alliance between France and the United Kingdom will continue to block all attempts to correct the democratic deficit in decision making, as it did before the Maastricht summit; and that, because of this, the institutions will remain weak, opaque and lacking in democratic legitimacy. If this prediction is borne out, the people of what is now supposed to be the European Union will remain apathetic and, at least to a certain extent, alienated from the whole process. All this will create fertile soil for 'fundamentalist' nationalism and populist demagogy, of the sort that surfaced in the French and Danish referendum campaigns on the Maastricht Treaty and that the miscalled 'Euro-sceptics' in both major British political parties have employed ever since membership first became a serious political issue.

A further and, in some ways, even more alarming implication follows as well. This is that a social democratic European project, of the sort envisaged by Wolfgang Streeck and Joel Rogers in their chapter of this book, will continue to be, in practice, utopian. It will be utopian because the nation-states of the Union have already surrendered too much power to supranational institutions to implement it on the national level, while the institutions of the Union will continue to be too weak to implement it on the supranational level. And if this is at all true, the clear implication is that Europe will continue to be dominated, in practice, by the political Right and centre-Right; that capital will continue to sit in the driving seat, with little to fear from the political Left or from organized labour – even if nominally Left or centre-Left governments hold office in certain capitals, as is the case at present in Spain. Though the Spanish socialists are still in office, it is worth remembering their programme is not very different from that of the neo-Thatcherites under John Major in the UK. And if this is all true, the likelihood is that European governments will continue to respond to international competition by hollowing out the welfare state, arguably the greatest achievement of European civilization in this century.

Last, but not least, eastern Europe will, on present trends, remain outside the new Union, an impoverished hinterland, cut off from the rich and complacent west by a new kind of Berlin Wall – a wall of patronizing indifference, tinged with suppressed fear, rather than of concrete. There is, of course, an argument for keeping the countries of eastern Europe out of the Union. It is a spurious one, but that does not make it any less persuasive to those who want, for other reasons, to accept it. It is that the economies of the eastern countries are too weak to sustain the competition implied by full membership; that if they were to become full members on terms that made it possible for them to escape the rigours of competition, the famous *'Acquis Communautaire'* would be fatally jeopardized in the existing member states; and that this would compromise the whole European project. The premise is true, although the conclusion does not follow; and because the premise is true, the argument has great resonance in the capitals of western Europe and still more, perhaps, in the strange Europe-half-capital that clusters around the Berlaymont building in Brussels.

The trouble is that it carries great dangers – dangers symbolized most poignantly and most powerfully by the word 'Sarajevo'. The problems of transition in eastern Europe have turned out to be enormously more difficult and the solutions enormously more painful than anyone expected in the euphoria of 1989. The Czech and Slovak Republics apart, the societies which will be suffering the pains have few or no democratic traditions to draw upon and, in almost all of them, ethnic hatreds and irredentist ambitions are rife. Fragile new regimes, long on hope but short on experience, necessarily dependent on the bureaucracies they have inherited from their Stalinist predecessors and encumbered by expectations they cannot satisfy, may well see in these ambitions their only reservoir of popular support. That is the inner meaning of the Bosnian tragedy; and there are plenty of other potential Bosnias in eastern Europe. These potential Bosnias are far more likely to suffer the fate of the real Bosnia if eastern Europe is excluded from the Union taking shape in the west than if it has a reasonable prospect of joining it in a timescale which is not impossibly remote. If they do suffer that fate, it is hard to believed that smug and prosperous western Europe could insulate itself from the ensuing conflicts, any more than the western Europe of 1914 could insulate itself from the consequences of what happened at Sarajevo then.

If there are plenty of potential Bosnias in eastern Europe, there are far more in the former Soviet Union, where the Stalinist terror was even more savage and did even more to destroy the mutual trust which provides the basis of a civic culture. Partly because of this, and partly because of the very nature of the Soviet regime, economic dislocation has already gone much further in its successor states than in the lands between the new united Germany and the former Soviet border, while ethnic conflicts and resentments are even fiercer. For the collapse of the Soviet Union has spelt more than the collapse of another economically irrational and politically illegitimate communist regime. It has also spelt the end of the last great European empire; and the end of empire is almost always a bloody business. So far bloodshed has been much rarer than it was in the Indian sub-continent after the end of the British Raj or in north Africa during the war against the French, but upheavals on that scale cannot be ruled out.

The paradoxes of the European project

Why should these trends, so gloomy compared to those that seemed to be in operation in the late 1980s and early 1990s, in the aftermath of the Single European Act and the dismantling of the Berlin Wall, appear to be in the ascendant now? I shall argue that the answer to that question lies in a series of confusions, or paradoxes, perhaps even of contradictions at the heart of the European project, at least in its contemporary form. In trying to explore these paradoxes and contradictions, I hasten to add, I imply no criticism of the founding fathers of the European Community.

On the contrary, I believe that Monnet, de Gasperi, Schuman and the rest were giants in their generation. They were statesmen of extraordinary inventiveness and extraordinary courage. If there is a criticism to be made, and I think there is, it should be directed not to them but to their latter-day followers who trod mechanically in their footsteps without realizing that times had changed.

What are these paradoxes? The first is a paradox of identity. We speak of the European Union, or the European Community, but what is meant by 'Europe'? Where are its boundaries? What are the essential features of a European identity? The founding fathers never asked these questions. They never defined what they meant by 'Europe'. They did not define it because they had no need to define it. Their Europe was, in practice, the Europe of Charlemagne, with the addition of southern Italy. It was the Europe of the Po Valley in northern Italy and of the lands clustered around the River Rhine: the Europe of Adenauer's Germany allied to the Europe of Charlemagne's France. And this Europe – the little Europe of Charlemagne – huddled in the shadow of American power, which it saw as its only feasible protector against the perceived threat from the East. Community Europe was in reality Carolingian Europe until Britain, Ireland and Denmark acceded to it twenty-one years later. Then, in the early 1970s, Community Europe expanded to include a northern addition; and in the early 1980s, it expanded again to include the Iberian peninsula and Greece. Apart from the last named, it is worth noting, this was, to a very considerable extent, Catholic Christendom (including, under that heading, formerly Catholic countries which became Protestant in the sixteenth and seventeenth centuries). To be sure, it did not include the whole of Catholic Christendom. Austria, Poland, what until recently we knew as Czechoslovakia, and the northern parts of what we used to know as Yugoslavia, were also part of Catholic Christendom in the Middle Ages, but did not belong to the Community either of the nine or of the twelve.

Now if 'Europe' does mean Catholic Christendom – and implicit in the arguments of many of the participants in the debate about further enlargement is the assumption that this is the most that Europe can ever mean – then clearly Poland, the Czech Republic, Hungary, Croatia and Slovenia, as well as Austria and Scandinavia, should, at least in principle and at least in due time, become part of it politically. But why should Europe be defined as Catholic Christendom? What about Orthodox Christendom? Greece, after all, is already in the Community and Greece is part of Orthodox Christendom, not of Catholic Christendom. And if 'Europe' includes Orthodox Christendom then there is no legitimate reason for excluding Romania, Bulgaria, Serbia if Serbia should eventually become a democracy of some sort, the Ukraine and perhaps Russia. Is Russia 'European' or not? If Greece is 'European', why is Russia not 'European'? Following the collapse of the communist regimes of eastern Europe and the subsequent collapse of the Soviet Union, these questions are now, at least by implication, on the table.

Secondly, there has been a paradox of territory. At the heart of this paradox lies a coincidence between economic convergence in the dynamic core of the Community and divergence in the periphery. Increasingly, the economic geography of late twentieth-century Europe is coming to resemble the economic geography of the late Middle Ages. At the heart of the Union is a grid of prosperity, where the line of Lombardy to the Rhine to the North Sea crosses the line of Munich to Marseilles and perhaps to Barcelona. That grid has become enormously, inconceivably more prosperous than ever before. But while economic integration has speeded up the development of this grid of prosperity, of the core of the Community, its impact on the periphery has been less benign. In absolute terms, of course, the periphery has also become more prosperous. In the boom years of the 1950s and 1960s, moreover, the gap between the periphery and the core narrowed significantly. But in the last twenty years or so, the gap between the periphery and the core has remained static at best, and widened at worst (see Cingolani, 1993).

This pattern is, of course, a familiar feature of all capitalist economies. Capitalism is centripetal. The free market rewards those who are well endowed for the marketplace, and punishes those who are badly endowed; and endowment includes geographical location. Nineteenth-century Britain was the classic case. The creation of a single market and monetary union between backward Ireland and advanced mainland Britain plunged the former into destitution and famine. In modern welfare democracies, however, there are strong countervailing tendencies. The tax and welfare system redistributes resources from richer to poorer territories as well as from richer to poorer persons – in large measure, of course, because there is a higher proportion of poor persons in poor territories than in rich ones. One reason why the tax and welfare system does this is that electoral competition gives the poorer territories political clout with which, at least to some extent, to redress the balance of market competition.

In the virtual one-party state which is the present-day United Kingdom, it should be noted, these countervailing tendencies have been blunted because the political party that represents the poorer territories has been out of power for so long that these territories have lost much of their political clout. But that merely underlines the point. In a normally functioning welfare democracy, the ballot box gives the poorer territories an instrument with which to mitigate the pressures towards ever-greater concentration that emanate from the capitalist free market; the reason that these pressures are not effectively mitigated in present-day Britain is that it has ceased to be a normally functioning welfare democracy. And that leads on to the really critical point. The mechanisms of territorial redistribution – electoral competition combined with a modern tax and welfare system – do not exist in the European Community. Plainly, the tax and welfare system remains under national control. In a strange way, the same is true of the electoral system. The European Parliament exists; political forces compete for representation in it; but it is not a European equivalent of a national parliament. The political forces which are represented in it organize and compete on a national, not on a European, level. In any case, it is so weak that electoral competition for representation in it has little more than a symbolic significance. Such political clout as poor territories possess – and it is not very impressive in quantity or quality – derives from the representation of poor *states* in the Council of Ministers, not from the representation of poor *people* in the European Parliament.

The problem is political, not technical. As long ago as 1977, the Mac-Dougall Report showed that a deliberately redistributive Community budget, accounting for as little as 5–7 per cent of total community GDP, could be as effective an agent of territorial redistribution as are the budgets of federal states which normally account for around 20 per cent of GDP (Commission of the European Communities, 1977). This, of course, was in a community of nine. In a Union of twelve the proportion would need to be larger. The real significance of the MacDougall Report, however, is that it quickly became a dead letter – not because of any technical imperfections in the case it set out, but because the political will which would have been needed to implement the kind of project it advocated simply did not exist. And herein lies the essence of the paradox of territory. The real obstacles to monetary union – the forces that actually generated the waves of speculation which have inflicted so much damage on the European Monetary System – are territorial. Monetary union between the core and the periphery would speed up the process of concentration. It would be good for the core. It does not follow that it would be good for the periphery, any more than monetary union between nineteenth-century Ireland and mainland Britain was good for Ireland or than post-unification monetary union between northern Italy and the Mezzogiorno was good for the Mezzogiorno. Until these economic realities have been addressed, there will be no monetary union, however fervently political leaders may proclaim their commitment to it, and half-way houses on the lines of the European Monetary System will always be vulnerable to speculative pressure. But they cannot be addressed through technical fixes. Here, as in so many areas of social life, only politics can countervail markets.

That brings me to the third paradox: the paradox of supranationalism. Supporters of the European project customarily proclaim that its object is to transcend the nation-state or national sovereignty. I suggest that the truth has always been more complicated. The founding fathers did wish to transcend the nation-state in certain crucial areas of policy, but they wished to transcend it because they also wished to reconstruct it. Above all, they – or at least the most important of them – wished to reconstruct the two key nation-states of Carolingian western Europe, Germany and France. Adenauer in one way, and the governments of Fourth Republic France in a slightly different way, both saw in the formation of the European Community a means to give their weak and insecure regimes greater legitimacy and greater efficacy. With extraordinary genius they saw that the best way to do this was to surrender control over certain key areas to supranational institutions. And, as Alan Milward (1992) has brilliantly argued in his latest book, they succeeded. On any reasonable definition, the nation-states of France and Germany are far stronger than they were when the Community was set up forty years ago. They are more respected. They are more firmly based in popular support. They are more efficacious; and they have greater legitimacy than they did at the beginning of the post-war period.

To be sure, the United Kingdom is an exception. The trajectory of the British state has been downwards not upwards. But it is a piece of Anglocentric insularity to imagine that, because the British state has lost strength, efficacy and legitimacy since the early 1950s, the same must necessarily be true of all nation-states. In most of western Europe, the reverse is the case. This, however, is where the paradox comes into the story. The nation-states of Carolingian little Europe, of the Europe of the six which is still and will, for the foreseeable future, remain the heartland of the Union, have become stronger because they have created a chain of interdependencies which has made it impossible, or at the very least extremely expensive, for them to act unilaterally in certain key areas – notably in the key area of macro-economic management and latterly even in the key area of industrial policy. The nation-states have not transcended sovereignty, exactly. They remain sovereign: indeed, they cling to their sovereignty. They also remain overwhelmingly the most important focus for political loyalty and political activity. Yet the very processes through which they have regained the legitimacy and efficacy which they lost during World War II have made it increasingly difficult for them to act in the ways in which the social democratic state of the post-war period used to act.

Politics as horse: economics as cart

That leads on to the fourth paradox. I shall call it the paradox of functionalism. By that I mean that the process of integration as it has been conceived up to now in Europe has gradually become self-stultifying – not because it has failed, but because it has succeeded. A brief historical reminder may be appropriate at this point. As everyone knows, the late 1940s saw a vigorous debate among supporters of European union between those who favoured a functional approach and those who wished to see the early creation of a federal system. As everyone also knows, functionalism prevailed. Functionalism prevailed because the interests of the nation-states and the aspiration for European unity could, so to speak, join forces in seeking gradual integration of key sectors of the economy. In the early 1950s, integrationists assumed that this process would set in motion an irresistible, ineluctable pressure for ever more integration, until in the end political union would come about almost of its own accord. It was a kind of bastard Marxism. Economics was the base, politics was the superstructure; to change the metaphor, economics was the horse dragging the cart of politics behind it.

From that key assumption flow some of the preconceptions which now bedevil debate on the future of the Union. The debate over 'widening' versus 'deepening' in relation to eastern Europe is the most obvious case in point. Wideners and deepeners have different aims, but they share a critically important assumption. Both those who want to see the Union enlarge first and engage in further integration later, and those who want more integration first and further enlargement later, if at all, take it for granted that politics follows economics. Wideners, for the most part, wish to slow down the process of integration in the existing Union. They are for widening because they are against deepening; for incorporating the eastern European countries because they want to weaken the forces making for further integration in the west. The deepeners object to widening for exactly the same reason. They fear that, as things are at present, widening would indeed inhibit deepening; and they are against it for that reason.

A parallel set of assumptions has shaped the debate about the single market and monetary union in western Europe. Central to the case for monetary union is that it is the logical, inevitable concomitant of a single market and the logical, preordained precursor of political union. On one level, that is true. A single capital market combined with stable exchange rates and with the free movement of capital across national boundaries is inconceivable, in the long run, without a single currency; and a single currency is inconceivable in the long run without an authority of some kind to run it. Ultimately, then, a single currency does entail a qualitative jump towards political union: to that extent, Thatcher and the British Euro-sceptics are right.

Unfortunately, this logic does not apply to the first step in the process. Though it is true that a single currency entails a qualitative jump towards political union, it does not follow that a single market *entails* a qualitative jump towards a single currency. The debacle which has overcome the European Monetary System and the stalling which has taken place in the various countries of western Europe since the Maastricht Treaty was signed point in a less comforting direction. So long as there is no political authority to ensure territorial justice, to overcome the centripetal tendencies inherent in a capitalist free market economy, the periphery will not be able to sustain monetary union; and so long as the periphery cannot sustain monetary union, monetary union will be incomplete. There is, in short, a contradiction between the monetary ambitions of the Union and its territorial divergences. Unless and until that contradiction is resolved, the Union is as likely to move backwards as forwards. And the contradiction can be resolved only by and through political institutions.

The implications are plain. The Maastricht Treaty, it is now clear, did not go nearly far enough. Indeed, in certain crucial respects it went in the wrong direction. For Maastricht was rooted in the technocratic economism of the Community's salad days. It was based on the assumption that a single market would lead ineluctably to monetary union, and a monetary union to political union. There was no need to mobilize consent for the eventual political union; it would emerge, of its own accord, from the bosom of history. By the same token, there was no need to examine the political obstacles to monetary union or to try patiently to overcome them. Monetary union was a technical matter, to be achieved by technical means.

As so often in history, developments since Maastricht have shown that economism of this sort is usually false, and often dangerous. The notion that politics can be a sort of cart, dragged along by the horse of economics, has no place outside the fairytale worlds of classical Marxism and classical economic liberalism. In the real world, politics is always the horse and economics the cart. Now that this ancient truth has been painfully rediscovered, the European Left, above all, should draw the obvious conclusion. Recognizing that its aims cannot be achieved in the half-way house created by the Maastricht Treaty, and that there is no future in reverting to the beggar-my-neighbour myopia of a *'Europe des patries'*, it should embrace a new version of the federalism of the forties, based on the good Christian Democratic principle of subsidiarity.

The kind of subsidiarity now needed, however, is not the kind implied in the Maastricht Treaty. Maastricht-style subsidiarity is offered as a principle of universal validity, to be realized in the same way in all parts of the emerging Union. In the Europe in which we live and will continue to live, that approach is likely to prove a blind alley. For a long time to come, the level of government on which decision making will be effective will vary, not just from subject to subject, but from country to country. In the Community's hard-currency core, whose members can already meet the Maastricht conditions in the monetary union without much difficulty, decision making in the monetary sphere would be conducted more effectively on a supranational level. In the weak-currency periphery, that is not yet true.

The real question is how much diversity an emerging political union can stand without dissolving into its constituent parts. Plainly, that question cannot be answered *a priori*. But it is worth noting that in the United States, arguably the world's most successful continental-size federation, the role of the federal government was, by the standards of contemporary European nation-states, extremely limited until well into the twentieth century, and that the states differed hugely both in economic performance and in the scope of public power. If the Community were to develop along the lines suggested here, there would have to be a significant redistribution of functions between the regional, national and supranational tiers. Responsibility for foreign and security policy would pass quite quickly to the Community. In the core countries, the same would be true of monetary policy. But since the pursuit of Community-wide free competition would have taken a back seat, at any rate as far as the new eastern and central European members were concerned, the deregulation and re-regulation needed to achieve a Community-wide 'level playing field' would not have to be extended to them; and the competences which Community institutions have had to assume in order to carry it out in the little Europe of the west could be left at the national level. And in the west European periphery, the same would be true of monetary policy for a long time to come. To put the point in another way, the model of Community federalism would be closer to that of the early nineteenth-century United States than to that of late twentieth-century Germany.

The result would be untidy. Politically, the Community would be a federation, but of a loose and limited kind. A wide range of functions would be devolved to the regional, rather than to the national level. Economically, things would be much less clear. In the little European heartland there would be a single (and social) market, on 1992 lines. To the east, to the south, and across the Channel, there would be a variety of economic regimes, all moving slowly towards full incorporation, but at different speeds. At first sight it would look rather like the Europe of 'variable geometry' which has sometimes been seen as a way of solving the British problem. But economic variation would be combined with political union, instead of being seen as an excuse for delaying it.

References

Cingolani, M. 1993: Disparités regionales de produit par tête dans la Communauté Européenne. *EIB Papers*, no. 19. Luxembourg. European Investment Bank.

Commission of the European Communities 1977: *Report of the Study Group on the Role of Public Finance in European Integration*. Vol. 1. Brussels: European Commission.

Milward, A. S. 1992: *The European Rescue of the Nation-State*. London: Routledge.

Comment: European Constitutional Patriotism

Jos de Beus

A European commonwealth can be seen as a special device for increasing either the wealth and welfare of all European peoples and residents or the capacity and advantages of European states and elites. From the viewpoint of the Left the primary virtue of a European commonwealth must lie in the protection and promotion of a transnational civil society and its common standard of living: liberties, rights, opportunities, and means for autonomy and well-being. Europe should be a community in which national institutions, such as the rule of law, democracy, a social market economy and multicultural tolerance, are strong of their own accord and effectively completed and strengthened, if necessary, by arrangements at higher institutional levels. Europe must mean more than mega-firms and soccer matches, and include European political parties, European interest groups, European mass media and a European public opinion.

The case for mutual reinforcement in the relations between national and supranational communities in Europe is deliberately utopian. Daniel Cohn-Bendit, one of the authors of *Heimat Babylon* (1992), calls it 'European constitutional patriotism' and 'one of the last utopias worth fighting for, without repeating the errors of old utopian struggles' (*Der Spiegel*, 1994). David Marquand rejects the notion that European union can rescue and revive traditional social democracy (macro-economic management, associative democracy) as utopian; I want to argue that Marquand's own notion that European union can itself be rescued by the federalism of the 1940s ('the good Christian Democratic principle of subsidiarity') is equally utopian. The issue is *which* political ideal of Europe will contribute to a feasible solution of common domestic and constitutional problems in the member states.

Marquand's defence of neo-federalism is based on a bleak view of

European development, both in the short run ('trends') and the long run 'paradoxes'). As to the short run, I am inclined to sharpen the bleak view. First, the refusal to yield rights to or share power with a European Parliament is not a French and English whim. The lack of willingness to face the democratic deficit and the lack of imagination in the plans to reduce it are present all over Europe, including in the pro-European Benelux countries. They are related to deep controversy and uncertainty with respect to the public goals, the legitimate procedures and the distributive consequences of a united Europe.

Secondly, the institutional structure of the European Union *is* at risk. Massive unemployment, a divergence of economic performance, regional inequalities, the growing pains of the united Germany, the rise of the xenophobic Right, and the gap between European policy makers and voters all continue to exist or grow. Suppose also that just outside the Union turmoil persists, in particular the former Yugoslavian war (and other secession conflicts), divergence in economic transformation and recovery in eastern Europe, and anti-liberal nationalism. Surely this setting will put impossible pressure on institutions: the monetary authority (the European System of Central Banks), the collective decision rules in the Council of Ministers, the functioning and standing of the Parliament, the rules for budgetary contributions and transfers, and so on. Consequently, the present trend of governments turning inwards and concentrating on domestic difficulties will become stronger (Hoffman, 1993). A combination of institutional deadlock, institutional vacuum and beggar-my-neighbour strategies will jeopardize both economic policy coordination and the single market.

What of the long run? The contradiction between Christianity in Europe and the incomplete Christian nature of the European Union (the paradox of identity) is only relevant when Europeans start to define their common identity in terms of religion. This is unlikely, since the old cleavage between Protestants and Catholics will not disappear, nor will the old tensions between Christians and secularists (Castles, 1993). Looking at the present degree of secularization of the Christian indigenous population and the future growth of the foreign population in Europe, and the mixed moral order which follows after immigration (in the Netherlands Islam is already the second largest denomination), one must anticipate a dilution of Europe's religious identity.

But suppose the global division between blocs of cooperating countries does have a religious aspect, as Samuel Huntington has recently suggested (Huntington 1993a, 1993b). What is the point of Marquand's paradox of identity? Does anybody want Europeans to unite on this cultural basis and start clashing with other 'civilizations'? From the point of view of the Left, the criterion for accepting a state as a member of the European Union should be its support of liberal constitutionalism (human rights, stable democracy). The contribution of Christian social thought to the Union's constitution is another thing. The core ideas of Christian Democracy, like macro-corporatism, works councils and a social market economy, are not exclusive. The principle of subsidiarity was formulated by the Protestant philosopher Johannes Althusius in 1603, and finally obtained constitutional status in Maastricht in 1991. If we introduce 'European Christendom' as a political concept, it is important to distinguish between its 'internal' role (constitutional harmony on a European scale) and its 'external' role (cultural conflict on a global scale). The internal role turned out to be constructive, the external role may easily become destructive.

The contradiction between market-based unequal development and the absence of a democratic distributive state function at the European level is urgent (the paradox of territory). Economic integration may trigger general economic growth, perhaps because distributive coalitions lose their power to block exchange within the old, small-scale jurisdiction (Olson, 1982). However, integration may also imply that some regions lose their competitive edge and stay behind other regions within the new, large-scale jurisdiction. Taking into account that the composition of the periphery may change (then Spain, now Britain) and that the counterfactual performance of poor countries is unknown, it seems safe to formulate the following propositions. First, poor countries will be losers from rapid monetary integration and from the introduction of high regulatory standards (for example, standards for pollution and social protection of workers). Second, monetary integration and harmonization of regulation are impossible without central redistribution from rich to poor member states, either to compensate vital losses or to build up new competitive advantages. To this Marquand adds a special proposition: redistribution will only come about when poor countries have gained political power in the European democracy; that is, more votes in the Council of Ministers, more seats in Strasbourg and, more ambiguously, more space for unanimity voting. Marquand's claim is based on an analogy between the emancipation of an industrial working class and the development of a post-industrial poor country.

This analogy is indeed striking, but Marquand neglects its practical meaning. Industrial workers never demanded special political weight, and justly so. They preferred implicit constitutional contracts ('social compromises'), coalition building in a majority rule setting (with the middle class, with non-socialist parties), social-policy-based economic growth and multilevel wage bargaining. The European periphery would be well advised to use social democratic means (such as civil and political rights) to establish economic equality and social rights, since formal means like the unanimity rule will never be sufficient. The case of structural policy clearly shows that the European periphery is engaged in a rational struggle against the paradox of territory, while the rich core, apart from the UK government, is convinced that *laissez-faire* – ecological and social dumping, and so on – is not a proper solution in terms of its self-interest (Lange, 1992, 1993; Marks, 1992, 1993).

The final paradox is a contradiction between the success of functionalism (the gradual spill-over of European cooperation from one policy area to another) and the failure of one-shot completion of integration. This paradox is artificial, because functionalist forces are already so weakened that they cannot fully explain the success or failure of integration strategies. The functionalist model of back-door community building by independent leaders (Walter Hallstein, Jean Monnet, Robert Schuman) is not tenable; publicity (conferences and projects as media events) and accountability (vigilance within national political arenas) are today so much greater than in the post-war years that 'integration by stealth' is not a viable strategy.

Marquand has no room to update the constitutional process of Maastricht. Of course, Brussels is a labyrinth and officials play their byzantine games there. But Marquand goes beyond the valid observation that European politics is highly technocratic and bureaucratic. He claims that the Maastricht Treaty was largely determined by the forces of functionalism and economism. This is very unlikely. Marquand barely refers to the early death of the EC diplomacy in the former Yugoslavia, the collapse of communism and the unification of Germany. These events forced the European elite to revise both their national policies and their supranational ones. Under normal circumstances the elite always falls back on functionalist and economist arguments, in order to pre-empt or conceal its internal disagreement about federalism and to postpone tough choices. However, after 1989 the elite began to understand that circumstances were abnormal, that the *Acquis Communautaire* were at stake, that instant answers were needed and that taking a chance was inevitable. This accounts for the bold decision of the big three to broaden the agenda and to cook up 'pillarization': the European Community treaties, the monetary union, the common foreign and security policy, and cooperation in the spheres of justice and home affairs (Buchan, 1993; Cafruny and Rosenthal, 1993).

This account does not deny, of course, the mirage of common-market capitalism without a common moral framework and the familiar pattern of 'cross-purposes among governments, inconsistencies between statements and actions, cleavages between elites and voters, and ambivalences and contradictions in official documents' (Nicoll, 1993: 21). It points, however, to the highly politicized nature of Maastricht. It shows that the debate on widening versus deepening is a continuation of the old political controversy by other arguments. The debate on flexible Europe ('different speeds', 'variable geometry') is yet another example of dis-agreement among functionalist believers. Will policy competition between member states lead to Anglo-American capitalism or to Rhenish capitalism (Siebert, 1991; Albert, 1991)? Will it lead to a retreat of the welfare state or to its global expansion (de Beus, forthcoming; de Swaan, forthcoming)? Functionalists fail to provide a common answer.

What is the upshot of all this for the Left? Some practise the wisdom of Eduard Bernstein: 'The goal is nothing, the movement is everything.' Marquand thinks that more must be said (and I agree). He wants us to return to the origins of the European movement. The Left should embrace the principle of subsidiarity, accept different speeds, take the American case of federation building as a role model and learn to live with a political union that is untidy but real. But subsidiarity cannot be applied by the European Court of Justice, says its most recent president (Nicoll, 1993: 23). And, if politicians apply it, subsidiarity means central-ization, opting out and regional *Alleingang* all at the same time. Different speeds are not an alternative for Maastricht, but a euphemistic description of current practices. The United States can only serve as a role model if one is willing to neglect the Civil War and the considerable differences between the state apparatus of nineteenth-century Virginia and the appar-atus of modern state intervention. It is hard to see how these ideas can help to resolve the paradox of supranationalism (Marquand's third paradox): the reconstruction of the capacity of states to realize their distinctive national interests by means of comprehensive interstate coop-eration and integration at the European level. But Marquand's analysis contains an important pragmatic precondition. The Left should learn that 'the European commonwealth begins at home.'

This begs the question of how to proceed. Six principles seem to me paramount to the Left:

1 Inform the electorate as frankly as possible about interdependence, about the way in which European markets, policies, actors and anony-mous mechanisms determine their daily lives in a world without safe or sacred boundaries.
2 Stand up for the ideal of an open society, both nationally (the rejection of class society and ethnic hierarchy) and internationally (the rejec-tion of 'fortress Europe' and protectionism in a wide sense).

3 Focus on the new constitutional problems, which go beyond old national or international cleavages and require a European approach: global competition, destruction of the natural environment, massive unemployment or low-quality jobs in a modern service economy, and suburbanization (the collapse of inner cities).

4 Do not deny the national benefits of decentralization (local government) and European state building, yet stick to the core business of the nation-state (public goods or control areas like legal ordering, public safety, infrastructure, welfare, education and health) as the strategic and intermediate variable in any process of administrative reform.

5 Recognize that national democracy and European democracy are interlocked and absolutely inseparable (Held, 1993); post-Cold War political unease and the democratic deficit of the European Union are intertwined, so the fundamental democratization of the nation and of Europe should go in tandem.

6 Make the party strategy with respect to European affairs credible by accepting visible pre-commitments and burdens (in particular with regard to a seat of the European Political Union in the Security Council of the UN, joint security action of Europe and NATO, and the membership of middle European nations).

This is not the politics of a European 'big bang', but a practical attempt, to use David Marquand's metaphor, to put the horse of public interest before the cart of market forces. On this at least, the Left should be able to agree. The challenge is how to achieve it.

References

Albert, M. 1991: *Capitalisme contre Capitalisme*. Paris: Seuil.
de Beus, J. forthcoming: On the convergence of formal rules: a reformulation of efficiency arguments. In H.-J. Wagener (ed.), *The Political Economy of Transformation*. Heidelberg: Physica Verlag.
Buchan, D. 1993: *Europe: the strange superpower*. Aldershot: Dartmouth.
Cafruny, A. W. and Rosenthal, G. G. (eds) 1993: *The State of the European Community*. Vol. 2. Harlow: Longman.
Castles, F. G. (ed.) 1993: *Families of Nations*. Aldershot: Dartmouth.
Cohn-Bendit, D. and Schmid, T. 1992: *Heimat Babylon*. Hamburg: Hoffmann and Campe Verlag.
Held, D. 1993: Democracy and the new international order. London: Institute for Public Policy Research.
Hoffmann, S. 1993: Goodbye to a united Europe? *New York Review of Books*, 61 (10), 27–31.

Huntington, S. P. 1993a: The clash of civilizations? *Foreign Affairs*, 72(3), 22–49.
Huntington, S. P. 1993b: If not civilizations, what? *Foreign Affairs*, 72(5), 186–94.
Lange, P. 1992: The politics of the social dimension. In A. M. Sbragia (ed.), *Euro-politics*, Washington, DC: Brookings Institute.
Lange, P. 1993: Maastricht and the Social Protocol: why did they do it? *Politics and Society*, 21, 5–36.
Marks, G. 1992: Structural policy in the European Community. In A. M. Sbragia (ed.) *Euro-politics*, Washington, DC: Brookings Institute.
Marks, G. 1993: Structural policy and multilevel governance in the EC. In A. W. Cafruny and G. G. Rosenthal (eds), *The State of the European Community*, vol. 2, Harlow: Longman.
Nicoll, W. 1993: Maastricht revisited: a critical analysis of the Treaty on European Union. In A. W. Cafruny and G. G. Rosenthal (eds.), *The State of the European Community*, vol. 2, Harlow: Longman.
Olson, M. 1982: *The Rise and Decline of Nations*. New Haven: Yale University Press.
Siebert, H. 1991: *The New Economic Landscape in Europe*. Oxford: Blackwell.
Der Spiegel 1994: Wer ist Links, Wer Rechts? Gespräch mit Daniel Cohn-Bendit. 1/3.1, 130–4.
de Swaan, A. (ed.) forthcoming: *Social Policy Beyond Borders*. Amsterdam: Amsterdam University Press.

11   Reinventing Politics

Manuel Escudero

European politics is in crisis. The symptoms are everywhere, from the emergence of new anti-system options from the populist and extreme Right, to the revival of exclusive nationalism, the emergence of racism as an important electoral force in several European countries, the sudden and unexpected disappearance of several traditional political parties, and corruption scandals that have captured public attention. In this chapter, I want to examine the causes of this crisis, and their consequences for the European Left, above all their consequences for the organization of parties of the Left. At the outset, it is important to stress a preliminary problem: the crisis of European politics that I describe potentially carries many more negative consequences for the Left than for the Right.

My central hypothesis is that the problems in the structure of politics stem from the increasing divorce between society and politics. In front of us there is a new society, based on new cultural principles – a new society which throughout the 1980s experienced a radical and silent revolution in terms of social power and structure. Unfortunately, European politicians and especially social democratic politicians seem not to have understood, or indeed noticed and analysed, these changes.

New cultural axioms

European society is undergoing transformation. Its first manifestation is the presence of a new, convincing and already dominant discourse. It rotates around three basic axioms: fragmentation, unpredictability and anthropocentrism, the last of which asserts that humankind is no longer creator but creature, centre of the universe, albeit at the cost of being unable to transform it.[1]

The plausibility of this post-modern discourse comes from the fact that has been abundantly and eloquently illustrated by the end of communism. With the Berlin Wall has fallen the idea of a stable totality, of a perfect order built by humankind: a triumph of the idea of fragmentation. With communism has fallen the belief in history as a planned path of unstoppable progress: a victory, then, for the notion of unpredictability. With the collapse of 'actually existing socialism' has ended the belief in human beings as a collective process: a battle won by anthropocentrism. The relevant question for the Left is how it should react to this new reality. Do we have to reject it?

The answer is that rejection would be a tremendous mistake. The new culture taking shape today is not a right-wing culture; it is not a cultural wave inspired by neo-liberalism, taking advantage of the fall of communism to undermine social democracy. Rather, the emergence of such categories as fragmentation or unpredictability, and the ensuing scepticism in relation to reformist projects, or the new centrality of individuals, are a natural consequence of political, scientific and technological change. Social democracy must accept the emerging cultural references at face value, as the new grounds on which to rewrite the political project of the Left.

The second key phenomenon that frames the challenge to the Left is the emergence of a new middle class, formed by white-collar workers as a result of the current technological revolution. Their main characteristics are the ownership and use of knowledge. Their number is growing and important, but these new groups have also crucial qualitative importance, to the extent that the upper segment of knowledge owners and users are becoming the dominant social group, though of course not the dominant economic group, in our societies. Social power is today more related to the possession of knowledge than to the possession of the means of production.

There is a relationship between these emergent socially dominant groups and the emerging dominant discourse, a two-way relationship of mutual support, reinforcement and reciprocal legitimation. The two new dominant groups and the new discourse, taken together, form the new driving force of social transformation in our societies. The task for social democracy is to analyse its position *vis-à-vis* this dramatic social revolution: what role is to be played by these dominant groups? Are they potentially part of a social block of support for the Left? Or are they the enemy, the new source of domination?

The reality is that the new dominant groups are politically undefined. In principle this new and growing 'social centre' is not politically biased to the Right or Left, either as a result of their class interest or as a consequence of their values and culture. In short, they are not politically predetermined. Moreover, any political suport that they grant to Left or Right will be contingent and unstable. Social democracy must make a radical effort to make compatible the political representation of its traditional base with growing attention to the aspirations and demands of these emerging groups.

The recent efforts of some social democratic parties to open themselves up to 'new social movements', to the values of feminism and ecology for example, represent a start, but they are not enough. The test for social democracy is the renovation of traditional politics to make compatible its historic values, as well as some of its traditional procedures and instruments, with the cultural references, procedures and aspirations which are becoming dominant in our societies as a result of the power of both the emerging dominant discourse and the emerging dominant social groups.

The agenda for social democratic reform

So what are the consequences for social democratic thinking and principles of the factors changing our societies? Six seem pre-eminent.

First, if social democracy is to come to terms with fragmentation as a basic category of reality and knowledge, then any temptation to build perfect overall systems, closed by dogma, must be avoided. Social democracy must renounce any predetermined moral superiority. In a fragmented, non-dogmatic world, social democracy can no longer rely exclusively on its 'programmatic will' as the way to achieve reforms, but must also count on its ability to reach social consensus and pacts. As a corollary, tolerance, pluralism and consensus must become basic assets of left-wing politics, parties and politicians.

Second, if social democracy is to come to terms with unpredictability as a basic category, then it must renounce any notion of historical progress. It should qualify the traditional view of the Left about planning as axiomatically a positive tool, and it must avoid the design of fixed, rigid paths for progress. In a sceptical world, where people participate in reformist politics for a multitude of reasons, politics must accordingly leave behind its tragic and heroic pathos, and recover an air of civic normality. Politicians must retrieve their original role as normal citizens performing a civic function; public policies should not be seeking to make provision for mass collective public participation, but to devise new instruments for accessible, normalized individual control.

Third, if social democracy is to recognize anthropocentrism as a value with firm roots in our societies, then it must base its appeal on the individual and his or her rights, duties and potentialities, rather than make a collective or class appeal. The new cultural reference points based on the individual do not preclude an appeal to the traditional social democratic value of solidarity, but give a new insight into it. Whether at the workplace or in any other activity, coordination and cooperation between individuals are a prerequisite. Social democracy cannot and must not therefore renounce its traditional commitment to solidarity, but must reconstruct it on the basis of the cooperative and committed dimension that is part of every individual. A consequence, for example, is that the welfare state needs to be rethought, placing the citizen, the client and his or her rights and freedoms at the heart of the system. The welfare state must become a rational organization of interest to all citizens, and not only to the poorest. Protective welfare will have to be combined with the need to encourage personal development and individual fulfilment.

Fourth, European societies have already become used to continuous change and innovation, and have rationally begun to adapt to it, in terms of both goals and procedures. Unfortunately, the political sphere remains associated with slow working routines, bureaucratic procedures, risk minimization, and almost non-existent evaluation and assessment methods. Political debureaucratization, flexibility and innovation should become the new criteria for the public sphere and for left-wing organizations.

Fifth, European societies are already operating through one transparent and accessible information and communication system. But the public sphere remains opaque and not easily controlled by the individual citizen; political institutions are still remote from and closed to the public. In the future, public institutions must be transparent and must guarantee citizens access. This will require the transformation of political parties into open organizations, answerable to and controlled by individual citizens, and of course transparent in their finances.

Finally, European societies are most of all producers and consumers of forms, and the European Left must place political forms, that is symbols, styles and crucially democratic procedures, at the centre of its political philosophy. For the European Left, the ends can no longer justify the means: the means – that is, democratic procedures – have become an essential part of the political message.

The reform of Left parties

There are a number of substantive policy and ideological challenges that face the European Left, many of them discussed elsewhere in this book. Economic renewal, the reform of the welfare state to promote efficiency, transparency and individual control, a solution to the interrelated problems of immigration and racism, and a radical strengthening of the political dimension of the European Union all spring to mind. But there is an equally important and urgent task, namely the reform of the social democratic movement itself, and above all the renovation of its political parties.

The fall of communism has meant the triumph of democracy, but paradoxically democracy has rarely shown its weaknesses so clearly. With no enemies, the flaws of democracy as traditionally conceived become more evident. At the core of its shortcomings is the exhaustion of the traditional model of the political party. Parties should be instruments for the organization of political participation, but they are now perceived to be introverted organizations, disproportionately small relative to the number of voters. They appear to the public to be excessively hierarchical, and prone to the generation of clientelist servitude, instead of being answerable to the public and controlled by citizens.

The reasons for placing this point at the top of the agenda are two-fold. On the one hand, political parties are the basis of democracy and civil liberties, and their loss of legitimacy is at the core of the crisis of European politics. On the other hand, the reform of Left party organizations does not need any consensus, pact or agreement with other political forces. It is simply a matter of political will for social democrats alone. If carried out, it will be the clearest signal of a consistent reformist attitude to overcome the crisis of European politics.

It can be argued that this issue, already pinpointed in countries like France and Italy, has been tackled superficially. In the wame way that the Left will not solve its problems of a growing divorce from society just by opening itself up to the 'new social movements', although that is, of course, a necessary condition, similarly the organizational forms of the Left will not become adequate by a call to these social movements to join the ranks of the political parties of the Left or to refound them. Beyond that, the traditional principles of Left organization will have to be changed by new principles, consistent with the new society, its values and procedures.

This reform, in terms of specific measures, is of course a matter of specific, national considerations. However, in a tentative way, four broad themes can be mentioned. First, Left parties must become more controlled by citizens and voters. The core of the alienation of political parties from society is the anomalous, autonomous nature they show today. There is a need for new forms of control and participation from society, so that those who take part in party decisions are not, as currently, a tiny percentage of voters.

Social democratic parties must, then, become participation parties – open, accessible and controlled by those citizens who agree with the general principles and proposals of social democracy, even if they are not inclined or willing to apply for full membership. A path to explore could be to extend some activities that have heretofore been considered as internal matters to those voter-sympathizers who are willing to register in a much broader census of party supporters. Citizen supporters should have the right to participate in the nomination of party candidates and in the management of party organization.

Second, Left political parties should prevent political oligarchy, and become less structured, even less professionalized, organizations. When parties are close-knit organizations of professionals, they become hierarchical and oligarchic, places where factions and their clienteles fight for power, the opposite to the mobility, flexibility and meritocracy which now govern our societies. Some measures can be suggested to hasten reform. For example, we need new ways of promoting a greater circulation of elites, opening up new possibilities of access to internal as well as external appointments. Thus both the process of nomination of electoral candidates and the election of the party's leadership should give more room for democratic competition, as well as be based on the principle of universal suffrage of rank-and-file members. A further possibility is to establish a limited number of re-elections for any given post within the party, as a symbol of commitment to renewal of the political class. The ultimate sanction would be to reduce the number of professional politicians and increase the number of part-time ones, consciously promoting the reality of a transient political class, linked to citizens in concrete ways.

Third, Left political parties should be at the vanguard in the generation of a democratic political culture. Representative democracy, if it is to become a cornerstone of social democratic thinking and proposals, has to be first of all applied to the organizations of the Left. This means a collective commitment to democratic political culture, that is to the values stemming from representative democracy. Some of the general ideas already suggested are consistent with this. But there are other consequences: a crucial one refers to the need for Left organization and politicians to stick to democratic legality as a moral issue. First and foremost, social democratic parties, as civic institutions formed by committed citizens, have to defend the rule of law and should never put the party's interests before the interests of the system. There are two corollaries of this principle: on the one hand, the finances of Left political parties should be transparent and subject to public scrutiny. On the other hand, Left politicians have to perform an exemplary role regarding the management of public funds.

To secure these changes, a fourth is necessary: Left parties must become 'parties of rights'. They must abolish the last vestiges of modes of organization and behaviour inspired by democratic centralism. Parties must become champions of representative democracy, and must guarantee to their own members the rights that citizens expect in the country at large; elementary rights, such as the right of free association within the party, the right to free and public expression, the right to individual and secret vote, and the right to fair and independent bodies to decide upon conflicts and to protect individual rights.

All this may seem obvious, but democratic centralism on the Left and other forms of authoritarianism on the Right have produced a situation where political parties are some of the least democratic institutions in advanced democracies. In short, if the European Left undertakes a radical transformation of its own organizational modes, it will solve more than a simple problem of forms and procedures: by coming to terms with a new society, it will set in motion a process of renewal and legitimation of European politics. Much is at stake, since a politically feeble Europe will not be able to weather its crisis of competitiveness and unemployment, or to fight off its domestic demons. In order to reorganize economic life and employment, without renouncing the basics of the European way of life, in order to exorcise the menaces of racism, neo-fascism and the revival of exclusivist nationalism, Europe needs a great deal of democratic and political muscle; the necessary reinvigoration will only be achieved by renovating, reinventing even, politics itself.

Note

1 The basic features of this emerging discourse are discussed in the inspiring work of Pedro de Silva (1993).

Reference

de Silva, P. 1993: *Miseria de la Novedad*. Ed. Nobel: Oviedo.

Comment: Turning Outwards: Towards a New Sort of Party

Margaret Hodge

Manuel Escudero bases his analysis of how Left political parties should develop on his views of how Left politics should adapt to the changed circumstances confronting society today. The uncertainty, chaos and fragmentation in society to which he refers have indeed undermined some of the certainties of Left politics. The collapse of communism has discredited collectivism. And the demands for personal independence cannot be ignored. But there are a number of other observations which it is important to make, before moving on to deal with Escudero's proposals for democratization of the political party as an agency of change.

While it is unquestionably true that the mobility of capital, among other things, has severely limited the autonomy of the nation-state as an arena of political change, Left parties are caught in a trap. On the one hand, it is difficult for any party of the Left to admit that its hands are tied, while on the other hand much popular disenchantment with politics arises because politicians promise what they cannot deliver. In Britain, the Conservatives promise to cut taxes, and then raise them; Labour promises full employment, but people are not yet convinced that we know how to do it. The way out of this trap is to distinguish between solutions which have failed, and values which endure.

People want their political parties to have clear values and goals. However much we need to change the means by which we move towards these goals, a distinct set of values remains crucial. Change must take place to extend distinctive values; we must not, as Escudero suggests, 'renounce any predetermined moral superiority'. We must believe that our values are not just right but needed. The challenge is to connect our values to everyday life. Young people in universities and colleges are joining single-issue societies rather than political clubs because they see in them a vehicle through which to take forward their idealism.

One way we can connect our values, as well as fail to connect them, is of course through our own conduct within our own parties, and that is why the issue of intra-party democracy is important. Unless our values – democracy, solidarity, equity – are reflected in our own practice, we will stand accused, with justification, of hypocrisy. It is not only popular perception that policies are agreed by an elite group of political activists and leaders; it is true, and Escudero is right to stress that the peculiarities of political practice, and the type of people who are attracted to it, do create distance between governors and governed. He is also right to say that politics must start from where people are at. When radical feminists concentrated on sexuality as an issue in the 1980s, they lost support and understanding from the majority of women who were simply trying to cope with the pressures of daily life – with too little money and not enough childcare. It is right to insist that the alternative to reform is ossification and obsolescence. But is democracy the alchemy of change?

Democracy is a central value for Left politics because it enables equal participation of individuals in the determination of the course of their own lives. But other values – equality and social justice – are important too. Formal democracy, undefined and undifferentiated, can coexist with vast inequalities, and as the basis for an ideology is not sufficient. Internally democratic parties can be based on a cadre of activists given privileges over the general public. Similarly, the end of communism cannot mean the end of collective action, and democracy can and must take collective forms too. While we must of course reject the centralized and disciplinarian culture of Leninism and (un)democratic centralism, we cannot stop doing things in a collective way. The answer is to make collectivism itself democratic, not to pretend that we can individualize and atomize all aspects of life. We must come to our values and our policies democratically, and then share them. Within a political party this sometimes means that you have to support things that you do not agree with, but this is very different from the domineering and coercive collectivism associated wtih the communist experience. The challenge for the Left is to define new relationships between the individuals and the party, and the individual and the community, without neglecting the value of both.

There is, however, a rub. It is simply unrealistic to believe that any political party will ever be wholly democratic. Self-selecting oligarchies are not acceptable; but elites will always exist, and the issue is how they are made accountable. Leadership is simply not the same as control and authoritarianism. People look to their leaders to lead them and not coerce them. Politicians must be taken down a rung or two, made aware of their pomposity, but not discouraged from providing leadership if politics is to regain credibility. Democracy and leadership do not always go hand in hand, but we need a balance of the two.

Let me raise three structural questions in this context, concerning the media, gender and the labour movement. The changes in communication and the role of the media inevitably lead to personalization of politics. Our party leaders appear on television in the living rooms of millions of voters, and their leadership skills, authority and personality have become crucial issues in election campaigns. We need to acknowledge that and work with it; disabling leadership by limiting freedom of manoeuvre will inhibit electoral success. Turning supporters into members is not necessarily the answer either. The American primaries are as much about image and money as about values and policy. They are not a good way of achieving accountable and representative parties. Equally, assuming that a leader can win without the backing and enthusiasm of a party will not work. For example, many aspects of the modernizing reforms in the Labour Party in the 1980s were driven through by a 'conviction leader', Neil Kinnock, but not ultimately owned by the party. They therefore lacked credibility with the public, and with a change of leadership the structural thrust towards modernization was not rooted in the culture of the party.

There are other ways of changing party structures to make them less hierarchical, to facilitate participation and encourage debate. We can reform the way we select leaders to ensure equality of opportunity and participation; of course we should eradicate corruption and abuse of power; and we must make our meetings less bureaucratic and boring. But we also need some fundamental shifts in the culture of politics. One example concerns the adversarial and confrontational elements built into political debate. The fact is that for many women, the traditional political knockabout is a massive turn-off. Women's participation is not just a technical issue. Parties need an egalitarian culture as well as a democratic one if they are to reach out to previously marginalized groups. If this requires reforms to the working hours and working practices of Parliament, then so be it. These are not peripheral issues to the 'crisis of politics' diagnosed by Manuel Escudero; they are at the heart of the disenfranchisement and disenchantment of the majority of the population.

Finally, Escudero does not mention trade unions at all. Clearly, the context in Spain is different from that in the UK, but the omission remains serious. To attack disadvantage of class, gender or race, the labour movement must be a strong ally of the political party. There is of course an important difference between being an ally of the trade union movement and being controlled by it, especially in countries where trade unionism is a minority pursuit, but it would be quite wrong to become detached from workplace struggles against exploitation and discrimination, especially in countries where capitalism becomes more brutalized by the day. There needs to be a new party-union settlement, and part of the answer must lie in reform within the trade unions. They are themselves in crisis and in need of reform. They are suffering from declining membership and an unhealthy concentration in the public sector; they too are in danger of not being representative of people they claim to represent. In Britain, we need to learn from abroad; in Scandinavia, continuing trade union membership rates of 80 per cent or more provide the basis for an inclusive and long-sighted trade unionism. The importance of funding political parties through the public purse may help attenuate some of the tension within the labour movement, and the mistrust of the general public.

The reality is that parties will only thrive when political ideology thrives. The danger of Manuel Escudero's recipe is that while superseding the past, he will not replace it with a positive future. The failures of collectivist paternalism clearly must be overcome, but we need a new synthesis of individual rights and collective responsibilities if we are to make progress. Existing parties are all we have got, and not all are ossified; 500,000 people voted in the election of Rudolf Scharping to lead the SPD, for example. Of course, the party must connect more closely to people's lives. That does not mean abandoning our values and principles; it may mean constantly reforming and renewing the way they translate into practice so they remain relevant. The question is whether there is the will to embark on this task, or whether too many of today's 'insiders' feel comfortable with the status quo, and do not see its limitations. The key may be to persuade them that applying the medicine of reform, democratic and egalitarian reform, will not kill the patient.

Part VI

Afterword

12 Dos and Don'ts for Social Democrats

James Cornford and Patricia Hewitt

Rather than conclude this book with another essay, we propose a more direct approach. The preceding chapters suggest to us *Ten Commandments for Social Democrats*.

First: don't imitate, innovate

The first commandment is innovate, don't imitate – either your opponents or your own past. Do not retreat before the tide of neo-liberalism: acquisitive individualism is a brutal and crippled view of humanity. The values of the Left remain potent, whatever the distortions and compromises of its history. But the context has radically changed. *Liberty* is as fragile as ever but needs new forms of expression and protection. *Equality* must encompass gender, race and culture; and hence *fraternity* must give way to wider *solidarities*. The environment must be integral to all policy, and posterity must be party to every decision. To change is not to abandon commitment: to reform is a sign of strength and not of weakness.

Second: think big

A social democratic programme must be universal, not particular. Social democratic parties should resist the temptation to represent particular classes or interests or to build coalitions of minorities. They must speak to the common as well as the specific interest of individual citizens: there has to be a view of the good society which embraces everyone.

Third: don't be fooled

Don't believe the myths assiduously peddled by opponents that prosperity or affluence have resolved the conflicts or eliminated the problems which brought socialism into being in the first place. There is still poverty in the midst of abundance: class matters; inequality and exclusion are as strong as ever; anxiety and insecurity are growing.

Fourth: don't rely on growth

Economic growth is a necessary but not sufficient condition of progress. Ecological constraints demand new ways of defining and measuring wealth. But no amount of growth, sustainable or otherwise, will eliminate all conflicts. More wealth will not end poverty, injustice or the abuse of power, although it can help.

Fifth: decide what kind of capitalist you are

The idea of replacing the market with state ownership and planning has breathed its last. But there are many kinds of market, and socialists have to decide what kind they want. Social democrats have to do more than recognize market failure when they see it: they have to advance an alternative conception of how market economies should work. The Left must be committed to the creation of wealth, albeit in sustainable ways, not just to its distribution. The Right offers a new world order in which capital moves freely and wages adjust; for Europeans that means up at the top and down at the bottom. The Left must offer an alternative in which responsibility, skills, ownership and power at work are taken by workers, in the interests of profitability as well as opportunity. The Left must construct markets which work by raising standards, not driving them downwards.

Sixth: redistribute work, not just income

Paid work is the main engine of distribution and is likely to remain so for many years to come. Unpaid work is the main source of inequalities between women and men. The Left needs a new vision of 'full employment': not full-time, lifetime jobs for men, but richer and more various ways of combining paid employment, family responsibilities, education and leisure for both women and men at different stages of their lives. The post-war welfare state redistributed income from employment to retirement: the post-industrial welfare state must redistribute work between men and women and across the life-cycle.

Seventh: build trampolines, not safety nets

People will fall sick, have accidents, get divorced, lose their jobs: the aim of all welfare provision must be to enable them not just to survive but to bounce back into health, work and active participation. With a few inevitable exceptions, welfare should be an investment in productive and capable people, not a last resort for the incompetent. This may mean spending more to enable some people to overcome their disabilities and more to upgrade the competence of others. So be it.

Eighth: don't confuse equality with sameness

Equality demands that people receive the same treatment where they are alike and different treatment where they are not. It is not 'equality' to demand that women behave like men or children like adults. There are rights to which every citizen is entitled, and these include the right to participate in the definition of rights themselves and in the decision as to when and how equality demands the same or different treatment. But however much they welcome difference, social democrats must accept that there may be limits to diversity, and those limits may not be easily agreed or finally drawn where they themselves would choose.

Ninth: pay attention to means

Politics is about means as well as ends: social democrats must remember that it is not (only) what you do, but the way that you do it that counts. The road to the gulag is paved with good intentions. Personal autonomy requires personal responsibility, self-control, self-government. This is not a harmless, warm sentiment: it involves radical change. Power is a positional good: the more equally it is distributed the less there is at the top. Orders must give way to persuasion and consultation must be for real. And this must be true across the whole range of social institutions, not something reserved for Sundays (or formal politics).

Tenth: think locally, act globally

This means taking *subsidiarity* seriously: interdependence is now so great that many important problems can only be resolved at international level. But social democrats should always have in mind the real effects of such decisions on individuals and communities, and remember William Blake: 'If you would do good, you must do it in minute particulars.'